The *Fabric & Fiber Sourcebook*

The Fabric & Fiber Sourcebook

Bobbi A. McRae

The Taunton Press

Cover photo: Susan Kahn

First printing: July 1989
International Standard Book Number: 0-942391-18-7
Library of Congress Catalog Card Number: 89-50484
Printed in the United States of America

A THREADS Book

Threads magazine® is a trademark of The Taunton Press, Inc.,
registered in the U.S. Patent and Trademark Office.

The Taunton Press
63 South Main Street
Newtown, Conn. 06470

TAUNTON
BOOKS&VIDEOS

...by fellow enthusiasts

Acknowledgments

For Rudy—

Ancient proverb say, "He who captures the heart of a chameleon and takes it for his companion will never want for love, for chameleons are very devoted creatures."

Many people helped me "keep everything together" while I was working on this book, but there are always those few who do more than their share. My special thanks go to my editor at The Taunton Press, Chris Timmons, who helped keep me organized and semi-unflustered during the time that the book was being written; to my parents, Bob and Barbara Neal; to Lisa Schobel, Sharon Wilson-Wilcox and Dianne Guest for their general support, love and advice; to the staff at Alphagraphics Printshops in Austin, Texas; to Michael C. McRae, attorney/poet, for legal "translation" services; and to all those weavers, shop owners, spinners, dyers, authors, knitters and other fiber artists who took time out of their busy schedules to send information and photos and to answer questions so that this book could be written.

Special love goes to my grandmother, Jennie Neal, who never quit asking, "Is the book done yet?"

Contents

Introduction

On New Year's Eve of 1984, when the first edition of this book, *The Fiberworks Source Book,* was just a germ of an idea, I sent letters to more than 500 yarn suppliers, publishers, college instructors, weavers, spinners and other fiber artists, telling them of my desire to put together a book of this type. I was astounded at the response. All the comments were positive and centered around one basic idea—the overwhelming need for a book of this kind.

The response to the published book was just as positive. And when several years later I was getting a steady stream of inquiries asking for updated information on fiber sources, I knew it was time for a new edition, thus *The Fabric & Fiber Sourcebook.*

In the pages that follow you'll find both large and small suppliers of fiber resources. Many of the latter are home-based fiber artists, craftspeople and business owners. Some are ranchers. Many live outside large cities and rely on mail order for their own supplies, as well as for their income. These suppliers offer a wide variety of materials, including looms, spinning wheels, wools, silks, Angora rabbit fur, thousands of handspun and naturally dyed yarns, natural and synthetic dyes, rubber stamps, natural fabrics, computer software for weavers and fabric designers, quilting and needlework supplies, books, and papermaking and basketmaking materials.

You'll also find listings of textile collections, professional organizations and educational programs in fiber, and periodical and book publishers in the U.S. specializing in the fiber arts.

I believe that this book should be about "discovery"— learn what clean wool straight from a sheep smells like, discover how soft the fiber from an Alaskan musk-ox can be, order a silk cocoon and reel your own silk thread, experience the pleasures of spinning your own knitting or crochet yarns, dye your own fabrics or yarns with natural materials or synthetic dyes. Thousands of books on all aspects of the fiber arts are also offered in these pages—buy one or several and learn an entirely new craft. How about making your own paper? Or making a basket for your home? Maybe hand painting an original design on a silk blouse or cotton T-shirt? I hope that once you see the vast array of interesting and unique materials and information listed in this book, you'll be inspired to explore areas of fiber that are now unfamiliar to you and to try some new techniques.

Whatever you decide to do, be daring. You can be sure that working in fibers is exciting, challenging and fulfilling. Fibers and fabrics are warm and sensuous. They feel good to touch and take on a life of their own. But beware—this stuff is habit forming!

Using This Book

This book is your guide to mail-order fiber supplies and services around the country. It is the most complete and comprehensive listing available of these materials and services.

As you will note in the Table of Contents, this book is divided into two parts. The first presents supplies and services; the second lists organizations, educational opportunities, textile collections and publications.

Each entry begins with a listing of the company, school or organization's name, address and phone number, and provides an overview of the supplies, services or program offered.

Only suppliers who conduct business by mail order are included in this book. However, a number of these suppliers also sell their products on a retail basis. If you plan to visit any of these retail stores, it's a good idea to call or write beforehand for the current business hours.

Where relevant, information is included on available discounts and whether the supplier sells only to resale accounts. If you qualify for discounts, be prepared to go through an application process with the company. Some simply require a large initial minimum order, in which case you may want to join with several friends or members of your guild to place a joint order and benefit from the discount.

Also included is the price (if any) of a supplier's catalog and/or samples. While a few suppliers do not have printed catalogs, all of them will be happy to respond to a simple request for prices or information. And even though some of the charges for samples may seem high, they're generally worth the price—many are large enough to be used in small projects.

Many suppliers ask that you send correspondence with a self-addressed, stamped envelope (SASE). Be sure to include one with your letter whenever it is called for; otherwise you may not get an answer.

Because many of the companies carry more than one type of supply, you will find a series of abbreviations in some chapter entries to help you find the supplies you need quickly. These abbreviations are explained in each chapter's introduction.

Also, to help you find what you're looking for, there's a subject index at the end of the book, as well as a geographical index of entries so that you can plan your fiber stops when traveling.

A Note to Readers and Suppliers

At the time this book went to press, all entries had been updated and checked for accuracy. Since publication, however, some of the suppliers listed may have changed their addresses or phone numbers, an inevitable occurrence in the mail-order business.

If you do not find your favorite yarn, company, supplier, school, museum or publication among the entries, they probably didn't return our questionnaire by the date requested. If your favorite supplier or material is unlisted, but you would like to see it included in future editions, please let me know. Although I cannot answer individual requests to find supplies and suppliers, I will try to list them in the next edition.

Also, while all transactions between the readers of this book and the suppliers listed are strictly between those parties, I would like to hear your comments, good and bad, about suppliers with whom you deal. It would also be helpful to hear your comments on how useful you find this sourcebook to be.

Suppliers of fiber materials or services who are interested in listings in future editions should send a SASE to me at the address below. And to those suppliers already listed, please keep me up to date on your new products and services, as well as any changes of address. Thanks.

I'd love to hear from you all. Write:

Bobbi A. McRae
P.O. Box 49770
Austin, TX 78765

Supplies
& Services

Yarns and Fibers   *1*

This chapter lists sources for thousands of fibers, yarns and threads for spinning, weaving, knitting, crochet, embroidery, lacemaking, tatting and rugmaking. You'll find an array of sources for spinning fibers, including everything from raw wool fleece and silk cocoons to the Alaskan musk-ox fiber known as quiviut. You'll also find many sources for handspun yarns, both in natural shades and hand-dyed in a rainbow of beautiful colors. Also listed are numerous sources for commercial wools, cottons, linens, luxury or exotic fibers, and some synthetics.

This chapter also contains listings of manufacturers and suppliers of fiber equipment. Whatever your needs—whether a spinning wheel, loom, knitting machine, knitting needles, crochet hooks, lacemaking tools or some hard-to-find accessory—you're sure to find a source. Letters identifying the principal supplies sold by each company have been added to the entry to help you find the suppliers you need quickly and easily. The legend for these identifying letters is found below:

KC knitting and crochet yarns and/or equipment
LC lacemaking supplies and equipment
R rugmaking supplies and equipment
SP spinning fibers and/or equipment
ST specialty stitchery suppliers
W weaving yarns and/or equipment

Aberdeen Yarn Company, Inc.

6 E. 37th Street
New York, NY 10016
(212) 889-8525

Wholesale only
Established in 1961
KC, W

The Aberdeen Yarn Company has New York's largest selection of yarns on cones for weavers and machine knitters. The company is primarily a dealer in surplus and odd-lot yarns and caters to yarn shops, schools, guilds, clubs and other large-volume buyers.

Qualified buyers should write or call for further information.

Arizona Knitting and Weaving Studio

7150 E. 4th Street
Scottsdale, AZ 85251
(602) 945-SILK

Mail order, retail, manufacturer
Established in 1981
KC, W

The Arizona Knitting and Weaving Studio is jointly owned and operated by the mother-daughter team of Joyce and Rebecca Mandall. The Studio offers a large line of handspun and hand-dyed yarns, including silks, wools, cottons, angoras and other exotic fibers. Other items include looms, imported knitting patterns, buttons, books and more.

Lessons in hand knitting, machine knitting, weaving and crochet are offered at the retail location.

Send for a free brochure.

Auntie Knits, Inc.

212 Rock Road
Glen Rock, NJ 07452
(201) 447-1331

Mail order, retail
Established in 1985
KC

Auntie Knits' full-color catalog includes a large number of knitting kits for men's, women's and children's sweaters, vests and coats by various designers, including Kaffe Fassett. Also available are several needlepoint and embroidery kits, as well as knitting needles from various manufacturers.

A 10% discount is given to senior citizens and embroidery-guild members. Write for details and a free catalog.

Aurora Designs

Wellscroft Farm
R.F.D, Box 158
Marlborough, NH 03455
(603) 827-3464

Mail order, manufacturer
Established in 1978
KC

Deborah Abbott, owner of Aurora Designs, offers a line of wool knitting yarns in worsted and sport weights in 19 rich, jewel-toned colors. The yarns are handspun from the farm's flock of black sheep, whose fleece has been developed especially for apparel yarns. Several of the yarns also have handwoven fabrics to match. Ms. Abbott also offers machine-washable sheepskins in natural shades and various sizes.

Wholesale prices are given to qualified resellers; write for details.

Send $2.00 for a current price list and yarn sample card.

Aurora Silk

5806 N. Vancouver Avenue
Portland, OR 97217
(503) 286-4149

Mail order, retail, manufacturer
Established in 1969
KC, W

Cheryl Kolander, owner of Aurora Silk and author of *A Silk Worker's Notebook* (Interweave Press, 1985), specializes in naturally dyed silks and offers more than 65 brilliant, fast colors. Ms. Kolander also offers a number of undyed silk yarns and fibers in blends, two-plys, tussahs, noil singles, cords, bouclés, chenilles and more.

Ms. Kolander will custom dye yarns to your specifications; write or call for details. *A Silk Worker's Notebook* is also available.

Send $15.00 for a complete catalog and yarn samples.

Harriet Converse Knox, owner of Autumn House Farm, has the largest flock of colored sheep in Pennsylvania. These sheep include many Karashires, a unique Autumn House Farm breed with variegated fleece. The Farm currently offers a number of carded wools and exotic fibers for handspinning, including Karashire rovings and batts in eight shades, karakul rovings in three shades, alpaca/lambswool blends, 100% alpaca, camel down, mohair, silks, linen and angoras. Also available is the Autumn House blend of Romney/Border Leicester wools, along with a number of handspun and hand-painted yarns.

Various discounts are given; write or call for information. Custom spinning and dyeing services are also available.

Send $1.00 for a current catalog.

Autumn House Farm

R.D. #1, Box 105
Rochester Mills, PA 15771
(412) 286-9596

Mail order, retail
Established in 1978
KC, SP, W

AVL (Ahrens & Violette Looms) designs and hand-builds looms for professional hand-weavers. The AVL basic modular loom is available in 40-in., 48-in. and 60-in. weaving widths, and with 4 to 12 harnesses. Production dobby looms in widths of 40 in., 48 in. and 60 in. are available with up to 16 harnesses. The AVL technical dobby loom comes in weaving widths of 40 in., 48 in. and 60 in. with up to 24 harnesses. AVL manufactures the Compu-Dobby computer attachment, which gives the weaver a fast, reliable means of accomplishing complex and sophisticated weaves with more ease. The Compu-Dobby system is compatible with all Apple II computers (except IIc), Macintosh, the IBM PC family and most 100% IBM MS-DOS-type compatible computers. Production-warping tools, computer software and optional equipment and are also available for use with the looms.

Send $2.00 for a current catalog.

AVL Looms

601 Orange Street
Chico, CA 95928
(916) 893-4915

Manufacturer
Established in 1977
W

The AVL technical dobby loom

Ayotte's Designery

P.O. Box 287
Center Sandwich, NH 03227
(603) 284-6915

Mail order, retail, manufacturer,
publisher
Established in 1958
SP, W

Ayotte's Designery, owned by Robert and Roberta Ayotte, offers a wide variety of weaving and spinning supplies. They state in their catalog, "We have been in the handweaving business for 30 years, and cater to our customers as a full-service handweaving business, mail order and shop." They have written and published a comprehensive weaving home-study course and offer memberships in their yarn club.

Send $1.00 for a current catalog and price list.

Bartlettyarns, Inc.

P.O. Box FW-36
Harmony, ME 04942
(207) 683-2251 or 2341

Mail order, manufacturer
Established in 1821
KC, R, W

Bartlettyarns spins locally grown wool on a spinning mule, a machine that's one of the last of its kind still operating in the country. Mule-spun yarns retain the softness of the natural wool and have a homespun appearance and durability. Their Fisherman yarns are rich in natural oils for softness and weather resistance. Other yarns offered include Glen tweeds, Donegal tweeds, Acadian tweeds, sport yarns, Navajo yarns, rug-hooking yarns and others. Several knitting patterns and accessories are also offered.

Send a #10 SASE for a free price list and samples.

The Batik and Weaving Supplier

393 Massachusetts Avenue
Arlington, MA 02174
(617) 646-4453

Mail order, retail
Established in 1982
SP, W

The Batik and Weaving Supplier carries a large number of supplies for weaving, dyeing, spinning and surface-design techniques. The current 36-page catalog includes such items as cottons, silks and luxury fibers for spinning; Ashford, Koala Deluxe, Lendrum, Schacht and Louët spinning wheels; Harrisville Designs, Schacht Spindle Company, Glimåkra, Norwood, Cranbrook, Leclerc and Louët looms, as well as a number of weaving and spinning accessories. Yarns include those by Harrisville Designs and other manufacturers. (See their listing of surface-design supplies on p. 105.)

Send $2.00 for a current catalog.

Bear Trap Fibers

Route 2, Box 110A
Ashland, WI 54806
(715) 682-5937

Mail order
Established in 1984
SP

Lucy Askue, owner of Bear Trap Fibers, offers a number of natural fibers for hand spinning. These include mohairs (raw and rovings), angoras (colored and white) and various wools. Ms. Askue also distributes a hand-crafted Turkish spindle and spinning kits with the spindle included.

Quantity discounts are given to individuals; write for details.

Write for current prices and more information.

Beau Monde

Noel Clark, owner of Beau Monde, offers a variety of colored and white raw fleeces, dyed rovings and handspun yarns from her flock of registered Cotswold, Romney, and Cotswold/Romney crossbreed sheep. Ms. Clark also stocks a number of natural dyes and mordants, felting batts, quilt and comforter battings, Ashford spinning wheels and accessories and Louët looms, spinning wheels and accessories

Beau Monde also offers custom carding, custom vegetal dyeing and custom handspinning services.

Send $2.00 for a current catalog and fiber samples.

Route 30, Box 687 (N. Rupert)
Pawlet, VT 05761
(802) 325-3645

Mail order, retail, manufacturer
Established in 1981
SP, W

Beck's Warp 'N Weave

Beck's Warp 'N Weave supplies a large assortment of supplies for weaving, spinning, dyeing and all types of needlework. Looms and equipment are available from Schacht, Harrisville Designs, Leclerc, Beka, Louët, Glimåkra, Norwood and Cranbrook. Spinning wheels from Ashford and Louët are also listed. Spinning fibers include domestic wool tops, cottons, silks and mohair. A large number of mill-end yarns, as well as yarns from Harrisville Designs, Bernat, Unger, DMC, Henry's Attic, Crystal Palace and others, are available. Other items include dyes and mordants, books, the Bond knitting frame, felting supplies, metallic threads, tatting threads and supplies.

Quantity and bulk discounts are given on yarns; write for details.

Send $1.00 for a current catalog and yarn samples.

2815 34th Street
Lubbock, TX 79410
(806) 799-0151

Mail order, retail
Established in 1976
KC, SP, W

Beggar's Lace

Beggar's Lace specializes in and carries a number of supplies for lacemaking, as well as a large number of books. Supplies include beginner's kits for Battenberg lace, bobbin lace, Carrickmacross lace, tambour embroidery, needle lace, tatting and Tenerife lace. A number of bobbins, pillows, pins, prickers and bobbin winders are also listed. Threads for lacemaking include DMC cottons; Egyptian cottons; Swedish, Irish and Belgian linens; silk threads and others. Other items distributed by Beggar's Lace include tatting shuttles, patterns and Battenberg and princess lace tapes.

Send $2.00 for a current catalog.

P.O. Box 17263
Denver, CO 80217
(303) 722-5557

Mail order
LC

An assortment of tatting shuttles available from Beggar's Lace

Bette Bornside Company

2200 Leon C. Simon Drive
New Orleans, LA 70122
(504) 366-8053

Mail order
Established in 1986
KC

The Bette Bornside Company offers a large selection of hand knitting yarns from national manufacturers at below-retail prices with free shipping. The yarns are from such suppliers as Berger du Nord, Bernat, Brunswick, Neveda and Reynolds. Ms. Bornside also lists a number of knitting patterns by Brunswick, Bernat, Neveda, Reynolds, Righetti and Straker; Boye Balene knitting needles; and a small number of knitting books.

Send $2.00 for a current catalog and yarn samples.

Black Sheep Knitting

133 Cherry Street
Black Mountain, NC 28711
(704) 669-2802

Mail order, retail
Established in 1986
KC

Black Sheep Knitting carries a number of natural-fiber yarns for hand knitting, including silks, cottons, wools and blends. These are available in bulky, worsted, fingering or sport weights in a variety of colors. Mohair, alpaca, wool and cotton blends are also listed.

A 10% discount is given on mail orders over $100.00; check the price list for details.

Send for a free price list.

Blue Star Ranch

R.R. 1, Site 17, #1
Princeton, BC V0X 1W0
Canada
(604) 295-7143

Mail order, retail shop,
manufacturer
Established in 1983
KC, SP, W

Max and Hilde Klein, owners of Blue Star Ranch, supply clean and carded 100% adult, fine or kid mohair in a variety of colors or custom-dyed shades, as well as mohair and wool blends from their flock of registered Angora goats. One-ply and two-ply handspun mohair yarns are also offered.

Send for a current price list and brochure.

The Blue Star Ranch logo

Brittany Company

3461 Big Cut Road
Placerville, CA 95667
(916) 626-3835

Mail order, manufacturer
Established in 1975
KC

The Brittany Company manufactures black walnut knitting needles and crochet hooks.

Write for a current brochure and price list.

Brown Sheep Company, owned by Robert G. Brown, is a family business that specializes in spinning and dyeing hand-knitting and hand-weaving yarns of American wool.

Qualified retailers should write for more information.

Brown Sheep Company, Inc.

Route 1
Mitchell, NE 69357
(308) 635-2198

Manufacturer
Established in 1980
KC, W

Owner Candace Carter offers a number of angora fibers and handspun yarns from her own herd of Angora rabbits. Angora spinning fibers include angora tops, clipped angora and various roving blends. The yarns are all made of top-quality, hand-plucked angora and are available in 100% angoras or blends of angora, silks, wools and rayon in both naturals or dyed colors. A large number of originally designed angora knitting and crocheting kits are also offered.

Ms. Carter has also written "The Angora Almanac," a collection of articles on raising Angora rabbits, harvesting the fibers, basic facts and figures, weaving with angora and other useful information.

A complete catalog is available for $5.00. "The Angora Almanac" can be ordered for $10.00. Write for further information.

Candace Angoras

49 Bassett Boulevard
Whitby, ON L1N 8N5
Canada
(416) 430-3590

Mail order, manufacturer
Established in 1981
KC, SP, W

The Caron Yarn Company specializes in 3-ply and 4-ply knitting yarns, brushed yarns and novelty yarns.

A current brochure and price list is free to retail shops only.

Caron Yarn Company

150 Avenue E and 1st Street
Rochelle, IL 61068
(800) 435-2938

Manufacturer
Established in 1916
KC

Chameleon, owned by Jean Nevin, is an authorized dealer for Passap, White, Knitking and Brother knitting machines. The company also offers an unusually wide variety of yarns on cones, including acrylics and natural fibers (wools, cottons, mohairs, linens, silks, rayons, alpacas, etc.). An extensive assortment of tools, accessories, patterns and books for all knitting machines is also available.

Any equipment or yarn purchase over $250.00 entitles the buyer to make all future purchases at wholesale prices (currently 30% off).

Send $2.00 for a current catalog.

Chameleon

6350 W. 37th Street
Indianapolis, IN 46224
(317) 290-1500

Mail order, retail
Established in 1985
KC

Charikar Karakuls

R.R. 2, Box 150
Elgin, NE 68636
(402) 843-2486

Mail order
Established in 1986
SP

Walter J. Koziol, owner of Charikar Karakuls, offers karakul fleeces for hand spinning with a no-questions-asked satisfaction guarantee.

Quantity discounts are given; write or call for details.

Write for current prices; enclose a SASE.

Charlie's Longhorn Weavers

1203 W. 11th
Coffeyville, KS 67337
(316) 251-8775

Mail order, retail
Established in 1983
SP, W

Charlie's Longhorn Weavers, owned by Charlene Keating, offers a large selection of mill-end yarns in addition to a variety of spinning fibers: wool, mohair, karakul, buffalo, camel, cotton, silk, qiviut and many blends. Charlie's also carries spinning wheels by Ashford, Peacock, Louët and Schacht, and looms from Norwood, Schacht, Beka and Cranbrook. A wide range of accessories and a large number of books are also carried.

Quantity discounts are given on orders over $100.00; shipping is free on all orders over $20.00.

Send for a free brochure.

Chester Farms

Route 5, Box 115R
Staunton, VA 24401
(703) 885-5210

Mail order, retail, manufacturer
Established in 1946
SP, W

Chester Farms, owned by Francis Chester, is the only sheep-farm to wool-mill operation in the U.S. The family-owned farm raises American Columbia and black karakul sheep, from which they produce 100% mule-spun yarns in various sizes and colors.

Send for a free price list and ordering information.

Chule's

2044 Redondela Drive
San Pedro, CA 90732
(213) 831-3850

Mail order, manufacturer
Established in 1975
W

Chule's, operated by Niko Culevski, carries high-quality wool yarns that are known for their softness. Chule's also offers custom weaving services and specializes in the traditional Yugoslavian "flokati" blanket.

Send for a free brochure and price list.

Dimitrije Culevski of Chule's weaving a 'flokati' blanket

Classic Elite Yarns is the only large-scale spinner of brushed mohair in the U.S. The company currently offers over 20 types of beautiful natural fiber and blended yarns in cottons, wools and luxury fibers in bright, vibrant colors, pastels and naturals. A large pattern collection of hand-knitted designs and a line of knitting and needlework books are offered through their current catalog.

Retail buyers should write for the name of the nearest dealer; wholesale buyers must send a business card and note on letterhead to Classic Elite's Sales Department to receive a credit application.

Classic Elite Yarns

12 Perkins Street
Lowell, MA 01854
(508) 453-2837

Manufacturer
Established in 1979
KC, W

  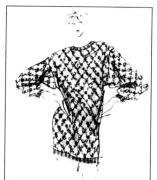 

Fashion knitting patterns available from Classic Elite Yarns

The Clear Water Dye Company, owned by Lee Gray, offers a selection of carded New Zealand Romney wool batts for spinning and felting in more than 60 beautiful, intense solid and heathered colors. Washed and carded white fleeces are also available.

Ms. Gray offers custom-carded batts, custom carding of your fleece and custom dyeing of fleece, yarns or yardage (natural fibers only).

Complete samples are $4.50; write for further details.

Clear Water Dye Company

1823 10th Avenue S.
Minneapolis, MN 55404
(612) 870-1473

Mail order
Established in 1986
SP

Clemes & Clemes manufactures a line of spinning wheels, drum carders, wool and cotton carders and drop spindles. The company also sells natural and dyed wools for hand spinning.

Dealer inquiries are welcomed; write for details.

Send for a free catalog; wool samples are $2.00.

Clemes & Clemes, Inc.

650 San Pablo Avenue
Pinole, CA 94564
(415) 724-2036

Mail order, manufacturer
Established in 1974
SP

Cloudspun Mohair

25358 Cherry Creek Road
Monroe, OR 97456

Mail order
Established in 1984
KC, SP, W

Sharon Chestnutt, owner of Cloudspun Mohair, offers top-quality raw, washed, dyed or carded mohair for hand spinning from her herd of champion registered Angora goats. Small quantities of naturally colored fibers are also available, as well as a number of beautiful handspun yarns.

A 10% discount is given on orders over 10 lb. All orders are shipped with a free scarf pattern and a copy of the pamphlet,"Knitting with Handspun."

Send $2.00 for a yarn and fiber sample card.

An Angora goat mother and kid

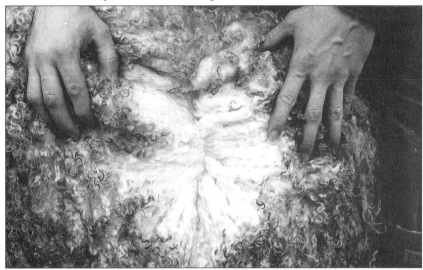

The long wool fibers of an Angora goat

Community Craft Cottage

7577 Elmbridge Way
Richmond, BC V6X 2Z8
Canada
(604) 278-0313

Mail order, retail
Established in 1971
KC, SP, W

The Community Craft Cottage offers a line of wools, silks, rayons, cottons, linens and blended yarns from various Canadian and British suppliers, among them, Condons, Briggs and Little, Le Mieux, and Merino. Fibers for spinning include New Zealand fleeces, alpaca tops and rovings, camel down, tussah silk bricks, mohair, cocoons, cashmere and various blends. Looms by Schacht, Leclerc, Rasmussen and Beka are distributed by the Community Craft Cottage, as are spinning wheels and equipment by Schacht, Louët and Lendrum. Also included are various dyes, mordants and miscellaneous chemicals for dyeing.

Quantity discounts are given on orders over $150.00; write for details.

Send $5.00 for a complete catalog and sample set.

Conshohocken Cotton Company

550 Brook Road
Conshohocken, PA 19428
(215) 825-4270

Mail order, manufacturer
Established in 1979
KC, W

Conshohocken Cotton Company is the manufacturer of the unique, patented SOFTBALL® cotton yarn and SOFTBALL COT'NWASH® cleaning liquid. These 100% combed cotton yarns are available in worsted and sport weights in many bright, vibrant colors.

Discounts are given to qualified retailers only.

Write for more information; send $25.00 for a current yarn sample card and price list.

Cotton Clouds, owned by Irene Schmoller, offers a large selection of cotton yarns, fibers, related tools, books and patterns by mail order—everything fiber artists "need for their dream studio." Just a few of the many 100% cotton yarns suitable for weaving, knitting or crochet include the Jewel of the Nile collection, made from long-staple Egyptian cottons in fifteen beautiful pastels and bright colors; the Pearly Perle assortment in over 60 colors; sock top loops in over 45 colors for making rugs; and the Aurora Earth line, an unmercerized textured yarn in 55 harmonizing shades. Several cotton/rayon blends are also listed in Cotton Cloud's extensive catalog. Spinning fibers include sliver cottons, pima, acala and puni cottons, brown cottons and more. Cotton seeds and instructions are included for those who want to "grow their own." Cotton Clouds also distributes Schacht looms, spinning wheels and accessories; Ashford spinning wheels; the Bond knitting frame; cold-water dyes; various knitting and crochet kits; patterns; and books and videos.

Quantity discounts are given to individuals with minimum orders; write for details.

Send $7.00 for a complete catalog with yarn sample cards (your name will also be added to the mailing list to receive future newsletters and notices of sales).

Cotton Clouds

Route 2, Desert Hills #16-FS
Safford, AZ 85546
(800) 322-7888
(602) 428-7000 in Arizona

Mail order, retail, manufacturer
Established in 1978
KC, SP, W

The Story of Rayon

Rayon is a fiber of economy. It was first developed over 100 years ago by silk weavers who needed an affordable substitute for their costly silk fibers. It wasn't until 1924 that the name "rayon" was officially adopted to replace the fiber's original name, "artificial silk." Rayon has the look and feel of silk and is spun in much the same manner as the silkworm spins its fiber. Whereas silk is a protein, rayon is a man-made cellulose fiber produced from regenerated cotton and wood. The fibers are reduced to a viscose (honey-like) solution, which is then forced through spinnerets (tiny holes) in a showerhead-like contraption to produce a thin thread of rayon yarn. The resulting yarn has an affinity for dyes, a high tensile strength and a sheen so brilliant that a dulling agent is often added to control luster.

Courtesy of Cotton Clouds

A spinning wheel, stool, lazy Kate and niddy noddy, available from The Country Craftsman

The Country Craftsman, owned by Cindy and Joseph Franzek, Jr., is a source for reproduction Saxony spinning wheels like those made in New England during the 17th and 18th centuries. The wheels are made from choice native hardwoods and are available unfinished or in several stained finishes. The Franzeks also offer other spinning accessories such as stools, lazy Kates, bobbins, niddy noddies and distaffs. All products have a lifetime warranty.

Send for a free brochure and price list.

The Country Craftsman

P.O. Box 412
Littleton, MA 01460
(508) 486-4053

Mail order, manufacturer
Established in 1972
SP

Coupeville Spinning & Weaving Shop

P.O. Box 520
Coupeville, WA 98239
(206) 678-4447

Mail order, retail
Established in 1974
KC, SP, W

The Coupeville Spinning & Weaving Shop catalog lists numerous supplies for weaving, dyeing, spinning and knitting. A large number of yarns are offered by Harrisville Designs, School Products, Borg's, Crystal Palace, Bemidji Homespun and others. Also listed in the current catalog are looms and accessories by Schacht, Howell, Glimåkra, Beka, Rasmussen and Harrisville Designs, as well as spinning wheels by Louët and Ashford. Synthetic dyes and paints include Lanaset dyes, Deka Series L dyes, Ciba Kiton acid dyes and Euro-tex fabric paints. Natural dyes include cutch, logwood sawdust, brazilwood sawdust, madder, osage orange, cochineal, and natural and synthetic indigo. Mordants and miscellaneous dyeing supplies are also offered (see the listing on p. 106). Coupeville carries a line of knitting needles, crochet hooks and accessories, as well as hundreds of books on weaving, spinning, knitting and dyeing. Publications from their book division, Shuttle Craft Books (see p. 201), are listed in the catalog.

Some discounts are given; check the catalog for details.

Send $2.00 for a complete catalog (refundable with your first purchase).

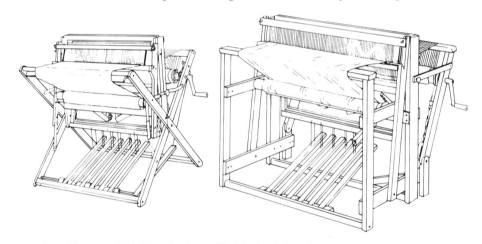

Several looms available from the Coupeville Spinning & Weaving Shop

Craft Gallery

P.O. Box 145
Swampscott, MA 01907
(508) 744-2334

Mail order
Established in 1971
KC, ST

The Craft Gallery, owned by Naomi Appleman, carries a full range of supplies for beginning and advanced stitchers. Ms. Appleman's current catalog contains needlepoint and cross-stitch kits, Brazilian embroidery kits, needlepoint canvases, sewing and stitchery accessories, DMC knitting and crochet yarns, needles, tatting supplies, fashion yarns, hundreds of books, knitting patterns and much more.

Discounts are given with a $25.00 minimum order.

Send $2.00 for a current catalog.

Creek Water Wool Works, owned by Don and Judi McGill, offers a large assortment of supplies and equipment for spinning and weaving. Spinning fibers include 20 different types of silk and silk blends, cashmere, alpaca, mohair, qiviut, camel top and down, flax, ramie, pima cotton, yak, white cashgora, angora/lambswool top, raw unwashed wools (merino/Border Leicester, Romney, merino, Romney/Perendale), processed wools and spinner's sample bags. A number of looms and accessories from Cascade are available—a Salish-Navajo frame tapestry loom, a box inkle loom, unique circular looms and a floor-model inkle loom. The Cascade Pacific folding loom is available in rock maple, cherry or oak in 36-in., 40-in. and 48-in. weaving widths. The Cascade Studio folding loom, made in rock maple, oak, cherry or black walnut, is available in 4-harness or 8-harness models with weaving widths of 24 in., 36 in., 40 in. and 48 in. The Atlantic multiharness professional loom comes in hardwoods with 4, 8 or 12 harnesses and in weaving widths of 46 in. or 54 in. Creek Water Wool Works also carries all looms and weaving accessories by Glimåkra, Louët, Schacht and Ashford, as well as spinning wheels by Louët, Clemes & Clemes, Ashford, Country Craftsman, Lendrum, Haldane, Schacht, Cascade, Restoration Arts, Joslin, Van Eaton, Redgates England, Fox and Reeves. A number of dyes and assistants are sold (see the listing on p. 106), as are books, patterns and products from Obadiah Tharp.

Send $3.00 for a current catalog and price list.

Creek Water Wool Works

P.O. Box 716
Salem, OR 97308
(503) 585-3302

Mail order, retail
Established in 1978
SP, W

A handcrafted 12-harness Cascade Atlantic floor loom with high castle, available from Creek Water Wool Works

'Cross Creek Fibers

P.O. Box 1235
Decatur, TN 37322
(615) 334-5963

Mail order, retail
Established in 1979
R, SP, W

'Cross Creek Fibers provides fleece from its flock of a rare breed of black sheep of Russian ancestry. The sheep are crossed with black Columbia or Lincoln/Finns for wool that ranges in color from black, dark and light grey and chocolate brown to salt and pepper. Weaving and spinning classes are offered in an authentic log cabin dating from the early 1800s, and rugmaking classes are taught on looms dating back to 1775. In addition, 'Cross Creek Fibers supplies precut wool or cotton strips for rugs or mats, odd-lot wools and wool-blend yarns, wool pencil roving, Leclerc looms and accessories and a selection of weaving books.

A 5% discount is given on full fleeces; write for prices.

Send $1.00 for a current catalog.

Crystal Palace Yarns

(A Division of Straw into Gold, Inc.)
3006 San Pablo Avenue
Berkeley, CA 94702
(415) 548-5241

Mail order, manufacturer
Established in 1971
SP, W

Crystal Palace Yarns offers a large number of weaving and spinning supplies including the beautiful Crystal Palace and Chanteleine yarns, among them, silks and silk blends, cottons, linens, rayons and wools. Crystal Palace also carries the entire line of Ashford products. Spinning fibers include tussah silks; Bombyx silk batts, noils, slivers, bricks and top; blended silks with rayon, linen or wool; and other fibers such as flax, ramie, camel down, and yak-hair top.

Discounts are given to qualified retailers; write for additional information.

Curtis Fibers

Star Route Box 15
Ritzville, WA 99169
(509) 659-1913

Mail order, retail
Established in 1984
KC, SP, W

Linda Curtis, owner of Curtis Fibers, offers a number of supplies for spinning and weaving. The spinning fibers include water-retted tow flax, pima cotton, raw brown cotton, wools (merino, Falkland Malvinas 56S top, Romney/Perendale heather slivers, natural color slivers, greasy carded batts, Wilde's dyed batts), silks, ramie, alpaca, camel, Texas mohair top, cashmere down, cashgora and many luxury fiber blends. Ms. Curtis also offers a number of yarns for weaving and knitting (including many cotton mill ends), the Bond knitting frame, the Bond ribber and accessories.

Send $1.00 for a current catalog.

Custom Handweaving

P.O. Box 477, Dept. SB
Redondo Beach, CA 90277-0477
(213) 316-0910 after 4:00 p.m. PST

Mail order
Established in 1978
SP, W

Custom Handweaving, owned by Nancy Boerman, offers "the largest selection of spinning fibers in Southern California." These include silk bricks, rovings, noils, slivers and waste; camel, mohair, alpaca and cashgora top; llama; ramie; flax sliver; pima cotton sliver; yak; Mongolian cashmere combed top; and many blends. Yarns include tussah and doupioni silks in a wide range of colors, white silk singles, baby camel hairs, spun silks, silk tweeds, cotton/wool worsted weights, 100% alpacas from Peru, 100% wool flake yarns from Ireland, 100% cashmeres, imported brushed mohair/wool/nylon blends, cashmere/wool blends and lots more. Ms. Boerman also offers sheepskin pieces for weaving or sewing projects.

Discounts are given on orders of $200.00 or more; write for details.

Send $5.00 for a complete set of yarn samples and current prices.

Deborah King, owner of Custom Knitwear and Exotic Fibers, offers a large assortment of yarns from various manufacturers at below-retail prices for hand knitting, machine knitting or weaving. These include wools and exotic fiber yarns from Lane Borgosesia, Rainbow Mills, Crystal Palace, Filatura Di Crosa, Anny Blatt, Tahki Imports, Euroflax, Melrose, Brown Sheep Company, Classic Elite, Ironstone and DiVe.

Ms. King also offers a "Needle Arts Project Journal" for those who crochet, knit, cross-stitch and/or do needlepoint. The journal has space for recording supplies used, pattern changes, measurements and gauge, as well as room for a photo of each project.

Quantity discounts are given; check the price list for details.

A complete sample set and one-year newsletter/catalog subscription is $10.00 (refundable with first order).

Custom Knitwear and Exotic Fibers

4859 Widner Street
Columbus, OH 43220
(614) 457-6037

Mail order, manufacturer
Established in 1985
KC, W

Cyrefco offers a number of looms and loom accessories including a standard 4-harness, 47-in. counterbalanced loom. Cyrefco has also developed and manufactures the Pegasus, a state-of-the-art 16-harness dobby system that converts counterbalance or countermarche looms into dobby looms. Pegasus uses paper dobby loops (instead of heavy and expensive pegged dobby bars), has countermarche action and provides for faster action than other dobby looms. The system fits traditional Cyrefco looms and is also available as a retrofit upgrade for other counterbalance and countermarche looms. The company also manufactures end-feed shuttles and other weaving accessories.

Send $2.00 for a current catalog.

Cyrefco

P.O. Box 2559
Menlo Park, CA 94026
(415) 324-1796

Mail order, manufacturer
Established in 1978
W

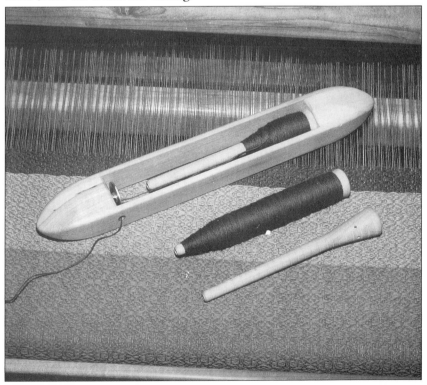

Cyrefco's end-delivery weaving shuttle

Daisy Chain

P.O. Box 1258
Parkersburg, WV 26102
(304) 428-9500

Mail order
Established in 1974
KC, ST

Daisy Chain carries a number of threads and yarns for embroidery and machine knitting. These include DMC cotton flosses, Balger French metallics, raw silks on cones and Au Ver à Soie French silk yarns for needlepoint, embroidery or knitting.

Send $2.00 for a current catalog.

David Stanley & Sons Leatherworks

1911 Austin Avenue
Brownwood, TX 76801
(915) 646-0141

Mail order, manufacturer
Established in 1985
KC

David Stanley & Sons Leatherworks is currently the only domestic manufacturer of the traditional Fair Isle knitting belt. The leather belt, which contains a pouch filled with horsehair, is worn around the knitter's waist. The right knitting needle is inserted into one of the perforated holes in the pouch, which holds the work securely and supports the weight of the fabric so you can knit comfortably while walking or standing.

Wholesale inquiries should be directed to Mary Stanley.

Write or call for more information and current prices. The Fair Isle knitting belt is also available from Meg Swansen at Schoolhouse Press (see the listing on p. 61).

Davidson's Old Mill Yarn

109 Elizabeth Street
P.O. Box 8
Eaton Rapids, MI 48827
(517) 663-2711

Mail order, retail
Established in 1921
KC, SP, W

Davidson's Old Mill Yarn offers a wide variety of mill-end yarns (mostly wools), as well as one of the largest selections of hand knitting, spinning and weaving supplies in the U.S. The company offers looms and weaving accessories by Leclerc, Schacht, Glimåkra, Norwood and Cranbrook. Many books are also listed.

Group tours and spinning and weaving classes are offered at the retail location.

Wholesale prices are given to commercial weavers with a minimum order of $300.00. Write or call Linton R. Davidson for more information.

Send a SASE for a free mill-end sampler; a complete catalog is $3.00.

D. B. Fisher Associates

P.O. Box 45
East Lempster, NH 03605
(603) 863-2960

Mail order
Established in 1986
KC, W

David B. Fisher of D. B. Fisher Associates is a source for first-quality mill-end yarns (mostly natural fibers) on cones. The company ships orders the same day they are received and guarantees 100% customer satisfaction. (Yarn selection changes, based on availability.)

Wholesale price quotes are given upon request.

Send for a free brochure and price list.

Detta's Spindle

Detta's Spindle, owned by Detta Juusola, offers a line of weaving and spinning supplies including yarns by Brown Sheep Company, Nature Spun, Bemidji Woolen Mills, Harrisville Designs, Green Mountain Spinnery, Crystal Palace and others. Spinning fibers include dog hair, mohair, cotton, silk, camel, yak, goat, ramie, flax, rayon, qiviut, angora and various wools. Spinning wheels are available from Rick Reeves, Rappard & Co. (New Zealand), The Country Craftsman, Schacht, Louët and Ashford. Looms are offered by Schacht Spindle Company. Other items include spinning stools, books, carders and spindles. A variety of fiber-arts classes are offered at the two retail locations.

Ms. Juusola is a very unusual woman. Not only does she have 13 children ranging in age from 10 months to 20 years, but she also specializes in spinning custom yarns from dog hair—Samoyeds, poodles, German shepherds, sheep dogs and Afghan hounds. Ms. Juusola doesn't consider any fiber too unusual to spin and has even made yarn from cat hair.

Send $1.50 for a complete catalog and price list, or write for custom spinning information (enclose a SASE).

2592 Geggen-Tina Road
Maple Plain, MN 55359
(612) 479-2886

Mail order, retail
Established in 1972
SP, W

Dyes & Wool

Dyes & Wool, owned by Gayle Bingham, supplies the entire line of Gaywool dyes (see the listing on p. 108), as well as premium Corriedale wools, Nooramunga spinning wools (merino/Border Leicester cross) and dyed Gaywool sliver from Australia.

Ms. Bingham also does custom dyeing and spinning for individuals or groups.

Send $1.50 for a complete catalog and price list.

19902 Panther Drive
Pflugerville, TX 78660
(512) 251-3502

Mail order
Established in 1987
SP

Earth Guild

Earth Guild is an all-around supplier for various fiber arts and crafts. The company's 52-page catalog includes a number of weaving, spinning and dyeing supplies. Spinning fibers include wools, camel top, silk noils, flax, ramie, cottons and rayon staple. Spinning wheels are available from Louët and Country Craftsman. A large number of yarns are offered, including mill ends, warp and textured cottons, Novitex linens, cotton carpet warps, Christopher knitting wools, Wilde & Wooley yarns, Harrisville Designs wools and others. Looms by Beka, Schacht, Glimåkra, Norwood and Cranbrook are also listed. Rugmaking and braiding supplies include braid-aids, fabric cutters, braidkins and linen threads. Earth Guild is a dealer for Brother knitting machines and accessories. (See p. 108 for their surface-design supplies.)

Quantity discounts are given to individuals; write for details.

Send $2.00 for a current catalog (refunded with first order).

One Tingle Alley
Asheville, NC 28801
(800) 327-8448

Mail order, retail
Established in 1970
KC, R, SP, W

23

Eaton Yarns

P.O. Box 665
Tarrytown, NY 10591
(914) 631-1550

Mail order, retail
Established in 1977
KC, W

Eaton Yarns offers a wide variety of Finnish wool, linen and cotton yarns in a large range of colors.

Some discounts are given; write for details.

Send $1.00 per yarn sample card desired.

Edgemont Yarn Service, Inc.

240 Edgemont Road
Maysville, KY 41056
(606) 759-7614

Mail order
KC, R, W

Edgemont Yarn Service, carries a wide variety of mill ends and other yarns, including cotton/rayon blends, 100% rayons, 100% cottons and 100% wools. The company also distributes the entire line of Maysville yarns, including Maysville 100% cotton carpet warp, mercerized perle cottons, rug fillers (rayon/cotton blend), mop yarns, sock loopers and 100% cotton rug rovings. Edgemont also carries the Model C cutting machine to cut strips for hooking or braiding rugs.

Send for a current price list. Yarn sample cards are $2.00.

Ehrman Needlepoint

(Westminster Trading Corporation)
5 Northern Boulevard
Amherst, NH 03031
(603) 886-5054

Mail order
Established in 1987
ST

Ehrman Needlepoint offers an extensive line of needlepoint and knitting kits designed by some of the best British designers, including Kaffe Fassett, Candace Bahouth, Anita Gunnett, Edwin Belchamber and Susan Skeen, as well as reproductions of pieces in the collections of the Victoria and Albert Museum. All needlepoint kits contain a full-color preprinted canvas, a needle, instructions and all the required wool yarns.

A full-color catalog is $2.00.

Fine Weaving

The ancient Egyptians made linens so sheer that they could be drawn through a finger ring.

—Courtesy of the Wool Education Center, Denver, Colorado

Elkhorn Mountains Weaving School

S.R. Box 165
Clancy, MT 59634
(406) 442-0354

Mail order, retail, school
Established in 1976
W

Joanne Hall, owner of Elkhorn Mountains Weaving School, offers several looms for sale through her company. These include six models of Swedish countermarche looms made of birch and 11 models of Leclerc looms made of maple. Ms. Hall also carries weaving equipment such as benches, warping frames, bobbin winders, shuttles, bobbins, reeds, umbrella swifts, repair heddles and more. (See the school listing on p. 177.)

Ms. Hall's self-published book, *Mexican Tapestry Weaving* (1976), is also available.

Send for a current loom price list.

Euroflax imports flax and linen for hand spinning from Belgium: long-line flax (natural and dyed) in stricks and 30 colors of flax rovings in hanks. The company also offers wet-spun linen yarns in 15 colors that can be used for hand or machine knitting. These yarns are machine washable and dryable and come in skeins or on cones.

Send $2.00 for flax samples and $2.00 for a linen color chart.

Euroflax, Inc.

P.O. Box 241
Rye, NY 10580
(914) 967-9342

Mail order, manufacturer
Established in 1985
KC, SP, W

Louise Walsh's herd of over 450 Angora rabbits makes Evergreen Enterprises the largest breeder of Angora rabbits on the East Coast. Ms. Walsh sells angora hair and is a dealer for Mitzy and Wee Peggy spinning wheels.

Send $1.00 for a current catalog.

Evergreen Enterprises

267 Burt Street
Taunton, MA 02780
(508) 823-2377

Mail order, retail, manufacturer
Established in 1980
SP

Louise Walsh, of Evergreen Enterprises, at her Mitzy Saxony spinning wheel with Valentine, her English Angora rabbit

Fairmount Farm Fleeces

Fairmount Farm, Thomas Road
Rindge, NH 03461
(603) 899-5445

Mail order, retail
Established in 1970
SP

Georgia Wolterbeek of Fairmount Farm Fleeces offers wools from her farm flock and enjoys helping her customers select the most suitable and beautiful fleece for their projects.

Send a SASE for wool samples and current prices.

Fallbrook House

R.D. #2, Box 17
Troy, PA 16947
(717) 297-2498

Mail order
Established in 1973
SP

Jean R. Case, owner of Fallbrook House, offers a very large line of silk fibers from cultivated *Bombyx mori* and semicultivated tussah. These are available in combed and carded forms in rovings, bricks, loose noil, mawata caps, raw and degummed reeling wastes, raw cocoons for reeling, batting and 14 exotic silk blends in combed rovings. Ms. Case also offers printed material on silk fiber and sericulture. In case you're wondering, she has even raised her own silkworms.

A 10% discount is given to guilds, museums and schools with a minimum order of $60.00.

Send $21.00 for a copy of Ms. Cases's "Silk Portfolio," which contains extensive information on the various forms in which silk fiber is available and complete procedures for reeling, making mawata, degumming and more. Also included are directions for drawing, spinning, blending, natural and synthetic dyeing and caring for silks. The 49 silk samples in the portfolio illustrate the various procedures and include all 33 silk fibers currently available. Send a SASE for general information and prices.

The Fiber Studio

P.O. Box 637
Henniker, NH 03242
(603) 428-7830

Mail order, retail
Established in 1975
KC, SP, W

The Fiber Studio, owned by Pamela Grob, supplies fibers and equipment for all aspects of the fiber arts. Ms. Grob currently carries mill-end and closeout yarns, as well as rug wools, cotton/linen blends, brushed mohairs, novelty synthetics, Irish linens, perle cottons, Shetland wools, English wool fancies and many more. Spinning fibers are also offered, as well as items by Leclerc, Tools of the Trade, Kyra, Schacht, Beka, Glimåkra, Louët and Mark V.

Quantity discounts are given; write or call for details.

Send $1.00 for a general catalog, $3.00 for yarn samples and $3.00 for spinning fibers.

Fibre Crafts

38 Center Street
Clinton, NJ 08809
(201) 735-4469

Mail order, retail, manufacturer
Established in 1971
SP, W

Fibre Crafts, owned by Kerry Adams, offers a large variety of yarns from such companies as Borgs, Harrisville Designs, Henry's Attic, Maysville and others. Ms. Adams offers all Leclerc looms and accessories, as well as equipment from Glimåkra, Tools of the Trade, Ashford, Louët, Clemes & Clemes, Norwood and Schacht. Raw fibers include wools, flax and ramie rovings, silks, cottons and cashmere. A number of books on the fiber arts are offered, as well as workshops and classes.

Send for a free brochure and price list.

Silk Terms

Jean R. Case, owner of Fallbrook House, has provided several definitions of terms applying to silk and sericulture:

Bombyx mori: White silk from the cultivated caterpillar of the same name.

Brick: Wide silk top folded into a small package.

Carded fibers: Fibers that have been carded several times to clean them, but which still contain noil (small balls of silk fibers).

Combed fibers: Fibers that have been cleaned further, and are smooth, shiny and without noil.

Mawata: Expanded, whole cocoons dried over a variety of shapes.

Raw silk: Silk fiber on which the gum is still present.

Roving: Silk top drawn into a long, continuous form 1 in. to 2 in. in diameter.

Tussah: Tan-colored silk from one of many varieties of wild silkworms.

Flag Hill Farm, owned by Sabra Ewing, specializes in "ultra-clean, ready-to-use" mohair for hand spinners from the farm's flock of registered Angora goats. The fleeces are well skirted at shearing, and only the finest fibers are selected for sale. The fibers are available raw, in rovings, washed or handspun into yarns.

Send $2.00 for fiber samples and current prices.

Flag Hill Farm

P.O. Box 31
Vershire, VT 05079
(802) 685-7724

Mail order
Established in 1985
KC, SP, W

Flag Hill Farm Angoras produce lustrous mohair fibers for hand spinning.

Fleece Artist

1865 Water Street
Historic Properties
Halifax, NS B3J 2V9
Canada
(902) 423-9311

Mail order, retail
Established in 1975
KC, SP, W

Fleece Artist offers a selection of British and domestic yarns in natural fibers and exotic mixtures; fabrics; weaving, knitting and spinning equipment; books and patterns; and exclusive knitwear and kits by Adrienne Thomas.

Mini-workshops on all aspects of the fiber arts are offered at the retail location.

Send $10.00 for a complete sample set and price list.

Flintridge Woodshop & Fibers

121 Woodcrest Road
Sister Bay, WI 54234
(414) 854-2919

Mail order, manufacturer
Established in 1975
SP

George and Ruth Jischke, owners of Flintridge Woodshop & Fibers, offer a number of handcrafted spinning wheels made to your specifications. These include the Saxony wheel, the Cottage wheel and the Irish Castle wheel. Spinning fibers include wools, line flax, tow flax, bleached Irish flax, ginned cottons and miscellaneous fibers such as alpaca and silks. Other spinning accessories and hand spindles are also included in the current catalog.

Send $.50 for a catalog and current price list.

From the Flintridge Woodshop & Fibers catalog

Frederick J. Fawcett, Inc.

1304 Scott Street
Petaluma, CA 94952
(707) 762-3362

Mail order
Established in 1879
KC, LC, R, SP, W

Frederick J. Fawcett is the largest U.S. importer of Irish linen threads for hand weaving, lacemaking, embroidery, crochet, rugmaking and so on. The company offers one of the widest selections of flax and linen products—from straw and hand-hackled fibers for spinning to yarns, threads (singles, plies, soft, waxed, polished, natural and dyed) and finished cloth. Fawcett also carries a number of cottons, wool hand-weaving worsteds, cotton/linen blends and 100% linen ropes for model riggings.

Quantity discounts are given on orders over $100.00; write or call for details.

Send $10.00 for a complete catalog with yarn sample cards (refundable with first order).

From Bolivia Yarns specializes in handspun and machine-spun naturally dyed alpaca yarns imported from Bolivia. The company also carries hand-spun alpaca in natural colors, machine-spun white alpaca and handspun wool in plant-dyed and cochineal-dyed colors.

Discounts are given to those who produce fiber works for resale; write or call for further information.

Send $3.00 for current samples and prices.

From Bolivia Yarns

P.O. Box 88-4951
San Francisco, CA 94188
(415) 387-1797

Mail order, retail, manufacturer
Established in 1985
KC, W

Gerald H. Whitaker specializes in supplying natural fibers and yarns on cones to qualified yarn shops and professionals. Spinning fibers include wool top, yak top, cashmere, alpaca top, cashgora, flax, mohair, ramie, camel, pima cotton top, silks and some blends. Weaving and machine-knitting yarns are available in mohair, cottons, Irish linens, cotton/linen blends, silk noils, cultivated silks and many more. Sterling silver and pewter jewelry and buttons are also available.

Qualified buyers should contact Gerald H. Whitaker for more information.

Gerald H. Whitaker Ltd./Inc.

1522 Main Street
Niagara Falls, NY 14305
(416) 937-1730

Manufacturer
Established in 1974
KC, SP, W

The Language of Linen

Flax: A bast (fiber-producing) plant, with fiber in the stalk. All linen comes from flax.

Line: The longest and best fiber of the flax plant.

Tow: Fiber byproducts of flax processing, produced at every stage and varying widely in quality and characteristics.

Wet spun: In the spinning process the fiber passes through 160°F to 180°F water, which softens the natural gums and waxes and allows the individual fibers to slip and lie down, producing a smoother, more even yarn. Most linen yarns are of this type.

Dry spun: Spun without water. Makes a softer, hairy, somewhat slubbier yarn.

Slubby: Uneven, having slubs or lumps. All linen yarns are slubby to some degree, which is part of their charm. —Courtesy of the Frederick J. Fawcett catalog

Gilmore Looms, owned by Mr. E. E. Gilmore, makes 4-harness and 8-harness looms in maple and other hardwoods in weaving widths from 26 in. up to 54 in. Other available accessories and parts include weaving benches, stainless-steel reeds, flat-steel heddles, horizontal warping reels, warping frames, raddles, swivel creels for sectional warping, warp tensioners, sectional warp beams, shuttles and bobbins.

Send for a free brochure or call E. E. Gilmore or Jim Lucas for more information.

Gilmore Looms

1032 N. Broadway
Stockton, CA 95205
(209) 463-1545

Mail order, retail, manufacturer
Established in 1936
W

Glimåkra Looms 'n Yarns, Inc.

(A Subsidiary of Viking Trading Company)
1304 Scott Street
Petaluma, CA 94952
(707) 762-3362

Mail order
Established in 1978
KC, LC, W

According to the owner, Lars Malmberg, Glimåkra Looms 'n Yarns is the largest importer of Scandinavian weaving equipment in the U.S. and the largest importer of hand-weaving yarns, especially those from Scandinavia (Borgs). The Standard counterbalance loom is available in five weaving widths from 44 in. to 64 in. in 4-harness or 6-harness models with a variety of accessories and add-on features (fly shuttle beater, double warp beam, opphämta attachment, Damask draw harness device, etc.) The Ideal loom comes in weaving widths of 24 in., 32 in. and 40 in. with up to 8 harnesses and treadles. Glimåkra also manufactures several tapestry looms. The Regina, an upright high-warp tapestry loom, is available in weaving widths of 49 in. and 60 in. The Sara model comes in 40-in. widths, the Tina is available in 19-in. widths, and the Eva's weaving width is 16 in. Other looms include the Victoria and the Emma, both table looms with optional legs. A new loom from Glimåkra is the Aktiv, a completely collapsible and movable model with a weaving width of 40 in., 8 harnesses and treadles. The Susanna rigid-heddle loom and the Belt loom round out Glimåkra's large selection. A number of weaving accessories (including the Viking stainless-steel reed) and lacemaking threads and supplies are also available.

Send $2.50 for a loom catalog; complete yarn and thread samples are $15.00.

Glimåkra Weaving Studio

1741 Allston Way
Berkeley, CA 94703
(415) 549-0326
KC, LC, W

The Glimåkra Weaving Studio, owned by Maj-Britt Mobrand, distributes the entire line of Glimåkra looms, weaving equipment and accessories. Borgs wool, cotton and linen yarns are also available.

Quantity discounts are given on yarn orders; write for details.

Send for a free brochure; a complete catalog is $3.00.

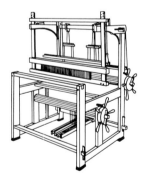

Looms available from Glimåkra

Golden Threads Knitting & Weaving Studio

Nicole McCoy's Golden Threads Knitting & Weaving Studio offers a large selection of designer yarns from various manufacturers, including DMC, Filatura Di Crosa, Reynolds, Susan Bates and more. Brother knitting machines, various videotapes, Schacht spindle looms and knitting kits are also offered in the current catalog.

Quantity discounts are given; write for details.

Send $2.00 for a current catalog and price list.

120 E. Main Street
Humble, TX 77338
(713) 446-8766

Mail order, retail
Established in 1979
KC, W

Grandor Industries Ltd.

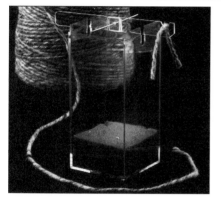
The McMorran yarn balance, distributed by Grandor Industries

Grandor Industries offers a variety of yarns, including pure wool berbers and rovings, textured cottons, linens and silks, warp yarns in linen, cotton, wools and blends. The company also distributes the McMorran yarn balance, a small device that figures the number of yards in a pound of yarn.

Discounts are given to qualified dealers only; write for information.

A current catalog and yarn samples are $5.00.

716 E. Valley Parkway, Unit 48
Escondido, CA 92025
(619) 743-2345

Mail order
Established in 1975
W

Great Northern Weaving

Great Northern Weaving specializes in supplies for rug weaving. The company carries colorfast cotton warps in 22 shades, cotton/rayon blend rug fillers in 11 colors, cotton rags, palm looms, loopers in 11 colors, 16-ply rug roping and miscellaneous books, tools and equipment.

Send $1.00 for a current price list and samples.

P.O. Box 361
Augusta, MI 49012
(616) 731-4487

Mail order
Established in 1985
R, W

Green Mountain Spinnery

Green Mountain Spinnery, managed by Diana Wahle, is the only U.S. manufacturer that will custom spin small (100-lb.) yarn lots of wools and precious-fiber blends for sheep breeders. The company also offers stock New England wool yarns and blends in a wide variety of shades. Vermont Designer patterns and kits for knitting are available and include socks, cardigans, vests and hats.

Send $6.00 for a complete catalog and set of yarn samples (deductible from your first order of $35.00 or more).

P.O. Box 568
Putney, VT 05346
(802) 387-4528
(800) 321-WOOL for phone orders

Mail order, manufacturer
Established in 1981
KC, W

Halcyon Yarn

12 School Street
Bath, ME 04530
(800) 341-0282

Mail order, retail, manufacturer
Established in 1972
KC, SP, W

From the Halcyon Yarn catalog

Halcyon Yarn, owned by Ms. Halcyon Schomp, offers a unique "Yarn Store in a Box" sample service. A suitcase-type box comes packed with a Halcyon Yarn yearbook/catalog; over 42 yarn sample sheets, which include printed suggestions on usage, sett, compatible yarns and other tips; literature on looms and equipment; helpful brochures; charts and more. Yarns offered by Halcyon include many naturals, exotics, blends and metallics made especially for the company, as well as yarns from Harrisville Designs, Oregon Worsted, Brunswick, Tahki Imports, Reynolds and others. Fibers for spinning, weaving and felting include wools, alpacas, silks, silk blends, mohair, camel down, cottons, flax and ramie. Weaving and spinning equipment is included from such suppliers as Harrisville Designs, AVL, Leclerc, Schacht and Louët. The Halcyon catalog lists a large number of books, patterns, videos (see the listing on p. 187) and computer software for weavers from AVL Designs.

Quantity discounts are given; write for details.

A general brochure is free; samples of the Halcyon Maine yarn collection are $15.00; a complete "Yarn Store in a Box" is $23.00 (including periodic newsletter updates, new sample sheets and more).

Harrisville Designs

Main Street
Harrisville, NH 03450
(603) 827-3333

Mail order, retail, manufacturer,
school
Established in 1972
KC, SP, W

Harrisville Designs, nestled in the Monadnock Highlands of southwestern New Hampshire, is the only surviving 19th-century textile village in the U.S. and is dedicated to preserving the tradition established in earlier times. Harrisville products include a popular line of hand-weaving looms, which are available in kits or assembled forms, as well as a line of beautiful wool yarns in singles, two-ply yarns, cotton/wool blends, tweeds and Shetlands. Dyed, carded fleeces are also available in a limited range of solid colors.

The Harrisville Designs Weaving Center offers a number of workshops and classes (see p. 178).

Send $4.00 for a yarn sample catalog and price list.

One of the looms available from Harrisville Designs

Heirloom Yarn Company specializes in the sale of coned yarns in contemporary fashion colors for knitting machines and for weaving.

A current catalog is free to retail shops only.

Heirloom Yarn Company

150 Avenue E
Rochelle, IL 61068
(800) 435-2938

Manufacturer
Established in 1916
KC, W

Henry's Attic, owned by Henry and Samira Galler, offers natural-fiber, undyed yarns for weaving and hand knitting. These include beautiful textures in silks, cottons, wools, linens, mohairs and blends. Orders are shipped promptly, and personal service is provided.

Henry's Attic sells only to stores and to professional weavers and knitters producing for resale. Others should write for the name and address of the nearest mail-order dealer.

A complete sample set is $15.00.

Henry's Attic

5 Mercury Avenue
Monroe, NY 10950
(914) 783-3930

Mail order, manufacturer
Established in 1972
KC, W

Herald Looms manufactures jack-type floor looms in weaving widths of 24 in., 32 in., 40 in. or 45 in. with 4 or 8 harnesses. All looms are made to order with natural or walnut finishes. Weaving accessories are also offered.

Send for a free brochure.

Herald Looms

118 Lee Street
Lodi, OH 44254
(216) 948-1080

Mail order, manufacturer
Established in 1954
W

Herrschners has one of the largest needlework catalogs in the U.S. and offers an extensive assortment of supplies and kits for all types of needlework. The current catalog includes kits for counted cross-stitch, needlepoint, crocheted afghans and braided rugs. Yarns and threads include acrylic afghan and sport-weight yarns, knitting worsted yarns, Paterna Persian wools, Bucilla tapestry wools, DMC machine embroidery threads, DMC embroidery flosses in over 100 shades, precut acrylic rug yarns, Aunt Lydia's polyester rug yarns, tatting cottons, crochet cottons and DMC perle cottons in over 50 colors. Other items include rugmaking tools and accessories, needlework framing devices, ballpoint paints for fabrics, quilting frames, needlepoint canvases, Loop 'n Loom weaving sets and tatting supplies.

Send for a free catalog.

Herrschners, Inc.

Hoover Road
Stevens Point, WI 54481
(715) 341-4554

Mail order, retail
Established in 1899
KC, LC, R, ST, W

Hub Mill Store

12 Perkins Street
Lowell, MA 01854
(508) 937-0320

Mail order, retail
Established in 1983
KC, W

The Hub Mill Store tries to satisfy the yarn needs of weavers and hand and machine knitters for high-quality yarns at reasonable prices.

Send $5.00 for a sample set and current prices.

Imagery Specialty Yarns, Inc.

P.O. Box 410
Danielson, CT 06239-0410
(203) 774-7227

Mail order, manufacturer
KC, W

Imagery Specialty Yarns offers a large number of weaving and knitting yarns at "direct-from-the-mill prices." These yarns include metallics in ten colors, beautiful mohair/wool/nylon blends, 100% rayons, rayon/Lurex® blends, perle cottons, braided metallics, cotton novelties and many others. All yarns are available in 50-g. skeins, on 1-lb. cones and mill cones, or in custom-size dye skeins or hanks.

Various discounts are given; write for details.

Send $7.00 for a complete yarn sample card folder (refundable with your first order.)

In Stitches

46-305 Ikiiki Street
Kaneohe, HI 96744
(808) 235-3775

Mail order, retail
Established in 1982
SP, W

In Stitches, owned by Charlene Anderson-Shea, is Hawaii's only weaving shop. The shop carries a large variety of yarns, looms, books, equipment, spinning wheels, dyes and other weaving supplies.

A catalog is not available at this time; write for specific information.

Ironstone Yarns

P.O. Box 365
Oxbridge, MA 01569
(508) 278-5838

Manufacturer
Established in 1972
KC, W

Ironstone Yarns specializes in mohair yarns in balls or on cones. The company also manufactures mercerized flake cottons, cotton/rayon blends, mohair/wool/nylon blends, cotton/rayon blends and many others in a number of brilliant colors and pastels. A line of knitting patterns is also offered.

Discounts are given to qualified buyers only; write or call for details.

Send $18.00 for a yarn sample book and price list.

Jacob's Well

P.O. Box 1222
Redmond, OR 97756
(503) 548-4089

Mail order, manufacturer
Established in 1987
SP

David L. Miller, owner of Jacob's Well, offers wool fleece from his flock of Jacob sheep, as well as Jacob sheep stock.

Quantity discounts are given to individuals; write for information.

Write for current prices.

JaggerSpun

JaggerSpun has been a spinner of worsted specialty yarns since the late 1800s. JaggerSpun Yarns offers an assortment of natural-fiber yarns including 100% merino wools and wool/silk blends on cones or in skeins in over 230 colors. The yarns are suitable for weaving or knitting, and the Maine line is appropriate for machine knitting.

Wholesale discounts are given on orders of $300.00 or more; write for details.

Send $5.00 for a current catalog and yarn samples.

(A Division of Jagger Brothers, Inc.)
P.O. Box 188
Springvale, ME 04083
(207) 324-4455

Mail order, retail
Established in the 1800s
KC, W

The JaggerSpun logo

Joan Toggitt

Joan Toggitt provides top-of-the line needlework fabrics and canvases, as well as Zweigart metallic thread.

Discounts are given to qualified buyers only; write for more information.

35 Fairfield Place
West Caldwell, NJ 07006
(201) 575-5410

Manufacturer
Established in 1874
ST

Jones Sheep Farm

Gary and Marilyn Jones, proprietors of Jones Sheep Farm, own the largest flock of colored sheep in the U.S. and provide hand-spinning wools from them. The sheep include Corriedale, Romney, Targhee, Navajo, Hampshire, Oxford, Suffolk, Finnsheep and Border Leicester.

An instructional booklet "Breeds of Sheep" is available from the Jones Sheep Farm.

Write for current prices and more information.

R.R. 2, Box 185
Peabody, KS 66866
(316) 983-2815

Mail order, manufacturer
Established in 1965
SP

Kaleidoscope Yarns

Kaleidoscope Yarns, directed by Jane Bernier, is a membership co-op organized by a small group of artists and designers. The company carries a variety of unique designer yarns from a large number of manufacturers, all at discounted prices. The co-op can match colors or help find suitable yarns for various projects, and co-op members are entitled to as much as 30% to 40% below-retail prices on all yarns (minimum orders are required).

Send $6.00 for a set of over 200 samples and information on co-op memberships, prices and services.

16 Church Street
Belfast, ME 04915
(207) 338-2902 (evenings only)

Mail order
Established in 1988
KC, W

Kathleen B. Smith, Textile Reproductions

P.O. Box 48
West Chesterfield, MA 01084
(413) 296-4437

Mail order, manufacturer
Established in 1982
ST, W

Kathleen B. Smith offers high-quality materials suitable for historical textile reproductions and other work requiring natural and vegetable-dyed fibers. Specializing in 18th-century furnishings, needlework and upholstery, Ms. Smith carries a variety of vegetable-dyed worsted, linen and silk threads; linen, cotton and wool fabrics; trimming tapes; samplers; tools; conservation supplies and dyestuffs. Also offered are vegetable-dyed felts, yarns and fleeces for handwork programs in the specialized Waldorf schools.

Ms. Smith specializes in accurate textile reproductions for museum and private period interiors and offers technical assistance in the research, design, fabrication and installation of these pieces. Write or call for further information.

Send $3.00 for a current catalog or $12.00 for a complete sample folder. The sample packet for Waldorf Schools is $1.50.

Knitking Corporation

1128 Crenshaw Boulevard
Los Angeles, CA 90019
(213) 938-2077

Mail order, manufacturer
Established in 1950
KC

The Knitking Corporation carries a large assortment of knitting machines and yarns and accessories for machine knitting. Machines available include sergers, the Compuknit III electronic knitter (an electronic standard needle machine with 555 built-in patterns), the Punch Card bulky knitter, the KK93 standard punch-card knitter, and the Simple Seven and Genie 710 knitters. A number of accessories, parts and tools are available for all machine models. Knitking also offers a number of yarns suitable for knitting machines, including synthetics, angoras, rayons, cottons, wools and blends. Books on machine-knitting design and technique are also available.

The Knitking Corporation publishes a quarterly magazine featuring at least 20 full-color garments with complete machine-knitting instructions. The current subscription rate is $20.00 a year for U.S. subscribers.

Send for a free catalog and current price list.

Knitting Concepts

P.O. Box 780544
Sebastian, FL 32978-0544
(407) 589-0024

Mail order
Established in 1987
KC, W

Knitting Concepts, owned by Sharon Wise, is a source for brand-name cotton, acrylic, rayon, mohair, wool, angora and novelty yarns on cones for machine knitting and weaving. Also available are first-quality mill ends and closeout yarns, knitting supplies, and Toyota knitting machines and accessories. Ms. Wise states, "I will go out of my way to find and buy what the customer needs. I give individual attention to each of my customers, and they appreciate this. I help them create their own unique yarn."

Various discounts are given; write for details.

Send $2.00 for yarn samples and current prices.

Knitting Machines of Florida distributes Brother knitting machines and looms and weaving accessories by Leclerc and Schacht Spindle Company. The company also carries Spindle Craft and Amberyarn coned yarns, as well as a large selection of mill ends.

Send for a free catalog.

Knitting Machines of Florida

380 Semoran Commerce Place, Suite 107A
Apopka, FL 32703
(407) 886-7300

Mail order, retail
Established in 1988
KC, W

Knots & Treadles, owned by Peggy Cost-Peltz, has western Pennsylvania's largest selection of yarns (Berroco, Classic Elite, Harrisville Designs, Tahki Imports and others), as well as looms by Schacht, Leclerc, Norwood, Tools of the Trade, Harrisville Designs, Cranbrook, Glimåkra and Beka. Also offered are books, dyes, "ewesful gifts" (mugs, stickers, T-shirts), fabrics and more.

Knots & Treadles has a VHS videotape rental library; write or call for information.

Send three first-class postage stamps for a current catalog. Swatches of "sheep print" fabrics are $3.00.

Knots & Treadles

101 E. Pittsburgh Street
Delmont, PA 15626
(412) 468-4265

Mail order, retail
Established in 1980
KC, W

Kruh Knits is a single-source supplier for a huge assortment of machine-knitting products. The 130-page catalog features over 2,000 items including machines, books, accessories and yarns. Knitting machines include those by Brother, Knitking, Passap, Studio, Singer, Superba, Toyota and White. Other items include overlock machines by Brother, Singer and Juki; instructional videotapes; threads; yarn winders; and yarns by Angora Corporation of America, BMS, Classic Elite, Delaine, JaggerSpun, Millor, Plymouth, Tamm and more. A line of furniture for sergers and knitting machines is also offered.

Quantity discounts are given to knitting machine dealers; write for information.

Send $2.00 for a current catalog.

Kruh Knits

P.O. Box 1587
Avon, CT 06001
(203) 674-1043

Mail order
Established in 1983
KC

La Lana Wools, owned by Luisa Gelenter, offers a beautiful assortment of handspun and plant-dyed yarns of wools, silks, mohairs, exotic fibers and mohair blends. Carded blends are also available for spinning and felting.

Ms. Gelenter offers custom knitting and rug weaving, as well as spinning and dyeing classes at the retail location.

Send $12.00 for a complete set of yarn samples and prices.

La Lana Wools

P.O. Box 2461
Taos, NM 87571
(505) 758-9631

Mail order, retail, manufacturer
Established in 1974
KC, SP, W

La Pajarosa

2010 Pleasant Valley Road
Aptos, CA 95003
(408) 724-2044

Mail order
Established in 1970
SP

La Pajarosa offers long-stapled, lustrous, clean fleeces for sale.

Send a SASE for a current price list.

The Lacemaker

(Formerly Frivolité)
23732-G Bothell Highway S.E.
Bothell, WA 98021
(206) 486-0940

Mail order, retail
Established in 1983
LC

The Lacemaker, owned by Alison Addicks, offers supplies and tools for lacemaking and other needle arts. These include various pillows, a lacemaker's beginner kit, conservation supplies, prickers, bobbin winders, tatting shuttles, needle tatting kits, Battenberg and bobbin lace patterns, Fresia linen threads from Belgium, Bockens linen thread from Sweden, a large number of silk and cotton threads, linen fabrics, bobbins and books on lacemaking, tatting, knitting and crochet.

Send $2.00 for a current catalog.

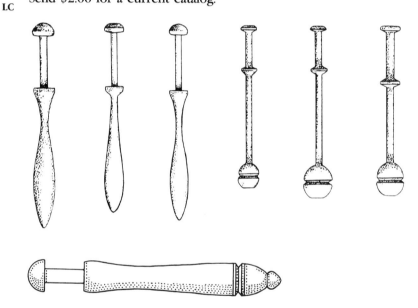

An assortment of lacemaking bobbins available from The Lacemaker

Laces & Lacemaking carries a large selection of supplies, lace tapes and patterns for making Battenberg and princess lace. Other items carried by this company include bobbins, pillows, 100% cotton threads, pillow stands, bobbin winders, pins, crochet hooks, fabrics, linen threads and instructional videos on lacemaking.

Laces & Lacemaking publishes *Lace Crafts Quarterly* (see the listing on p. 207).

Send a large SASE with two first-class postage stamps for a current catalog.

Laces & Lacemaking

3201 E. Lakeshore Drive
Tallahassee, FL 32312
(904) 385-5093 or 386-1159

Mail order, manufacturer
Established in 1984
LC

LACIS, owned by Jules and Kaethe Kliot, is a complete textile-arts center specializing in antique lace and textiles, as well as the tools, equipment and services geared to the lesser-known fiber arts like tatting. Lacemaking supplies include a large line of threads (cotton, silk, linen and metallic), lace pins, bobbin lace kits, bobbins, pillows and a variety of tools. Other tools and supplies are available for making Battenberg, point, filet and Tenerife laces and nettings. In addition, LACIS carries tatting, knitting, crochet, embroidery, smocking, rug-making and weaving supplies, including the Kliot tapestry and bow looms. An extensive booklist includes volumes on the history and identification of lace, needlework and lace techniques and the conservation of textiles.

Send $1.00 for a current catalog.

LACIS

2982 Adeline Street
Berkeley, CA 94703
(415) 843-7178

Mail order, retail, manufacturer, distributor
Established in 1965
KC, LC, R, ST, W

What is Battenberg lace?

Battenberg lace is a simple technique that forms an open-lace fabric by using only a needle and thread and variations of the buttonhole stitch. When these stitch-es are used with a premanufactured tape that outlines the design, the resulting fabric is referred to as Battenberg lace.

—Courtesy of the LACIS catalog

Laines Anny Blatt USA offers an extensive line of beautiful yarns in a large range of colors. The yarns are predominantly blends, but include some 100% cottons, wools, angoras, alpacas, silks and polyesters. The company also supplies unusual yarns made from beaver fur, as well as yarns with blends of feathers, beads and various fibers.

Interested resellers should write or call for more information.

Laines Anny Blatt USA, Inc.

24770 Crestview Court
Farmington Hills, MI 48331
(313) 474-2942

Manufacturer
Established in 1977
KC, W

Lanas Margarita specializes in mohairs and novelty yarns from Spain on cones or in balls.

Send for a current price list.

Lanas Margarita, Inc.

P.O. Box R
Island Heights, NJ 08732
(201) 929-3232

Mail order, manufacturer
Established in 1978
KC, W

Las Manos

P.O. Box 515
Lower Lake, CA 95457
(707) 994-0461

Mail order, manufacturer
Established in 1982
KC, W

Las Manos supplies an assortment of yarns for weaving, knitting and crochet.

Quantity discounts are given to individuals; write for details.

Send $2.00 for a current catalog.

Lauralyn Wool Farm

Sandy Branch Road
Bakersville, NC 28705
(704) 688-2317

Mail order, manufacturer
Established in 1985
SP

Mickey and Pete Bickett, owners of Lauralyn Wool Farm, offer clean, well-skirted prime fleeces for hand spinning.

Spinning groups are welcome at the farm for tours and hands-on selection of fleeces.

Write or call for further information and current prices.

Leclerc Corporation

R.R. #1, Box 356 A
Champlain, NY 12919
(518) 561-7900

Manufacturer
Established in 1876
W

The Leclerc Corporation, a family-owned company, has been manufacturing looms and weaving equipment for over 112 years and has earned a well-deserved reputation for high-quality items. The company offers a complete line of looms in all sizes, from their 15¾-in. Dorothy table loom to their 120-in. Kebec II 4-harness loom. Other available items include dobby-head mechanisms and multiple-shuttle beater assemblies; Gobelin tapestry looms in weaving widths of 45 in., 60 in. and 80 in.; benches; swifts; bobbin winders; cone holders; tension boxes; sectional warp beams; combs; bobbins; shuttles and more.

Leclerc sells directly to dealers only. Others should write for the address of the nearest mail-order outlet, and interested retail sellers should write for wholesale information.

Send for a free catalog.

Livingston's

14799 E. Augusta Drive
Augusta, MI 49012

Mail order
Established in 1972
SP

Marilyn Livingston specializes in the sale of angora wools and several wool blends for hand spinners.

Send $1.00 for current prices and fiber samples.

Loomcraft

P.O. Box 65
Littleton, CO 80160
(303) 798-6111

Mail order, manufacturer
Established in 1970
W

John and Virginia Post, owners of Loomcraft, offer 4-harness, 6-harness and 8-harness looms in 30-in., 40-in. and 45-in. weaving widths. The looms are built from either maple, cherry or walnut, with an exclusive optional double-warp beam feature that allows the weaver to control warp tension by sensitive hand levers. Loomcraft also offers a weaver's bench with a tilting, rocking or level seat in 25-in. and 26-in. heights.

A free brochure and ordering information is available.

The Looms specializes in complex weaving equipment and serves as a dealer for AVL, Leclerc, Harrisville Designs and Glimåkra looms. The company also carries unusual tools for weavers such as end-feed shuttles, nylon maillons, automatic denters, raddles, loom sleyers, easy leases, warp menders and more.

The Looms sponsors a number of workshops and an annual conference on complex-weave structures.

Send for a free brochure and booklist.

The Looms

P.O. Box 61
Mineral Point, WI 53565
(608) 987-2277

Mail order, retail, school
Established in 1965
W

Louët Sales is the North American distributor for all Louët products, which are made in the Netherlands. The company manufactures a number of looms, spinning wheels and other weaving and spinning supplies, including skein winders, spindles, bobbins, and drum and hand carders.

Qualified resellers should write for more information. Others may send for a list of local Louët dealers.

Send $1.00 for a current catalog.

Louët Sales

Box 70
Carleton Place, ON K7C 3P3
Canada
(613) 257-5793

Manufacturer
Established in 1981
SP, W

The Louët gear-driven and maintenance-free drum carder

The Mannings Creative Crafts

P.O. Box 687
East Berlin, PA 17316
(717) 624-2223

Mail order, retail, school
Established in 1960
SP, W

The Mannings Creative Crafts offers a large number of weaving and spinning supplies, including yarns, looms, spinning wheels and accessories, books and spinning fibers. Natural dyes, mordants and synthetic dyes are also available.

The Mannings teaches weaving and spinning on a year-round basis and gives spinning workshops and seminars in June and October (see the listing on p. 179). The store also sponsors an annual hand-weavers show and exhibit in April through the beginning of May.

Send $1.00 for a complete catalog.

Maple Ridge Sheep Farm

R.F.D
Roxbury, VT 05669
(802) 728-3081

Mail order
Established in 1980
KC, SP, W

The Maple Ridge Sheep Farm, owned and operated by Tut and Linda Doane, is a supplier for premium-quality natural-color Shetland and Romney wools for hand spinners. These are offered in white, gray, black, eesit and moorit shades. Handspun natural-color yarns are also available.

The Doanes have more than 100 of the first Shetland sheep in the U.S. and offer pelts and breeding stock.

Send $2.00 for yarn and fiber samples and current prices.

A Shetland sheep from the flock of Maple Ridge Sheep Farm

Maple Springs Farm, owned by Robert and Sandra Rego, is a source for various sizes of wool battings, which can be used in quilts and comforters. Sheepskin pelts are also available.

The Regos offer a recarding service for wool battings from old quilts or comforters; write or call for details.

Send $1.50 for a current catalog and a brochure that lists helpful hints for working with wool batting.

Maple Springs Farm

1828 Highway PB, Dept. W
Verona, WI 53593
(608) 845-9482

Mail order, retail
Established in 1982
SP

Margaret Perl offers a line of handspun and hand-dyed yarns of worsted-weight wools for knitting, weaving or crochet. The yarns are available in six naturals, 21 beautiful hand-dyed colors and four hand-painted shades. Ms. Perl also offers various knitting kits for hats, mittens, vests and sweaters.

Send for a free brochure; complete yarn samples are $2.00.

Margaret Perl Yarns

Box 21F, Big Laurel Road
Sias, WV 25563
(304) 778-3772

Mail order
Established in 1977
KC, W

Madalen A. Bertolini, owner of The Mariposa Tree, carries a wide assortment of supplies for knitting, crochet, weaving and spinning. Yarns from Classic Elite and a variety of specialty fibers for spinning are listed, among them, cashmere/silk top, mohair, alpaca, merino, angora, flax rovings, cotton sliver and camel down top. Silk fibers, blends and yarns are also offered including combed silks in brick form, mawata squares and caps, thrown silk waste, blended rovings in lamb's wool and silk, carded rovings and a number of yarns. Ms. Bertolini even has a "reel-your-own-silk" kit that includes white *Bombyx mori* cocoons and complete instructions on how to reel the silk from the cocoons and make mawata flakes or caps from them.

Weaving and spinning equipment include looms and spinning wheels from Ashford, cherry-wood tapestry looms, kits and equipment, Clemes & Clemes carders (wool and cotton) and other accessories. The Classic Elite pattern collection is offered, along with Brittany knitting needles and crochet hooks, the Knitter's Rule®, yarn ball winders, books and Cushing dyes. Many natural dyes and mordants are listed in the catalog, as well as various potpourri mixtures.

Send $1.50 for a complete catalog and a sample of Ms. Bertolini's wonderful lavender petals.

The Mariposa Tree, Inc.

P.O. Box 040336
Staten Island, NY 10304-0006

Mail order
Established in 1982
KC, SP, W

Marr Haven

772 39th Street
Allegan, MI 49010
(616) 673-8800

Mail order, manufacturer
Established in 1984
KC, W

Marr Haven, owned by Barbara and Gene Marr, claims to supply the "only American wool yarn made of 100% fine Rambouillet wool, with no blends of coarse or medium-grade wools." These yarns are available in worsted or sport weights in eight colors on cones or in skeins.

The Marrs' farm is open to the public on the first Saturday in October. The farm animals are on display, and demonstrations are given on sheep shearing, skirting of fleeces and hand and machine knitting.

Send a SASE for a current price list.

From the Marr Haven catalog

Martha Hall

46 Main Street
Yarmouth, ME 04096
(207) 846-9746

Mail order, retail
Established in 1978
KC

Martha Hall carries a wide assortment of yarns for knitting including natural fiber yarns from Maine, Maritime wools and exotics of cashmere, silk, alpaca and mohair. Many knitting kits are available for sweaters, vests, cardigans, hats and mittens. Miscellaneous supplies include needles, bags, buttons (including adorable ceramic animal buttons), needlecases and mothproof sachets. A large selection of books on knitting, needlepoint, weaving and spinning are also listed, as well as videotapes by Elizabeth Zimmermann.

Send $2.00 for a full-color catalog.

Mary Lue's Knitting World

101 W. Broadway
St. Peter, MN 56082
(507) 931-3702 (ext. 30)

Mail order, retail
Established in 1965
KC, W

Mary Lue's Knitting World is a good source for coned yarns to use with knitting machines, as well as other yarns for weaving and tapestry. Mary Lue's is also an authorized sales outlet and warranty service center for Brother knitting machines.

Quantity discounts are given; write for more information.

Send $2.00 for a current catalog and yarn sample cards.

McFarland Custom Carding

N3967 N. O'Connor Road
Columbus, WI 53925
(414) MA-FIBER

Mail order, retail
Established in 1983
SP, W

In addition to custom carding services, Susan McFarland offers spinning wools from Romney, Lincoln and Border Leicester sheep, as well as spinning wheels from Schacht, Louët and Haldane. Ms. McFarland is a distributor for Haldane and Louët looms and Patrick Green carders. Many books are also available.

Send for a current price list and further information.

Melrose Yarn Company offers a large line of designer-style hand-knitting yarns to qualified retailers and yarn shops.

A yarn sample set is $25.00; write for more information.

Melrose Yarn Company

1305 Utica Avenue
Brooklyn, NY 11203
(718) 629-0200

Manufacturer
Established 1926
KC

The Mountain Loom Company, owned by Larry and Sheila Sutherland, offers a number of good-quality, inexpensive table and floor looms, including the pique loom in various sizes with double-warp beams and counterbalance and countermarche looms in 36-in. and 45-in. weaving widths. All looms are made of maple with an oiled finish and are 100% guaranteed. The company also offers a variety of loom stands and weaving accessories.

Send for a free loom catalog.

Mountain Loom Company, Ltd.

P.O. Box 182
Curlew, WA 99118
(604) 446-2509

Mail order, manufacturer
Established in 1986
W

Mudra offers an assortment of supplies for weaving and spinning, including looms by Harrisville Designs, Beka, Dorset and Louët, as well as spinning wheels and accessories by Louët. Spinning fibers include combed tussah silks and caps, *Bombyx mori* caps, New Zealand wools and combed flax tops. Yarns are available from such suppliers as Brown Sheep Company, Harrisville Designs, Henry's Attic, Ironstone, Lily, Scott's, Silk City Fibers and Tahki Imports. A large number of books on spinning and weaving are also available.

A 10% discount is given on orders over $100.00; write for details.

Send $1.00 for a current catalog.

Mudra

219 W. Gurley Street
Prescott, AZ 86301
(602) 778-5947

Mail order, retail
Established in 1982
SP, W

Nancy Ellison Roberts works at her spinning wheel.

Nancy Ellison Roberts offers supplies for weaving, spinning and felting, including the entire line of spinning wheels, looms and accessories from Louët, Gaywool dyes from Australia and natural-colored wools. Ms. Roberts also produces a number of handspun yarns from her flock of Angora goats and Columbia, Scottish blackface, Lincoln and Lincoln crossbred sheep.

Send $2.00 for a current price list and catalog.

Nancy Ellison Roberts

Box 325
Lake City, MN 55041
(612) 345-5241

Mail order, retail
Established in 1978
SP, W

Natural Fiber Nook

R.R. 1, Box 55
Primghar, IA 51245
(712) 757-3875

Mail order, retail
Established in 1982
KC, SP, W

Sheryl Wilson, owner of the Natural Fiber Nook, sells clean Corriedale wool and angora fibers from her flock of sheep and Angora rabbits. Ms. Wilson is also a dealer for Beka, Harrisville Designs, Louët, Schacht and Tools of the Trade looms, as well as Ashford, Louët and Schacht spinning wheels. The Nook also stocks a number of yarns from Brown Sheep Company, Harrisville Designs, Schoolhouse Yarns, Edgemont, Crystal Palace, Chanteleine, Grandor and others.

A 10% discount is given on orders over $100.00; write or call for details.

Send $2.00 for a current catalog (applied to the first order).

Sheryl Wilson in her shop, the Natural Fiber Nook

The Norrises of Storrs

52 Willowbrook Road
Storrs, CT 06268
(203) 429-2986 or 536-3945

Mail order, manufacturer
Established in 1975
W

The Norrises of Storrs make looms patterned after the uniquely designed Rollo Purrington loom. These include folding floor looms in 20-in., 26-in. and 32-in. weaving widths. Table looms in 14-in. weaving widths with 4, 8 or 12 harnesses or 18-in. weaving widths with 4, 8, 12, or 16 harnesses are also available. The Norrises also manufacture a unique 10-in. Sampler loom that is identical to larger table looms except for the weaving width. Ideal for testing weaves or to take to workshops, the Sampler loom comes in 4-harness, 6-harness and 8-harness models. All looms are individually made from select hardwoods (maple, cherry and walnut) and are signed by the maker.

The Norrises offer a free bed-and-breakfast to those who pick up loom orders at their Studio.

Send a SASE for a free brochure.

A 16-harness table loom with an 18-in. width and optional holding legs, from The Norrises of Storrs

Norsk Fjord Fiber, owned by Noel A. Thurner, specializes in unique spinning fibers from Scandinavia—wools from the primitive breeds of sheep indigenous to these countries. Ms. Thurner is now the sole importer of Norwegian Spelsau and Swedish Gotland wools (raw fleeces, washed batts and rovings), 100% Spelsau Norsk Kunstvevgarn yarns, NOVI knitting needles and government-graded Spelsau and Gotland sheepskins.

Various discounts are given; write for further details.

Send $1.00 for a complete catalog.

Norsk Fjord Fiber

Route 2, Box 152
Lexington, GA 30648
(404) 743-5120

Mail order
Established in 1985
KC, SP, W

Valuable Animals

In early colonial days, it was illegal to kill sheep for food. The animals were needed too badly to produce offspring and wool for clothing. —Courtesy of the Wool Education Center, Denver, Colorado

Martin and Cynthia Blumenthal, owners of Northwest Looms, make the Pioneer model table loom in four different models—the 10-in. Sampler, the 15-in. Designer, the 20-in. Craftsman and the 25-in. Super. All looms are available with 2, 4 or 8 harnesses. These unique hardwood looms have an open reed and open top heddle system that allows for quick and easy warping right on the loom. The loom frame also comes with front and rear extenders that enable it to hold a warp of up to 84 in. If a longer warp is desired, a Pioneer warping attachment is available, permitting continuous-thread warping of up to 9 yd. directly on the loom.

Send for a free brochure.

Northwest Looms

P.O. Box 78583
Seattle, WA 98178
(206) 772-1793

Mail order, manufacturer
Established in 1967
W

The Pioneer loom by Northwest Looms

Norwood Looms, Inc.

P.O. Box 167
Fremont, MI 49412
(616) 924-3901

Mail order, manufacturer
Established in 1947
W

Norwood Looms offers a selection of beautiful folding floor looms hand-made from clear northern cherry or hard rock maple. These looms are available in weaving widths of 30 in., 40 in. and 50 in. with 8 harnesses, or in 22-in., 30-in., 40-in. and 50-in. weaving widths with 4 harnesses. A lightweight folding loom is available with 4 harnesses and a 16-in. weaving width, and a workshop model is available with 4 harnesses and a 22-in. width. Norwood Loom accessories include extra warp beams, spool racks in two sizes, workbox benches, tool shelves, shuttles, bobbin winders, warping boards, bobbins and heddles. Norwood also manufactures Cranbrook countermarche looms in weaving widths of 46 in., 62 in., 73 in. and 97 in. in 4-harness or 8- harness models. A Model 120 Cranbrook loom with a 10-ft. weaving width is available by special order.

Send $1.00 for a current catalog.

The Norwood 8-harness loom

Oak Grove

Oak Grove, owned by Linda Mac-Millan, represents a number of New England farms (including its own) with products ranging from raw fleece and handspun yarns to knitted garments. All of the yarns are handspun and hand-dyed by local artists. A small sampling of the available yarns includes Oak Grove Farms yarns of angora/merino blends, 100% angoras and 100% merinos dyed to match. Penfrydd wool yarns include hand-dyed 100% wools and mohair/wool blends in a full range of colors. Bonnie Harris handspun yarns are unusual blends of natural wools and colors in a one-ply novelty yarn.

Custom-dyed handspun or mill-spun yarns from farm flocks are also available.

Send for free information; complete yarn sample cards are $10.00.

P.O. Box 531
Putney, VT 05346
(802) 387-5205

Mail order, retail
Established in 1987
KC, SP, W

Linda MacMillan of Oak Grove at her spinning wheel

Obadiah Tharp Products

Obadiah Tharp Products, now owned by Don McGill of Creek Water Wool Works (see the listing on p. 19) supplies the "world's finest" non-petroleum, water-soluble carding and spinning oil. Also available from Obadiah Tharp is the "Lexicon & Syllabus on The Procurement of Suitable Fleece for the Endeavoring Spinner" by Katy Turner.

Discounts are given to retail shops and custom carders; write for information.

(Creek Water Wool Works)
P.O. Box 454
Salem, OR 97308
(503) 585-3302

Mail order, manufacturer
SP

Old Orchard Farm

Mary Jane Coble of Old Orchard Farm specializes in a large variety of carded rovings for spinners in many blends and different colors featuring Michigan grown fibers.

Ms. Coble also does custom spinning; write or call for details.

Write for current prices and further information.

1815 N. Steinbach
Dexter, MI 48130
(313) 426-3342

Mail order, manufacturer
Established in 1980
SP

O'Neill Stock Ranch

Route 1, Box 179
Rice, WA 99167
(509) 738-6310

Mail order, manufacturer
Established in 1983
R, SP, W

Julie O'Neill, owner of the O'Neill Stock Ranch, raises karakul sheep in colors ranging from black to grey, occasionally creamy beige, grey-brown or white. Karakul fleece is long, lustrous and very strong. The adult karakul is double-coated with a woolly undercoat and a hairy overcoat. Yarns made from these fleeces are usually classified as "rug weight" and are excellent for blankets, rugs, upholstery fabrics and heavy garments. Fleeces are usually available in the spring.

A 10% discount is given on orders of 10 lb. of fleece or more.

Send a SASE for details and current prices; the minimum order is one fleece.

On the Mountain

Route 1, Box 76
Shady Valley, TN 37688
(615) 739-5077

Mail order
Established in 1978
SP

On the Mountain is a home-based, family business managed by Todd V. Eastin. Mr. Eastin raises Angora goats and provides high-quality mohair fleece for hand spinners. The fleeces are offered in the grease, washed or as rovings from adults, yearlings or kids.

Some discounts are given; write for details.

Send $2.00 for a current catalog and samples.

Oomingmak, Musk Ox Producers' Co-op

604 H Street
Anchorage, AK 99501
(907) 272-9225

Mail order, retail
Established in 1969
SP

Sigrun Robertson, manager of Oomingmak, offers qiviut fibers from the domestic musk-ox. These fibers are extremely warm, soft and light, and do not shrink when washed.

The co-op also distributes handknit items by Eskimo women; check the free catalog for details.

A musk-ox, in the natural history collection of the British Museum
(from The Bettman Archive)

Karen D. Wilts, owner of Oregon Romney Wools, offers a large number of Romney wools, wool blends and yarns from her award-winning flock of Romney sheep, as well as fleece from other breeders (including Shetland, merino/Border Leicester, Sharlea, American Cormo, Jacob, and Icelandic wools). Ms. Wilts also offers an extensive selection of carded and dyed silks, angoras, mohairs and lamb's wool blends. Handspun yarns are available in five different weights and in an array of beautiful colors. Luxury spinning fibers include cashmere, cashgora, llama, alpaca/tussah silk blends, camel down, ramie and yak. Ms. Wilts also distributes Louët spinning equipment, Penny Straker and QuickKnit knitting patterns, knitting and crochet needles and accessories, and a line of unique gifts for fiber artists.

Various discounts are given; write for information.

Send $2.00 for a catalog or $4.00 for a catalog and set of yarn sample cards.

Oregon Romney Wools

1780 Cleveland Hill Road
Roseburg, OR 97470
(503) 673-7913

Mail order, manufacturer
Established in 1982
KC, SP, W

The Oriental Rug Company offers the 2-harness Orco loom with a 36-in. weaving width and the Orco 4-harness loom with a 36-in. weaving width. Also available is the Peacock table loom with a 12-in. weaving width. These looms come fully assembled, warped and ready to weave. A line of yarns, rug fillers, rags, carpet warps, shuttles, bobbins and other accessories is also available.

Send for a free price list.

The Oriental Rug Company

P.O. Box 917
Lima, OH 45802
(419) 225-6731

Mail order, retail
Established in 1923
R, W

Myal Griffin, of the Otter Creek Store

Myal Griffin, owner of The Otter Creek Store, specializes in designing custom handspun yarns. She currently spins over 100 lb. of yarn per year (mostly bulky-weight yarns for designers of knitted coats and jackets). She also offers various yarns from suppliers such as Aarlan, Wilde Yarns, Classic Elite and Rainbow Mills, as well as mill ends. Spinning fibers are also available and include wools, angoras and silks.

For custom yarns, send a description of the yarn (or color) needed, an ounce of your fibers and $5.00. Ms. Griffin will send back three yarn samples and a cost estimate for spinning the yarns.

Send $2.00 for a current catalog and mill-end samples.

The Otter Creek Store

106 S. Diamond Street
Mercer, PA 16137
(412) 662-2830

Mail order, retail
Established in 1980
KC, SP, W

Partridge Creek Farms

R.R. 2, Box 38
Eagle Bend, MN 56446
(218) 738-4341

Mail order
Established in 1984
SP

Partridge Creek Farms, owned by Larry and Clara Moyle, specializes in wools for hand spinners from their flock of black and white sheep. They also raise Angora goats and offer mohair in a large range of colors.

Some quantity discounts are given; write or call for details.

Send $1.50 for a price list and wool samples.

Passap Knitting Machines

271 W. 2950 S.
Salt Lake City, UT 84115
(801) 485-2777

Manufacturer, wholesale only
Established in 1939
KC

Passap Knitting Machines offers the Passap Electronic 6000 knitting machine, the Goldy®, the Monomatic 20 and a variety of modular features that can be added to the machines.

Passap only sells to authorized dealers. Store owners and other retailers should contact Peter Foss for additional information.

Patrick Green Carders Ltd.

48793 Chilliwack Lake Road
Sardis, BC V2R 2P1
Canada
(604) 858-6020

Mail order, manufacturer
Established in 1974
SP

Patrick Green Carders, owned by the husband-and-wife team of Patrick Green and Paula Simmons, designs, manufactures and sells a variety of fiber-processing equipment. This includes the Paula's Picker wool picker, the Cottage Industry carding machine and Paula's Rover, intended for hand spinners as cottage-industry tools. Drum carders are available in three different sizes, as well as hand carders, pickers, felting brushes and carding cloth fillet.

All of Paula Simmons' books are available, autographed, from the author.

Send for a free catalog and price list.

Paula Simmons with a wool batt made on the Cottage Industry Carder (left), and with Paula's Picker for teasing wool (right), both from Patrick Green Carders

Linda Skolnik, owner of Patternworks, offers a wide range of hard-to-find supplies for knitters, including circular needles, European Quick-Knit needles, French RCN color-coded needles, needle/hooks for picking up stitches, suede leather mitten palms and a knitting calculator wheel. Also available is the Bond knitting frame and accessories.

Send for a free catalog.

Patternworks, Inc.

P.O. Box 1690
Poughkeepsie, NY 12601
(914) 454-5648

Mail order, manufacturer
Established in 1979
KC

Peacock Alley offers an extensive collection of originally designed needle-point canvases and kits. All designs are hand-painted on single-mesh, white imported canvas. Each kit includes Paternayan Persian wool yarns, a needle and full instructions. The wool can be ordered in nonstock colors for an additional fee.

Peacock Alley specializes in custom designing. Write or call for a price estimate.

Send $2.00 for a current full-color catalog.

Peacock Alley

650 Croswell, S.E.
Grand Rapids, MI 49506
(616) 454-9898

Mail order, retail, manufacturer
Established in 1966
ST

The Pendleton Shop, owned by Mary Pendleton carries a full line of weaving and spinning supplies, including a number of Navajo rug-weaving supplies and looms by Pendleton, Schacht, Norwood, Glimåkra, Brittany and Leclerc. Spinning wheels from Ashford, Clemes & Clemes and Louët are distributed by this source, and spinning fibers, yarns, weaving and spinning accessories and books are also offered. Ms. Pendleton is the owner of the Pendleton Fabric Craft School (see the listing on p. 180).

Quantity discounts are given with a minimum order of $125.00; write for further information.

Send $1.00 for a current catalog and price list.

The Pendleton Shop

P.O. Box 233
Sedona, AZ 86336
(602) 282-3671

Mail order, retail
Established in 1948
SP, W

Dempsy and Brenda Perkins, owners of Perkins Farm, offer prime hand spinner's fleeces and pure white wool roving from their flock of Louisiana native sheep crossed with Perendale, North Country Cheviot and Border Leicester x Finn rams. Also available are a number of handcrafted items, including a Yarnmaster spinning wheel, a swift with grooved slats, a warping mill, a loom bench, a hand-turned bobbin winder, boat and rag shuttles, drop spindles and an Early American 4-harness loom. All items are made from select hardwoods with hand-rubbed natural oil finishes.

Perkins Farm sponsors an annual Wool Days open house each April, when the farms' sheep are sheared and Mr. Perkins's woodshop is open to visitors.

Send for a free price list and information on Wool Days.

Perkins Farm

P.O. Box 1
Reeves, LA 70658
(318) 666-2252

Mail order
Established in 1976
SP, W

Phildar USA

6110 Northbelt Parkway
Norcross, GA 30071
(404) 448-7511

Manufacturer
Established 1978
KC

Interested shop owners and qualified professionals should contact Marc Ducloz, president of Phildar USA, for more information.

The Pitman

4868 Rhoads Avenue
Santa Barbara, CA 93111
(805) 964-7457

Mail order, retail, manufacturer
Established in 1971
SP

Edith Ogella, owner of The Pitman, offers various fibers and fiber blends for spinning. The fibers include wools, mohair, dog hair, silks, goat hair, cashmere, alpaca, camel, silk, flax and cotton. Blends of mohair/wool, mohair/dog, cotton/silk and others are available.

Ms. Ogella specializes in custom spinning of yarns and will also spin unusual animal fibers upon request.

Send $1.50 for fiber samples and a current price list.

PlumHill Farm

W9418 Woodside Road
Cambridge, WI 53523
(608) 423-4425

Mail order, manufacturer
Established in 1978
SP

Linda Ball, owner of PlumHill Farm, offers wool battings for spinning, quilts or comforters from her small flock of white and natural colored Suffolk and Finn x Columbia sheep.

Ms. Ball will recard older batts of 100% virgin wools.

Send $2.00 (refundable) for a price list and samples of batts.

Wool batts, available from PlumHill Farm

Plymouth Yarn Company, Inc.

P.O. Box 28
Bristol, PA 19007
(215) 788-0459

Mail order, manufacturer
Established in 1964
KC, ST, W

The Plymouth Yarn Company offers a wide variety of 100% alpaca yarns in many sizes and hundreds of colors. Also available are over 250 different colors of needlepoint yarns on cones or in skeins, as well as a wide selection of knitting yarns.

Retail shops and resellers should contact Richard W. Power, Jr., for more information.

Send $20.00 for a complete sample-card album.

Possum Valley Farm Weaver's Shop, owned by Jacqueline S. Moore, is an exclusive dealer for Leclerc looms and accessories and White-Superba knitting machines and accessories. The shop also carries Ashford, Wee Peggy and Louët spinning wheels and Clemes & Clemes, AVL and Glimåkra accessories. Spinning wools include Australian and New Zealand fleeces, Alaskan qiviut and domestic cottons. Yarns include imported mohair/silk blends, as well as yarns by Berroco, Chester Farms, Christopher Farms, Condon, Fort Crailo, Harrisville Designs, Henry's Attic, Oregon Worsted, Tahki Imports, Unger, Fawcett and G. Whitaker. Books and instructional videotapes are also available.

Mrs. Moore also teaches classes in spinning, weaving, quilting and knitting.

Send a SASE for a current price list.

**Possum Valley Farm
Weaver's Shop**

Route 2
Martin, TN 38237
(901) 587-3489

Mail order

KC, SP,W

Pamela Bryan, owner of Pucker Brush Farm, is probably the largest producer of fleeces for hand spinning in the Appalachian chain. She currently has over 400 animals and emphasizes softness, luster, color variation and ease of processing in her wools. Spinning fibers from Pucker Brush Farm include raw wools in various colors; dyed and uncarded wools; washed and carded wools; and raw, washed, dyed or carded mohair. Other available spinning fibers include flax, angoras, silks, llama and cotton. A line of handspun yarns is also available in natural or dyed wools, mohair, mohair and wool blends, wool and silk blends, brushed mohairs and other fibers. The farm also offers tanned skins from Karashire sheep. Custom washing, carding, dyeing and spinning of fibers are available.

Send for a free catalog; a yarn sample card is $2.00.

Pucker Brush Farm

R.D. #3, Box 130A
Shelocta, PA 15774
(412) 349-6623

Mail order, retail, manufacturer
Established in 1975

KC, SP, W

Dominique Jewett, owner of Rabbit Rendez-vous, offers beautiful angora fibers in rare colors from English and French Angora rabbits. She also offers custom carding services, angora blends, spinning instruction, seminars and rabbit stock.

Quantity discounts are given with a minimum order of $50.00.

Send $1.00 and a SASE for samples and a current price list.

Rabbit Rendez-vous

1253 Valley High Avenue
Thousand Oaks, CA 91362
(805) 497-7641

Mail order
Established 1980

SP

Rainbow Mills, owned by Stanley and Carole Klein, supplies a number of handspun and hand-dyed yarns for hand and machine knitting and weaving. These include silks, wool/mohair/rayon blends, cottons, cotton/rayon blends, exotics such as camel and cashmere, merino wools and others in an assortment of hand-dyed, space-dyed or spatter-painted yarns.

Wholesale inquiries are accepted on business letterhead with a resale number.

Send $28.00 for a complete set of samples and prices.

Rainbow Mills, Inc.

5539 Fair Oaks Street
Pittsburgh, PA 15217
(412) 422-7012

Mail order, manufacturer
Established in 1981

KC, W

Renaissance Yarns

P.O. Box 937
Norwalk, CT 06856
(203) 852-8823

Manufacturer
Established in 1985

KC, W

Renaissance Yarns, owned by James T. Whitin, is the sole importer for Swiss Froehlich Wolle yarns. Renaissance also offers their own line of 100% wool and cotton yarns and blends with natural fibers such as ramie, mohair, silk and cotton, as well as a two-ply worsted yarn made especially for knitting machines.

Qualified buyers should contact Mr. Whitin for more information.

Send $20.00 for a yarn sample set.

Terms of the Wool Trade

The R. H. Lindsay Company has provided a brief explanation of some of the everyday terms used by suppliers when referring to wools:

Scoured: Wool that has been washed commercially and from which most of the dirt, grease and vegetable matter has been removed.

Carded: Wool that has been put through a carding machine. A commercial carding machine is large, with several round drums. Each drum has many metal pins that grab the wool and "comb" it, aligning the fibers in a more-or-less parallel fashion.

Combed: Wool that has been combed after carding to clean it, extract the short fibers and align the remaining fibers even more.

Top: Wool that has been scoured, carded and then combed.

Sliver: One form in which carded wools can be delivered. Wool is drawn through a tube, which rolls the wool together and pulls it out a bit further, helping the fibers become more parallel.

Batts: Another form of carded wool, which is taken as it comes directly off the carding machine.

R. H. Lindsay Company

393 D Street
Boston, MA 02210
(617) 268-4620

Mail order, manufacturer
Established in 1936

SP

The R. H. Lindsay Company is a third-generation family-owned business specializing in wools and stocking over 8,000 lb. of varying types for prompt shipment. The company can supply at least nine different types of greasy-fleece wools—colored crossbred, Romney, Border Leicester, Perendale, Coopworth, Lincoln, British Jacob, Australian merino and skirted domestic fleeces. Romney/Perendale fleeces can be ordered in greasy and carded or scoured and carded forms. Other special-breed fleeces are available scoured and carded—Drysdale, Falkland/Malvinas 56s Top and merino. Romney/Perendale blends are available in 21 dyed, scoured and carded colors. Scoured New Zealand Romney fleece and Texas mohair top are available in naturals; the mohair is also offered in six different colors.

Quantity discounts are given on orders of 15 lb. or more.

Send $3.00 for a current catalog.

Rachel Brown, author of *The Weaving, Spinning and Dyeing Book* (Knopf, 1984), is the owner of Rio Grande Weaver's Supply. She carries over a dozen different types of yarns in more than 200 hand-dyed and natural-fleece colors. These yarns include wools and blends for apparel, rugs, tapestries and warps. The warp yarns include wools, cottons and linens. Acid dyes are offered for wools and silks in 20 different "Southwest colors," including turquoise, slate, indigo, mauve and rust. Natural dyes include brazilwood chips, cochineal, indigo, madder root, osage orange extract, fustic extract and logwood sawdust. Spinning equipment includes the Rio Grande wheel and others by Schacht, Ashford and Peacock. Looms include the Rio Grande loom (also available in kit form) and others by Glimåkra and Schacht. Other items include warping tools, weaving and spinning accessories, books, videos and notepaper.

Send $1.00 for a current catalog. Sample cards are $5.00 for apparel yarns, $3.00 for rug yarns, $3.00 for tapestry yarns and $2.00 for warp yarns.

Rio Grande Weaver's Supply

P.O. Box 2009
Taos, NM 87571
(505) 758-0433

Mail order, retail
Established in 1985
KC, R, SP, W

The River Farm, owned by Jerry and Priscilla Blosser-Rainey, is located on the bank of the Shenandoah River. The farm makes a perfect setting for the annual intensive-study sessions taught by Ms. Blosser-Rainey on beginning spinning, dyeing and using wool yarn. In addition to these classes, she also offers Fiber Weekends at the farm and shorter weaving and knitting workshops. The River Farm supplies clean colored and white fleeces from the large flock of Corriedale and Corriedale/Suffolk/Rambouillet sheep. Supplies offered through the extensive catalog include yarns and fibers; gifts; books; Ashford, Louët, Schacht and Country Craftsman spinning wheels; spinning and carding accessories; and Dorset, Schacht and Harrisville Design looms and accessories, Australian sheepcovers and sheep stock.

Discounts are given during the annual fleece sale at the Farm.

Send for a free catalog.

The River Farm

Route 1, Box 401
Timberville, VA 22853
(800) USA-WOOL
(703) 896-9931 in Virginia

Mail order, retail
Established in 1973
SP, W

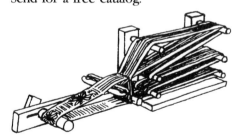 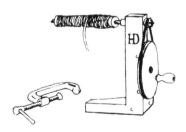

Some weaving looms and accessories available from The River Farm

Robin & Russ Handweavers

533 N. Adams Street
McMinnville, OR 97128
(503) 472-5760

Mail order, retail, manufacturer
Established in 1946
LC, SP, W

Robin & Russ Handweavers carries a large assortment of weaving, spinning and lacemaking supplies and equipment. Looms are available by Oregon Trail (manufactured by Robin & Russ), Norwood, Leclerc, Macomber and others. Yarns and threads in wools, cottons, linens, silks, metallics and other exotics are offered, as well as carded, dyed wool tops for spinning. Lacemaking supplies include pillows, prickers, bobbins and patterns. More than 500 books on all aspects of the fiber arts are listed in the company's extensive catalog.

Send for a free catalog and price list.

Robin's Bobbins & Other Things

Route 1, Box 1736
Mineral Bluff, GA 30559
(404) 374-6916

Mail order, retail
Established in 1978
LC

Robin S. Lewis, owner of Robin's Bobbins, offers an extensive line of supplies for lacemaking. These include pillows in various sizes and shapes, pillow stands, threads in linen, cotton and metallics, many styles of bobbins, tools, bobbin winders, pattern stock, pins and tatting shuttles. Also listed are patterns and books on lacemaking techniques, lace history and identification, crochet, embroidery and needlework, needle lace, smocking and tatting.

Discounts are given to teachers; write or call for details.

Send $1.00 for a current catalog and price list.

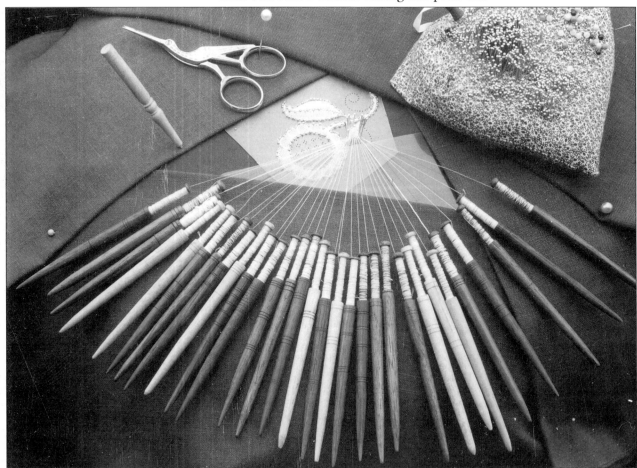

A Honiton bobbin-lace pillow in progress, from Robin's Bobbins

A punch needle for rugmaking, available from The Ruggery

The Ruggery offers an impressive number of supplies and patterns for punch-needle rugmaking. These include cotton backing fabrics in various sizes, Meriwell mothproofed rug yarns, Paternayan rug yarns in over 200 colors, Craftsman's dyes, Cushing Perfection dyes, the Craftsman's punch needle, Tru-Gyde® shuttle hookers, frames, fabric cutters and needles. A number of rug-hooking patterns and finished rugs designed by George Wells are included in the current catalog.

Several custom-design services are offered; check the catalog for details.

Send a business-sized envelope with $.45 postage for a catalog and price list.

The Ruggery

565 Cedar Swamp Road
Glen Head, NY 11545
(516) 676-2056

Mail order, retail, manufacturer
Established in 1921
R

Rumpelstiltskin, owned by Linda Urquhart, offers a variety of fiber supplies, including domestic and imported yarns, basketry supplies, looms, spinning wheels and knitting machines. Classes in the fiber arts are offered at the retail location.

No catalog is available at this time; write or call with specific requests.

Rumpelstiltskin

1021 R Street
Sacramento, CA 95814
(916) 442-9225

Mail order, retail
Established in 1973
KC, SP, W

St. Peter Woolen Mill is one of the few mills left in the country that will custom card your wool. The mill will also wash or recard wools and acrylics for spinning or quilt batting. St. Peter makes wool mattress pads, pillows and hand-tied comforters.

Send for a free brochure.

St. Peter Woolen Mill

101 W. Broadway
St. Peter, MN 56082
(507) 931-3734

Mail order, retail, manufacturer
Established in 1867
SP

Ruth Ohlsen, owner of the Salt Lake Weaver's Store, offers a complete inventory of weaving and spinning supplies and equipment. Classes are given in weaving, spinning, knitting and basketmaking.

Discounts are given to local guild members.

Send for a free catalog and price list.

Salt Lake Weaver's Store

1227 E. 3300 S.
Salt Lake City, UT 84106
(801) 486-1610

Mail order, retail
Established in 1987
SP, W

Ron and Teresa Parker, owners of Sammen Sheep Farm, supply heavily skirted, prime spinning wools from their sheep. They feature Sammen Selection silver and Sammen Selection black, which are very bright, lustrous and wavy Lincoln/Finn wools. The entire line of Schacht spinning equipment and accessories is also available.

Send a SASE and $1.00 for a current price list and wool samples.

Sammen Sheep Farm

Route 1, Box 153
Henning, MN 56551
(218) 583-2419

Mail order
Established in 1976
SP

San Francisco Fiber

3435 Army Street
San Francisco, CA 94110
(415) 821-2568

Mail order, retail
Established in 1980
SP, W

San Francisco Fiber, owned by Lou Grantham, offers a large number of supplies for weaving, spinning, dyeing and natural basketry. The selection includes yarns by Brown Sheep Company, Crystal Palace, Borgs and Lane Borgosesia; looms by Harrisville Designs, Leclerc, Schacht, Glimåkra and Ashford; and various spinning fibers such as New Zealand rovings, raw fleece, bleached flax and mohair.

San Francisco Fiber also sponsors a number of fiber-arts classes (see the listing on p. 181). Check the catalog for the schedule.

Send for a free newsletter and price list.

School Products Company, Inc.

1201 Broadway
New York, NY 10001
(212) 679-3516

Mail order, retail
Established in 1949
KC, SP, W

The School Products Company offers a variety of looms, yarns, equipment and accessories for hand weavers and spinners. Equipment includes the Dorothy table loom, Schacht looms and accessories, the Beka rigid-heddle loom, Leclerc floor looms and benches, Ashford spinning wheels, the Penguin spinning wheel, carders and hand spindles, a tapestry loom, beaters and combs. A large assortment of miscellaneous weaving and spinning tools and accessories include warping mills and boards, electric bobbin winders, bobbin racks, ball and cone winders, skein holders (umbrella swifts), shuttles, temples, reed and heddling hooks, shed sticks, warping paddles, reeds, pick-up sticks, heddles, raddles and sleying hooks. Yarns include a number of linen and cotton warp yarns, perle cottons, Shetland wools, handspun mohair, cotton/linen blends, waxed linens and others. Dylon dyes, instructional videotapes, Brother knitting machines and books are also listed.

Send $2.00 for a current catalog and price list.

A Schacht Spindle Company loom, available from School Products

Schoolhouse Press

6899 Cary Bluff
Pittsville, WI 54466
(715) 884-2799

Mail order, manufacturer
Established in 1959
KC

Schoolhouse Press, owned and operated by the mother-daughter team of Elizabeth Zimmerman and Meg Swansen, offers a variety of supplies, books and videotapes (see the listing on p. 190) for hand knitters. Supplies, tools and accessories include 16-in. and 24-in. circular needles in sizes 0 to 10.5, 11½-in. needles in sized 3 to 10, lace needles in sized 0000 to 0, large wool needles with blunt or sharp tips, knitting sticks, knitting belts and many knitting books. Schoolhouse Press specializes in Shetland wools and is one of the few suppliers in the U.S. of Shetland cobweb-weight wool. Other yarns include eight types of imported wools from Scotland, Iceland, England and Canada in hundreds of colors.

Schoolhouse Press produces Elizabeth Zimmerman's knitting videotapes, including a knitting-glossary video and a series of knitting-workshop tapes. The company also produces "Wool Gathering," a twice-yearly subscription newsletter published in March and September, which contains news of books and supplies, as well as full directions and illustrations for a knitting project of Elizabeth's and Meg's design. "Wool Gathering" is now available on videotape.

Send a SASE for a current price and book list. A complete yarn sample card is $2.00.

The Sensuous Fiber™

P.O. Box 44, Parkville Station
Brooklyn, NY 11204
(718) 236-4562

Mail order, manufacturer
Established in 1978
KC, SP, W

Arlene Mintzer, owner of The Sensuous Fiber™, offers an exclusive line of handspun "jeweled yarns." These yarns are one-of-a-kind skeins made with a combination of handspun and hand-dyed exotic fibers embellished with coral branches, fresh-water pearls, carnelian, agates or amethyst stones. The yarns themselves are blends of alpaca, mohair, angoras or silks and have been featured in *New York* magazine, *Women's Wear Daily* and *W*. Ms. Mintzer also offers the yarns in a nonjeweled series, as well as the entire line of Takumi bamboo knitting needles and crochet hooks and a number of unusual tools for knitters, crocheters and needleworkers.

Send $2.00 for a current catalog; a sample of the jeweled yarns is an additional $2.00 (deductible from your first order); a complete sample card of the nonjeweled series is $9.50.

Shadeyside Farm

P.O. Box 48
Chenango Bridge, NY 13745
(607) 656-4737

Mail order, retail
Established in 1981
KC, SP, W

Nancy Morey and Rick Westerberg of Shadeyside Farm specialize in rainbow-dyed fibers, yarns and fleeces for hand spinning from their flock of Border Leicester, Lincoln and crossbred sheep. Other dyed fibers include blends and rovings from kid mohair, thrown waste silks, German angoras, alpacas and cottons. Undyed spinning fibers include wools, mohair in the grease, mohair top, cashgora top, alpaca top, carded cashmere, pima cotton, yak top, camel top, ramie top and many silks. Also listed in the current catalog are dyes and assists for dyeing protein fibers.

Send $5.00 for a complete Colorways Portfolio, which includes prices and samples of various fibers dyed in the Farm's stock colors.

Shannock Tapestry Looms

10402 N.W. 11th Avenue
Vancouver, WA 98685
(206) 573-7264

Mail order, manufacturer
Established in 1980
W

Laura and John Shannock, owners of Shannock Tapestry Looms, build "the strongest tapestry looms available anywhere." The loom frames are constructed of welded, square steel tubing, and the roller beams are designed to withstand 40 lb. of tension per inch of weaving width. The standard looms are available in two styles and four basic sizes—with weaving widths of 36 in., 48 in., 72 in. and 96 in. A new collapsible and portable frame loom is available with a maximum weaving size of 24 in. by 35 in. The Shannocks will custom-make larger high-warp tapestry looms in any size, including 12 ft. or more in width, with custom features such as automatic shedding systems and built-in beaters. Various weaving accessories are also included.

Quantity discounts are given on bobbin orders.

Send for a free brochure and current price list.

A 4-ft. wide tapestry loom (left) and an 8-ft. wide tapestry loom (above), from Shannock Tapestry Looms

Shepherds of Goose Pass

10341 Springport Road
Springport, MI 49284
(517) 531-3261

Mail order
Established in 1987
SP

Deborah and Philip Simon, the "shepherds of Goose Pass," offer top-quality, prize-winning spinning fleeces from clean white Corriedale and crossbred sheep, mohair (in the grease or washed) and blends in rovings and batts. The Simons specialize in cream and brown colors from their registered Tunis, Corriedale and karakul sheep and from their commercial Angora goats.

Various discounts are given; write for details.

Send a SASE for a free price list and flyer.

Ann L. Kreckel's Shuttle & Ewe Studio offers a large number of wools, cottons and exotic fibers for spinning. These include alpaca tops in black, brown or cream; angoras in agouti, beige, grey or white; camel down; cashgora top in white; cashmere in fawn; ginned cotton; pima sliver cotton; bleached or natural flax sliver; honey or white mohair top; ramie; silks in cultured noils, Bombyx or tussah top; various blends; and wool sliver in white, grey or brown/black. Sampler packs of various fibers are also available. The studio is an authorized distributor for Louët spinning equipment.

Ms. Kreckel offers custom handspun and/or dyed yarns and custom fiber blending; write or call for information.

Send a SASE for a free price list; request the Louët price sheet for spinning equipment.

Shuttle & Ewe Studio

P.O. Box 133
Webster, NY 14580
(716) 671-3793

Mail order, manufacturer
Established in 1983
SP

Sievers Looms, owned by Ann H. Young, offers a number of table and floor looms made from birch lumber harvested on Washington Island. These include 22-in. and 36-in., 4-harness folding floor looms; a 15-in., 4-harness table loom; a 10-in., 4-harness sampler-workshop loom; and an inkle loom. A number of weaving accessories are available, including hardwood shuttles, warping boards, weaving benches, reeds, bobbin and ball winders and a loom-accessory shelf. Sievers also has explicit, low-cost plans for those who want to build their own looms, quilting frames, loom benches, spinning wheels and accessories.

Many fiber-arts classes and workshops are available through the Sievers School of Fiber Arts (see the listing on p. 182).

Send $1.00 for a current catalog.

Sievers Looms

Jackson Harbor Road
Washington Island, WI 54246
(414) 847-2264

Mail order, retail, manufacturer, school
Established in 1973
SP, W

The Sievers folding floor loom

Sight/Feel Cards offers unique contoured, coded weaving cards or tablets. According to the manufacturer, the cards are the "first real advance in card weaving in 4,000 years." By changing traditional cards from straight edges to distinctive contoured edges (each edge is a different shape), the process of card weaving becomes much easier and faster.

Quantity discounts are given; write for details.

Write for a current price list and sample.

Sight/Feel (S/F) Cards

P.O. Box 176
Comptche, CA 95427
(707) 937-4298

Mail order, manufacturer
Established in 1982
W

Silk City Fibers

155 Oxford Street
Peterson, NJ 07522
(201) 942-1100

Mail order, distributor
Established in 1981
KC, W

Silk City Fibers offers a large number of color-coordinated yarns and fibers for weaving, crochet and hand and machine knitting, including silks and silk bouclés, silk ribbons, mohairs, novelty metallic yarns, alpacas and mohair/wool blends. Mokuba knitting tapes are also available in linen blends, cottons, synthetics and leathers.

Quantity discounts are given with a minimum order of $300.00; write for information.

Send $65.00 for a complete set of samples and a current price list.

The Silk Tree

(A division of Select Silks, Inc.)
Box 78
Whonnock, BC V0M 1S0
Canada
(604) 462-9707 or 687-SILK

Mail order
Established in 1979
KC, SP, W

The Silk Tree specializes in high-quality, undyed silk yarns and spinning fibers. Spinning fibers currently include cultivated silks, tussah fibers, noil fibers, tussah noil fibers, silk/cashmere blends, silk/linen blends, silk/wool blends and baby camel down/tussah blends. Yarns include cords, singles, bouclés, bourettes, noil flecks, silk/wool blends, tussahs, silk/linen blends, silk/viscose blends and lots more.

Quantity discounts from 10% to 20% are given; write for details.

Send $4.00 for a complete set of samples and price list.

Silver Cloud Farm

1690 Butler Creek Road
Ashland, OR 97520
(503) 482-5901

Mail order, manufacturer
Established in 1979
SP

Silver Cloud Farm, operated by Kent Erskine and Dona Zimmerman, offers top quality, heavily skirted, lustrous Romney fleeces and mohair. The wools are available in colors ranging from white and silver to black.

Breeding stock for top-quality wool and mohair production is also available.

Send for more information and current prices.

Silver Crown Farm

R.D. 1, Box 363
Chester, NJ 07930
(201) 879-2508

Mail order, manufacturer
Established in 1976
SP

Silver Crown Farm, owned by Barbara R. Wheeler, carries a variety of wools from Shetland, Jacob, Welsh and Orkney sheep. Also offered is a line of natural fibers, including alpaca tops, camel hair tops, linen sliver, mohair, qiviut, merino and silk tops. Imported wools include Jacobs, Welsh, Herdwick, Swaledale and Wenslydale.

Ms. Wheeler will also custom spin one-ply or two-ply yarns.

Send a large SASE for a current price list.

Sandra Bradshaw, of Sinkut Fibre Company

Sandra Bradshaw, owner of Sinkut Fibre Company, has developed a palette of beautiful hand-dyed, handspun yarns from Canadian and New Zealand wools, as well as many exotic fibers. Ms. Bradshaw's wool yarns are available in two weights in solids, blended hues and custom blends, whites and naturals. The exotic yarns include silks, dyed silks, camel, alpaca, wool/mohair blends or wool/silk blends. Metallics are formed by plying any of Sinkut's yarns with gold, silver or copper threads. Wool batts and rovings are available in white, naturals, solids, blended colors or layered batts. Exotic fibers include baby camel down, alpaca, white silk brick, tussah silk brick, white angora, mohair or silk/lamb's wool blends. A line of acid dyes for protein fibers is also listed.

Quantity discounts are given; write for details.

Send $3.00 for a complete set of yarn samples or $2.00 for fiber samples.

Sinkut Fibre Company

P.O. Box 1592
Vanderhoof, BC V0J 3A0
Canada
(604) 567-9383

Mail order
Established in 1985
KC, SP, W

Speed Stitch carries a large assortment of supplies for "sewing machine arts and crafts," including the Sulky® brand rayon threads in over 190 popular colors and 12 metallics. Ribbon Threads are available in 28 vibrant colors and 15 metallics. Also listed in the extensive Speed Stitch catalog are DMC machine embroidery threads, Kanagawa and Madeira metallic threads, Natesh® rayon embroidery threads, coned polyester threads, Battenberg lace tapes and more.

Send $3.00 for a catalog (refundable with your first order).

Speed Stitch

3113-D Broadpoint Drive
Harbor Heights, FL 33983
(813) 629-3199

Mail order, manufacturer
Established in 1979
LC, ST

Spin 'n Weave

3054 N. First Avenue
Tucson, AZ 85719
(602) 623-9787

Mail order, retail
Established in 1980
KC, SP, W

Spin 'n Weave offers a variety of natural fibers for spinning including cotton lint, pima cotton puni, Corriedale cross and New Zealand dyed and heathered Romney/Perendale fleeces, natural colored rovings, flax, llama, ramie, angora, camel down, mohair and many silks. The company sells spinning wheels by Ashford, Louët, Lendrum and Schacht Spindle Company, as well as a line of looms by Norwood, Cranbrook, Harrisville Designs, Leclerc, Schacht, Kyra and Beka. Spin 'n Weave also offers dyes, weaving and spinning accessories and a large number of national-brand natural-fiber yarns.

Various classes are also offered at the retail location.

Send a SASE for a current catalog and price list.

Spinner's Hill Shop

Lakeview Farm
R.D. #1, Box 118
Brackett Lake Road
Bainbridge, NY 13733
(607) 843-6267 or (607) 967-8325

Mail order, retail, manufacturer
Established in 1981
SP, W

The Spinner's Hill Shop, owned by Lisa Ann Merian, offers mohair for sale from her farm-raised Angora goats, as well as various spinning fleeces from Tunis, Dorset, Finn, Rambouillet, Corriedale and crossbred sheep. Other items include Euroflax in 31 colors, Createx liquid fiber-reactive dyes, dye plants and mordants, Louët spinning wheels and accessories, buttons, Glimåkra and Beka looms and accessories and much more.

A custom spinning, blending, carding and washing service is also available. Write or call for details.

Send $3.00 for a current catalog; $3.00 for samples.

Spring House Yarns

649 Wexford Bayne Road
Wexford, PA 15090
(412) 935-5266

Mail order, manufacturer
Established in 1985
KC, W

Catherine L. Thompson, of Spring House Yarns, offers a large collection of natural-colored and dyed handspun yarns in wools and exotic fibers in sport, worsteds and bulky weights. Over 100 shades are hand-dyed in the fleece before the carding and spinning process to ensure an even distribution of color throughout the fiber. Ms. Thompson also offers small sample skeins of each yarn.

Quantity discounts are given; write for details.

A catalog and price list is $1.50; check for prices of sample cards and sample skeins.

Steel Heddle Mfg. Company

P.O. Box 550
Greenville, GA 30222
(404) 672-4238

Mail order, manufacturer
Established in 1899
W

The Steel Heddle Mfg. Company is the world's largest manufacturer of precision equipment for the weaving industry. The company offers made-to-order reeds for hand weaving. The reeds are available in carbon, pitch-bound or stainless steel and can be made in heights up to 6 in. with 2 to 30 dents per inch. The Ultra pattern reed is also available and is made to the dent configuration of your choice with certain wires removed to provide space for large yarns or cords.

Send for a free brochure and ordering instructions.

Stonewood Farm & Fibers, owned by Sheila Clement, offers a beautiful color range of rainbow-dyed mohairs and mohair-blend fibers for hand spinning. Ms. Clement also produces angora fibers blended with silk, wool, mohair, alpaca, camel and other precious fibers. Fibers for felting include wool, mohair, rainbow-dyed wools and rainbow-dyed mohair.

All fibers are subject to seasonal availability.

Send a SASE with two first-class postage stamps and $3.00 for samples of fibers. (State your intended use for these so that Ms. Clement can send appropriate samples.)

Stonewood Farm & Fibers

Route 1, 202 Highway DD
Kewaskum, WI 53040
(414) 626-4650

Mail order, retail
Established in 1974
SP

Sue Drummond of Stony Lonesome Farm provides raw mohair fibers and Louët spinning and weaving equipment. She has self-published a book entitled *Angora Goats—The Northern Way*, which can be ordered directly from her.

Discounts are given on book orders of ten or more.

Write for more information.

Stony Lonesome Farm

1451 Sisson
Freeport, MI 49325
(616) 765-3056

Mail order, manufacturer
Established in 1980
SP, W

Susan Druding, owner of Straw into Gold, claims to be "a textile junkie who loves yarns and fibers." The company offers a large number of weaving and spinning supplies, including the entire line of Crystal Palace and Chanteleine yarns in silks and silk blends, cottons, linens, rayons and wools, as well as the entire line of Ashford products. Spinning fibers include Bombyx silk batts, noils, slivers, bricks and top; tussah silks; blended silks with rayon, linen or wool; and other fibers such as flax, ramie, camel down and yak hair top. (See their listing for books on p. 201)

Bulk discounts are given on some items; write for additional information.

Send a SASE with $.45 postage for a current catalog and price list.

Straw into Gold, Inc.

3006 San Pablo Avenue
Berkeley, CA 94702
(415) 548-5241

Mail order, manufacturer
Established in 1971
KC, SP, W

Studio 35, owned by Doris Walton, offers a number of hard-to-find supplies for needleworkers and knitters. These items include knitter's pins, blocking cloths, Japanese tacks, stitchery knives, needlepoint stitch-fixers, sterling silver knitting needles, hand-finished Appalachian black walnut knitting needles and crochet hooks, 22K gold-plated tapestry needles and solid 9K gold tapestry needles. Studio 35 also offers a number of books on knitting and other needle arts.

Send a large SASE for a current price list.

Studio 35

P.O. Box 1177
Brooklyn, NY 11202-0026
(718) 625-5661
(from 4:00 to 6:00 p.m.)

Mail order
Established in 1975
KC

Tahki Imports Ltd.

11 Graphic Place
Moonachie, NJ 07074
(201) 807-0070

Manufacturer
Established in 1970
KC, W

Tahki Imports, owned by Diane Friedman, offers 100% wool and cotton yarns and a full line of beautiful blends.

Interested shop owners should contact Ms. Friedman for more information.

The Tahki Imports logo

Tails & Yarns of Alaska

P.O. Box 41
Hope, Alaska 99605
(907) 782-3115

Mail order, manufacturer
Established in 1983
KC, SP, W

Tails & Yarns of Alaska, owned by Diane Olthuis, offers a variety of Alaskan fibers and yarns. Diane's own flock of Angora goats provide mohair fibers and yarns. Also offered is picked qiviut, qiviut and tussah-silk blends, handspun qiviut yarns, designer dog-hair yarn (one-third each dog hair, red mohair and black wool), mohair/moose-hair yarns, Russian trade beads from Kodiak Island, knitting patterns for qiviut and many other items.

Ms. Olthuis also offers a custom carding, spinning and knitting service.

Send a SASE for a current price list.

Talisman Clay & Fibre Company

1370 7th Avenue
Prince George, BC V2L 3P1
Canada
(604) 564-5244

Mail order, retail
Established in 1983
KC, SP, W

Talisman Clay & Fibre Company is a specialty yarn house that offers many yarns not commonly found elsewhere. These include a number of linens, heathers, tweeds, fine merinos, brushed wools, silk blends, rug yarns, cottolins, metallics, rayons and bouclés. Talisman also distributes Bramwell yarns for machine knitting, as well as a number of weaving and spinning supplies.

Send $1.00 for a current catalog.

Tatsy

P.O. Box 1401
Des Plaines, IL 60018

Mail order, manufacturer
Established in 1976
LC

Tatsy supplies threads, tools, kits and patterns for tatted lace. Some of these include contemporary shuttles for use with yarn or thread, mini hooks for joining, perle and crochet cottons in various colors, and original kits and patterns for holiday ornaments, tatted lace baskets and more.

Send $1.00 for a current catalog.

Texas Fibers

919 Lake Drive
Weatherford, TX 76086
(817) 598-0731

Mail order
Established in 1985
SP

Robin Cummings, owner of Texas Fibers, carries Rambouillet-top wools and kid mohair top grown in Texas. She also offers a number of exotic fibers, including silks and camel down, as well as a line of Ashford spinning wheels.

A 5% discount is given on spinning wheels.

Send $2.00 for a current price list and samples.

Maggie Backman, owner of Things Japanese, carries an assortment of supplies for Japanese needlework. These include Tire® Silk filament threads in 171 colors, Soie et Soie Japanese knitting yarns, Rozashi brocade threads, metallic and silk/blend threads, silk ribbons, supplies for Oriental gauze embroidery and an assortment of needlework kits.

Send $2.00 for a current catalog.

Things Japanese

9805 N. E. 116th Street
Suite 7160
Kirkland, WA 98034
(206) 821-2287

Mail order
Established in 1983
ST

Tochay's Fibers, owned by Christine and Tom McKay, supplies wool and wool/mohair blended rovings for hand spinning in natural and hand-dyed colors. These are available from Cotswold, Romney, Corriedale and Rambouillet sheep.

The McKays offer a custom spinning and dyeing service; write for information.

Send $1.00 and a SASE for a current price list and samples.

Tochay's Fibers

5700 N. Bunn Road
Jonesville, MI 49250
(517) 849-2630

Mail order
Established in 1985
SP

The Tomato Factory Yarn Company, owned by David Codling and managed by Liz Vierow, carries a number of yarns, including Rowan, Jamieson & Smith and Emu Superwash. The catalog offers Fair Isle knitting supplies, books, general knitting supplies and notions, and eight designs of Liberty of London fabrics with matching knitting patterns.

Send $1.00 for a price list and shade-card information.

Tomato Factory Yarn Company

8 Church Street
Lambertville, NJ 08530
(609) 397-3475

Mail order, retail
Established in 1984
KC

Tools of the Trade offers a line of floor and table looms, that are entirely hand-built of northern hard maple, red oak or cherry woods by Arthur Weitzenfeld, owner of the company. Large jack-type floor looms are available with 4, 8 or 12 harnesses in widths of 15 in. to 60 in. Small-frame floor looms are available in widths of 25 in. and 32 in. and table looms come in 15-in., 25-in. and 32-in. weaving widths. Benches and accessories are also available.

Write for a free price list.

Tools of the Trade, Inc.

P.O. Box 4533
Burlington, VT 05401
(802) 878-7168

Mail order, retail, manufacturer
Established in 1970
W

Traditional Handcrafts, owned by Gloria and John Teeter, carries a selection of weaving and spinning supplies, including yarns and looms by Harrisville Designs.

Write or call for specific information.

Traditional Handcrafts

571 Randolph
Northville, MI 48167
(313) 349-7509

Mail order, retail
Established in 1972
SP, W

Treenway Crafts

725 Caledonia Avenue
Victoria, BC V8T 1E4
Canada
(604) 383-1661

Mail order
Established in 1978
KC, W

Treenway Crafts offers a variety of silk yarns.

Send $3.00 for a current catalog and price list.

Turn of the Century

1676 Millsboro Road E.
Mansfield, OH 44906
(419) 529-TURN

Mail order, manufacturer
Established in 1971
KC, LC, SP

Turn of the Century offers a number of handturned wooden tools for needleworkers by William Schmidt and Diana Andra. These include crochet hooks and knitting needles in various sizes, thimbles, darning eggs, tatting shuttles, bobbins for lacemaking and spinner's hooks. All tools are made from exotic woods and select American hardwoods such as cherry, walnut and maple.

Send a SASE for a current price list.

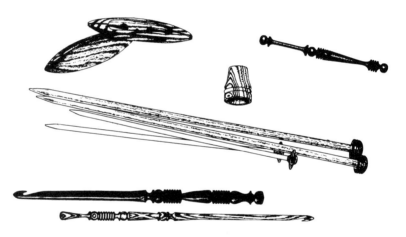

Items available from Turn of the Century

Two CottonWoods

P.O. Box 686
Clint, TX 79836
(915) 851-1530

Mail order, retail shop
Established in 1976
KC, SP, W

Joan Nussbaum, owner of Two CottonWoods and recently appointed Texas representative of the Handweaver's Guild of America, is an exclusive distributor for Texas mohair yarns. These yarns are available in balls or on cones in 12 colors. Ms. Nussbaum also offers natural sliver roving, scoured fleece and raw kid fleece.

Discounts are given on minimum orders of $150.00.

Send $1.00 for a current price list and samples.

The Unique, owned by Eva Gerd-Asher, imports a number of traditional Norwegian yarns—ski sweater, tapestry and rug wools for weaving, knitting, crochet and stitchery. The company stocks the full line of Rauma and Roros Norwegian Spel-Sheep yarns, as well as other wools from Sweden, England, Scotland and domestic sources. The Unique also distributes products by Schacht, Leclerc, Glimåkra, Harrisville Designs, Clemes & Clemes, Ashford and others.

Quantity discounts are given; write or call for information.

Send $5.00 for a current catalog and yarn samples.

The Unique

21½ E. Bijou
Colorado Springs, CO 80903
(719) 473-9406

Mail order, retail
Established in 1966
KC, SP, W

Dawn M. Brocco, owner of The Unique Sheep, offers a number of beautifully colored plant-dyed and wood-dyed yarns and fibers. These include Romney wools, merino wools, mohairs, linens, lamb's wools, cottons, silks, alpacas and rayons. Ms. Brocco also carries yarns made from camel hair, goat hair and horse hair.

Various quantity discounts are given; write for details.

Send $2.00 for a complete set of yarn sample cards (refundable with first order).

The Unique Sheep

88 McEwen Street
Warwick, NY 10990
(914) 986-1951

Mail order, manufacturer
Established in 1987
KC, SP, W

Yarns available from The Unique Sheep

Andrea Amodeo, owner of Vermont Homespun, offers a number of fibers for spinning, including wool rovings, angora, alpaca, llama and silk, as well as handspun designer yarns and yarns spun to order in hand-dyed or natural colors. Also offered are spinning and weaving supplies and Learn-to-Spin kits.

Write for more information.

Vermont Homespun

R.F.D #1, Box 34
Readsboro, VT 05350

Mail order, manufacturer
Established in 1987
KC, SP W

Warps End

1504 Mountain Springs Circle
Huntsville, AL 35801
(205) 534-3210

Mail order, retail
Established in 1984
KC, W

Jane Reuther, owner of Warps End, carries most of the major brands of weaving equipment and yarns.

Write for further information.

The Weaver's Knot, Inc.

121 Cleveland Street
Greenville, SC 29601
(803) 235-7747

Mail order, retail
Established in 1975
KC, SP, W

Ellen Shaw and Kerstin Craven, partners in The Weaver's Knot, carry a full line of supplies for weaving, spinning, basketry, knitting, dyeing and needlework. They are also agents for Glimåkra, Harrisville Designs, Leclerc, Louët and Schacht looms. Spinning wheels are available from Ashford, Louët, Country Craftsman, Reeves, Ertoel and Schacht. Spinning fibers include cotton roving, flax, Perendale and Romney fleeces, prepared wools, camel, mohair, alpaca, ramie and various silks. A huge selection of yarns is offered from such suppliers as Aarlan, Borgs, Brown Sheep Company, Brunswick, Candide, Crystal Palace, Harrisville Designs, Henry's Attic, JaggerSpun, Lane Borgosesia, Manos del Uruguay, Paternayan, Reynolds, Tahki Imports and many others. Basketry supplies include reeds, hoops, handles and kits. Natural and synthetic dyes and mordants are also available, as are a large selection of videotapes and books.

Quantity discounts are given to schools, institutions and professional fiber artists.

Send $1.00 for a current 35-page catalog.

Weavers Shed

1616 Mabry Street
Tallahassee, FL 32310
(904) 576-4485

Mail order
Established in 1977
KC, W

Diana Roth, owner of Weavers Shed, offers unique, handspun bulky and textured wool yarns at reasonable prices. The yarns are available in solid colors and blends, as well as in a rainbow blend of six colors.

Ms. Roth is a demonstrator for AVL Looms and does custom wall baskets and Scandinavian rugs.

Send $1.00 for a current price list and samples.

From the Weavers Shed catalog

The Weaver's Studio offers a large selection of yarns, looms, spinning wheels and accessories.

No catalog is available at this time; write or call with specific requests.

The Weaver's Studio

115 W. Main Street
Ligonier, PA 15658
(412) 238-2540

Mail order, retail
Established in 1986
SP, W

Mohair Magic

Wash your newly knitted, woven or crocheted mohair items with a conditioning shampoo—it will leave them soft and glossy.

Weaver's Way, owned by John and Jean Durant, offers a number of yarns for hand weaving. These include the Alternatives line of modacrylic/viscose blends, the Weaver's Lace line of Carolina cottons, unmercerized cottons in 48 colors, perle cottons and more. John Durant states that his Carolina cottons are special because, to his knowledge, they are "the only line of perle and novelty cottons custom-produced and dyed in the U.S. for hand weaving." Other yarns are available from suppliers such as Borgs, Plymouth, Oregon Worsted Co., Berroco, Old Mill Yarn and Harrisville Designs. Weaver's Way is also a distributor for weaving and spinning equipment from such manufacturers as Leclerc, Schacht, Macomber, Harrisville Designs, Norwood, Cranbrook, Lendrum, Louët and Mark IV.

Same-day service is offered on all orders.

Send $3.00 for a current catalog and yarn sample cards.

Weaver's Way

P.O. Box 70
Columbus, NC 28722
(704) 894-8568

Mail order, retail, manufacturer
Established in 1975
KC, SP, W

The Weaver's Way logo

Gail Kenney and Eric Redding, co-owners of The Weaving and Knitting Shop, offer yarns by Harrisville Designs, Glimåkra, Brown Sheep Company, Candide and others. They are also representatives for Schacht, Glimåkra, Harrisville Designs, Norwood, Cranbrook and Louët looms.

Quantity discounts are given with a minimum order of $200. Free shipping in the continental USA, yarn sample packets and a $50 gift certificate for yarns are included with the purchase of every loom.

Send $7.50 for a current catalog and yarn sample packet.

The Weaving and Knitting Shop

1702 Walnut Street
Boulder, CO 80302
(303) 443-1133

Mail order, retail
Established in 1970
KC, W

The Weaving Works, Inc.

5049 Brooklyn Avenue N.E.
Seattle, WA 98105
(206) 524-1221

Mail order, retail
Established in 1974
KC, SP, W

The Weaving Works offers an extensive listing of supplies for weaving, spinning, basketry, dyeing, knitting and crocheting. The company distributes yarns by Berga, Borgs, Brown Sheep Company, Condon, Harrisville Designs, Henry's Attic, Ironstone, JaggerSpun, Novitex, Silk City and many others. Knitting machines by Brother and Singer, as well as a large number of knitting needles, crochet hooks and miscellaneous supplies are also listed. Looms by Cranbrook, Glimåkra, Leclerc, Louët, Harrisville Designs, Norwood, Rasmussen, Schacht and Whalecraft are distributed by The Weaving Works. Other items include spinning fibers (alpaca, angora, camel, cashgora, cashmere, cotton, flax, mohair, ramie, silk, wool and blends), spinning wheels by Ashford, Louët, Peacock, Pipy and Poly, carders and accessories.

A 10% discount is given on yarn orders over $150.00; write for details.

Send $1.00 for a complete catalog (refunded with first purchase).

Morning Dew

"Morning Dew" was the name given to the incredibly sheer cotton cloth woven in ancient India from yarns spun as finely as 250 miles to the pound. This cloth was so sheer that when it was laid out on the grass, it looked like a light mist of dew.   —Courtesy of Cotton Clouds

Weaving Workshop

920 E. Johnson Street
Madison, WI 53703
(608) 255-1066

Mail order, retail
Established in 1971
KC, SP, W

The Weaving Workshop, owned by Gloria Welniak, offers "the largest selection of natural fibers for weaving, knitting, spinning and basketry in the upper Midwest." This selection includes yarns from such suppliers as Stanley Berroco, Brown Sheep Company, Drop Spindle, Filature Le Mieux, Harrisville Designs, Henry's Attic, Ironstone Warehouse, Tahki Imports and others. Spinning fibers include Romney and merino fleeces, mohair, alpaca, camel top, cashmere, angora, silks, raw silk cocoons, cottons, ramie and flax. The Weaving Workshop is a distributor for Glimåkra, Harrisville Designs, Norwood, Herald, Kyra, Leclerc and Schacht looms; and for spinning wheels by Ashford, Country Craftsman and Louët. Books, small tools, natural and synthetic dyes and dye assistants are also listed.

Quantity discounts are given on orders of $125.00 or more; write for details.

Send $1.00 for a current catalog and price list.

The Weaving Workshop logo

Webs

Webs, owned by Barbara Elkins, is a full-range fiber-arts supply source. The company sells looms, loom kits and spinning wheels, as well as a complete assortment of spinning, knitting and weaving tools. Webs also represents manufacturers such as Susan Bates, Harrisville Designs, Tools of the Trade, Leclerc, Schacht, Glimåkra, Cranbrook, Norwood, Ashford, Louët, Phildar and Clemes & Clemes. Mill-end and closeout yarns, including worsteds, cottons, silks, rayons, blends and rug wools, are also offered.

Various quantity discounts are given; check the catalog for details.

Send for a free catalog and price list.

P.O. Box 349
Amherst, MA 01004
(413) 253-2580

Mail order, retail
Established in 1974
KC, SP, W

Wethersfield Farm

Wethersfield Farm produces white and colored Romney sheep wools for hand spinning.

Send $1.00 for fiber samples and current prices.

R.R. 1, Box 440
Pugsley Hill Rd.
Amenia, NY 12501
(914) 373-8413

Mail order, retail, manufacturer
Established in 1980
SP

The Whitaker Reed Company

The Whitaker Reed Company manufactures custom-made reeds for hand looms in any normal combination of length, height and dents-per-inch with carbon-steel or stainless-steel dents. Metric dentages are also available.

Send for a current brochure and price list.

P.O. Box 172
Worcester, MA 01602
(508) 752-8385

Mail order, manufacturer
Established in 1869
W

White Knitting Machines

White Knitting Machines manufactures the White Easy Knitter, the Double Bed Electronic Machine, the Single Bed Electronic Machine and the Bulky Knitter. A line of machine-knitting accessories is also available.

Send for a free brochure and price list.

11760 Berea Road
Cleveland, OH 44111
(216) 252-2310

Manufacturer
Established in 1876
KC

Whitin Yarns

Whitin Yarns provides a line of natural-fiber, high-quality hand-weaving yarns to retail yarn shops.

Qualified buyers should write for more information; color cards are available.

P.O. Box 937
Norwalk, CT 06856
(203) 852-8823

Manufacturer
Established in 1984
W

Wilde Yarns

P.O. Box 4662
Philadelphia, PA 19127
(215) 482-8800

Mail order, manufacturer
Established in 1880

KC, SP, W

Wilde Yarns offers a line of 100% wool yarns in various weights and styles. Some of these include naturals in two-ply, four-ply and six-ply; berbers in heavy two-ply and four-ply; natural whites in eight weights; fine two-ply in 28 colors; soft clothing yarn in 18 muted colors; brushed wool loop yarn and nubby wool bouclés. Carded wools are offered in five natural shades and nine dyed colors. Wilde Yarns also does custom spinning, dyeing and carding, and offers occasional mill tours.

Various discounts are given to qualified retail stores or those producing for resale; write to Jennie Wood for more information.

A current price list is free; yarn sample packs are $5.00.

The Wilde Yarns logo

Windsor Farms

Route 1, Box 76
Amesville, OH 45711
(614) 448-2771

Mail order
Established in 1976

SP

Ron Chacey of Windsor Farms offers high-luster, long-staple, prize-winning fleeces for hand spinners from his flock of champion longwool sheep.

Send for a free brochure.

Woodland Woolworks

17340 N.E. Woodland Loop Road
Yamhill, OR 97148-8420
(503) 662-3641

Mail order, manufacturer
Established in 1987

SP

Melda Montgomery, owner of Woodland Woolworks, supplies wools and fiber blends for hand spinners, including raw wools, rovings and batts in 100% wool; or wool with mohair, angora or silk blends. These are available in a variety of natural or dyed colors.

Ms. Montgomery also offers custom washing, dyeing, picking, blending of colors and/or fibers, carding and hand spinning.

Send for a free brochure and price list.

The Wool Gallery

1555 Fir S.
Salem, OR 97302
(503) 363-5197

Mail order
Established in 1979

KC, W

The Wool Gallery, owned by Caryl Gertenrich, offers Swedish Nya Berga yarns.

Discounts are given to individuals with a $500.00 minimum order.

Send for a free price list; yarn sample sets are $20.00.

Wool 'N Quilts

Michelle Reilly of Wool 'N Quilts specializes in clean Romney and Border Leicester wools and fleeces in all colors, as well as handspun yarns in a large variety of colors, wool batts and wool dusters.

Ms. Reilly also registered Romney sheep and breeding stock for sale through her Triple 'R' Farm; write or call for information.

Write for current fleece and yarn prices.

Triple 'R' Farm
4614 Locust Grove Road
Rohrersville, MD 21779
(301) 432-2009

Mail order, retail
Established in 1976
KC, SP, W

The Wool Room

The Wool Room offers a number of supplies for weaving and spinning including looms, spinning wheels and spinning fibers.

Send for a current brochure.

Laurelton Road
Mt. Kisco, NY 10549
(914) 241-1910

Mail order, retail
Established in 1982
SP, W

The Wool Shop

Ellen Morrow, owner of The Wool Shop, hopes "to fill part of the need for classic wool knitting yarns." Ms. Morrow offers a variety of wool yarns that include 100% Shetland sport weights, knitting worsteds and double-twist worsteds.

Send $1.00 for prices and yarn sample cards.

Route 3, Box 554-A
Buchanan, VA 24066
(703) 254-1902

Mail order
Established in 1987
KC

The Woolery

Marianne and Tim Horchler, owners of The Woolery, believe that they are the most competitively priced mail-order fiber-arts firm in the country, and one of the few that keeps a full complement of equipment and supplies in stock for fast delivery. The Woolery carries the leading brands of spinning wheels (Ashford, Louët, Schacht, Peacock and the imported Charkha wheel), looms (Harrisville Designs, Leclerc, Glimåkra, Beka, Norwood, Cranbrook, Schacht) and knitting machines (Studio/Singer). The Woolery also offers many spinning and weaving accessories including some exclusives, such as the production fiber picker, the Woolery picker and Woolery drop spindles. Natural dyes (madder, henna, cochineal, indigo, walnut hulls), dye assistants and synthetic dyes are also available. Fibers in many forms, blends and colors are listed: angora, wool, silk, cashmere, camel, mohair, alpaca, yak, ramie, cotton, flax and rayon. For the knitter, the company has various knitting needles and crochet hooks, patterns, buttons, cotton and linen yarns and The Woolery's own natural-dyed and rainbow-dyed wool and angora yarns. Supplies and kits for basketmaking and bobbin lacemaking are sold, along with a number of books.

Most prices in The Woolery's catalog are discounted; additional quantity discounts are given to professionals. Write for information.

Send $1.00 for a current catalog and price list.

R.D. #1
Genoa, NY 13071
(315) 497-1542

Mail order, retail, manufacturer
Established in 1981
KC, LC, SP, W

Woolstons' Woolshed

651 Main Street
Bolton, MA 01740
(508) 779-5081

Mail order
Established in 1986
KC, SP, W

Woolstons' Woolshed, owned by Richard and Ada Woolston, probably has North America's largest selection of spinning and felting fibers, as well as a good number of yarns. The yarns include blends of wools, angoras, mohair, silks and rayons. Spinning fibers include alpaca, llama, angora, ramie, rayon, camel, cashmere, yak, mohair, silk, synthetics, many types of wools and exotic blends. These blends are made of such fibers as tussah silk/lamb's wool lap, silk/merino, tussah silk/camel down, Angora rabbit blends, mohair blends, alpaca/llama blends, deer hair/wool top, raccoon fur/wool top and many others.

Various quantity discounts are given; write for details.

Send $2.00 for a current catalog.

Wooly Acre Farm

Route 2, Box 39
Royal Center, IN 46978
(219) 889-2662

Mail order
Established in 1942
SP

Wooly Acre Farm, owned by Louis E. Zimmer, offers "the best Corriedale wool in the Midwest." These prize-winning wools were the Grand and Reserve White Champions at the 1988 Indiana State Fair, the Reserve Colored Champions and first place winners in all seven classes in the Fair.

Quantity discounts are given to individuals; write for information.

Write or call for current prices.

Wooly Hill Farm

R.D. 1, Box 366
Bridport, VT 05734
(802) 758-2284

Mail order, retail
Established in 1977
KC, SP, W

Wooly Hill Farm, operated by Nancy Low and Greg Pahl, offers a number of fibers for hand spinning: Corriedale fleeces; washed, carded natural or dyed Corriedale wools; exotic blends of wool with silk, mohair, alpaca or camel down; Corriedale machine-washable pelts; and two-ply sport-weight yarns. Wooly Hill Farm is also a distributor for Louët spinning wheels and accessories.

Send for a free brochure or $2.00 for wool samples.

Angora goats, owned by Sharon Chestnutt of Cloudspun Mohair

The Wooly Sheep Company, owned by Page M. Jacobs, offers karakul and merino fleeces, as well as mohair fibers and rovings for hand spinning. Ms. Jacobs also sells custom-spun yarns and sheep pelts.

Write or call for current prices.

The Wooly Sheep Company

9877 N. Attaway Road
Coolidge, AZ 85228
(602) 723-3132

Mail order, retail, manufacturer
Established in 1980
KC, SP, W

The Wooly West, owned by Nancy Bush, offers a variety of yarns in alpacas, wool blends, cottons, linen/rayon blends, Irish wools and more. The entire line of Aarlan Yarns is also available.

Send for a free price list and ordering information.

The Wooly West

208 S. 1300 E.
Salt Lake City, UT 84102
(801) 583-9373

Mail order, retail
Established in 1980
KC, W

Yarn Barn, owned by Susan Bateman, carries a large selection of supplies for weaving, spinning, dyeing, basketry, knitting, lacemaking, rugmaking, papermaking and crochet. Looms are available from such manufacturers as Schacht, Norwood, Loomcraft, Harrisville Designs, Glimåkra, Macomber and Leclerc. Spinning wheels are available from Ashford, Louët and Reeves. Spinning fibers include a number of tops and slivers (silk/wool, tussah silk, flax, alpaca, ramie, cashgora, mohair, pima cotton, wools) as well as Bombyx and tussah silk bricks, cocoons, flax stricks and more. Raw fibers include cashgora, mohair, camel down, cottons, wools and flax. Knitting tools, lacemaking and rug-braiding supplies are also available from the Yarn Barn.

Quantity discounts are given to individuals; check the catalog for details.

Send $1.00 for a current catalog. A subscription to the Yarn Barn Mill-End Sample Club is $4.00 per year.

Yarn Barn

918 Massachusetts
Lawrence, KS 66044
(913) 842-4333

Mail order, retail
Established in 1971
KC, LC, R, SP, W

Wanda Grassmyer, owner of The Yarn Basket, offers a large selection of undyed natural-fiber yarns, including rayons, cottons, linens, wools and blends. Ms. Grassmyer also carries a number of metallics from one-ply to six-ply in 14 different colors.

Ms. Grassmyer offers a yarn-search service for those needing large volumes of any natural yarns. Simply send her a one-yard reeling of the desired yarn.

Quantity discounts are given; check price list for details.

Send $3.00 for complete set of sample cards and a current price list (applied to first order).

The Yarn Basket

2723 Coltsgate Road
Charlotte, NC 28211
(704) 366-6091

Mail order
Established in 1987
KC, W

Yarn by Mills

Box 28
Wallback, WV 25285
(304) 587-2561

Mail order
Established in 1985
KC, W

Margy Mills offers a line of handspun, hand-dyed yarns from cashmeres, silks, angoras and other exotics blended with fine merino wools for knitting or weaving.

Quantity discounts are given; write for details.

Send $2.50 for a current price list and yarn samples.

Margy Mills, of Yarn by Mills

Yarns...

P.O. Box 434
Uxbridge, MA 01569
(508) 278-7733

Mail order, retail
Established in 1987
KC, W

Yarns... offers a wide range of yarns for knitting or weaving, including mohairs, wools, cottons and alpaca/silk blends and a selection of mill ends.

Send for a free price list and yarn samples. Additional samples are sent to customers every five to six weeks.

Yarns + More

2249 S. Brentwood
St. Louis, MO 63144
(314) 961-4377

Mail order, retail
Established in 1983
KC

Yarns + More, owned by Marjorie Ivey and Frances Slusher, offers knitting yarns by Lane Borgosesia, Silk City, Muench, Manos of Uruguay, the Stacy Charles Collection, Joseph Galler, Rainbow Mills, Bernat, Berger du Nord and Susan Bates. Many of the yarns are available on cones to use with knitting machines. Also available is a large number of Marjorie Ivey knitting patterns and kits.

Yarns + More offers a custom design and knitting service; write or call for details.

Send $2.00 for a current catalog.

Fabrics 2

This chapter contains sources for all types of fabrics—fashion fabrics for sewing, lingerie fabrics, materials for quilt making and rughooking, and natural unfinished fabrics ready for dyeing or other surface-design work. Also included are sources for bridal fabrics, imported ethnic fabrics, felts, garment leathers and exotic skins.

A. R. Lawrence and Associates

Asian Textiles Division and Batik
Imports Division
P.O. Box 4096
Fullerton, CA 92631
(714) 525-7069

Mail order, importer
Established in 1957

A. R. Lawrence and Associates offers a variety of 100% silk fabrics, as well as Indian tussahs and cotton greige goods. The company seeks out fabrics that are unique and mails customized samples to their customers.

Send for a current price list and further information.

Baltazor Fabrics and Laces

3262 Severn Avenue
Metairie, LA 70002
(504) 889-0333

Mail order, retail
Established in 1929

Baltazor Fabrics and Laces carries a wide variety of textiles and trims, and specializes in bridal and fine fabrics. The offerings include batistes and broadcloths, lawns, organdies, linen batistes and a wide array of woolens. Bridal veilings and nets include nylon illusion, silk illusion, cotton English net and point d'esprit. (See the listing of surface embellishments on p. 117.)

Quantity discounts are given to qualified buyers; write for more information.

Send $2.00 for a current catalog.

Berman Leathercraft

25 Melcher Street
Boston, MA 02210
(617) 426-0870

Mail order, manufacturer
Established in 1905

Berman Leathercraft, operated by Robert S. Berman, president, is a family-owned business that has been in operation for more than 83 years. The company offers leather hides in various types and weights, garment leathers (chamois, sueded pigskin, etc.), snakeskins, leather lacings, wool shearlings, calfskins and rabbitskins. Leather scraps are also available, as well as tools for leatherworking, dyes, solvents, preservatives, stamping tools, kits and books.

Various discounts are given with a minimum order of $75.00; write for details.

Send $3.00 for a current catalog.

Blue Ginger Designs offers yard goods of hand-blocked, 100% cotton batik fabrics—more than 200 different fabrics in all.

Send $2.00 for a current catalog and price list.

Blue Ginger Designs

1221 Honoapillani Highway
Lahaina, HI 96767
(808) 667-5433

Mail order; retail
Established in 1983

Blueprints—Printables, owned by Barbara Hewitt and John Basye, provides "wearable canvases" to the fiber artist. Presewn garments (made in the San Francisco Bay area) that are ready to dye or decorate with other surface-design techniques include shirts, jackets, jumpers, skirts, pants, kimonos, shorts and caftans in white or solid-color cottons and silks. Eleven of the garment styles are pretreated with blueprinting solution. The company also offers several Design and Print kits for T-shirts and quilt squares.

Initial orders for a few items are available at wholesale prices. This allows you to check the fit of the garment, inspect the sewing and determine if the style fits your design requirements. Follow-up orders require a $100.00 minimum.

Send $2.00 for a current catalog folder with descriptions of all clothing.

Blueprints—Printables

P.O. Box 1201
Burlingame, CA 94011-1201
(800) 356-0445 for orders
(415) 594-2995

Mail order, manufacturer
Established in 1982

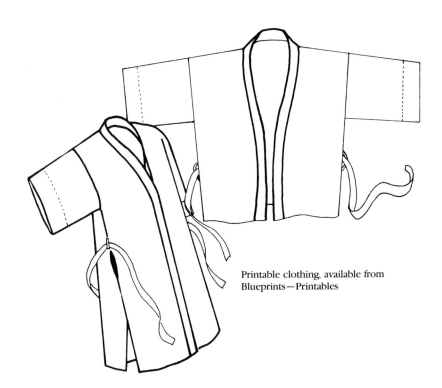

Printable clothing, available from Blueprints—Printables

Britex by Mail

146 Geary Street
San Fransisco, CA 94108
(415) 392-2910

Mail order, retail

A favorite retail store for fabric lovers in California, Britex offers an extensive collection of fine domestic and imported fabrics by mail order.

Send $3.00 for fabric samples; specify the type and colors needed.

Cabin Fever Calicoes

P.O. Box 550106
Atlanta, GA 30355
(404) 873-5094

Mail order
Established in 1977

Cabin Fever Calicoes, owned by Fay Swennes, offers more than 200 solid colors of cotton fabric, as well as prints suitable for quilt making and other sewing projects.

Discounts are given to individuals with a $50.00 minimum order.

Send $3.00 for prices and swatches of solid-color cottons.

Stamp design courtesy of Stampberry Farms (see p. 115)

Central Shippee, Inc.

P.O. Box 135A
Bloomingdale, NJ 07403
(800) 631-8968 for orders
(201) 838-1100 in New Jersey

Mail order, manufacturer
Established in 1928

If you're used to finding 12-in. by 12-in. squares of felt in only three or four colors, take a look at the color card from Central Shippee. These felts come in 6-ft. widths and two weights. The colors include sweet cantaloupe, ice mint, seafoam, curry, copper and claret—more than 80 in all. The company also offers industrial felts for block printing or other heavy-duty use, drapery and upholstery felts and wallcovering felts.

There is a 3-yd.-per-color minimum order on all felts.

Send for a free price list.

Chantilly Boutique

11505 Pencewood Drive
Austin, TX 78750

Mail order
Established in 1980

Chantilly Boutique offers a selection of calico and solid 100% cotton fabrics for quilt making. Christmas prints are also available.

Send $5.00 for samples (approximately 2 in. by 2 in.) of calicoes and solids; send $2.50 for Christmas prints.

Clothworks

Clothworks offers a line of white, ready-to-dye 100% cotton fabrics, including 62-in. wide cotton fleece fabrics, 38-in. wide cotton canvas, 80-in. wide cotton sheeting and others. The company also manufactures the Polyfab® textile dye in 11 mixable colors.

Quantity discounts are given to individuals; write for details.

Send for a current brochure and price list.

132 Powell Street
Vancouver, BC V6A 1G1
Canada
(604) 669-0127

Mail order, retail, manufacturer
Established in 1980

Cotton Patch

Carolie A. Hensley, owner of Cotton Patch, says that if you can "imagine 25 different greys, 10 blacks and 30 to 40 pink to burgundy shades of fabric" then you can get an idea of the solid-color cotton fabrics she offers that will "coordinate with anything."

Send for a free price list; fabric swatches are $3.00.

1025 Brown Avenue
Lafayette, LA 94549
(415) 284-1177

Mail order, retail
Established in 1978

D'Anton

D'Anton, owned by Judy Antone, offers a variety of high-quality garment leathers in a range of colors, finishes and weights. These currently include sueded pigskin in shirting weight, smooth or embossed pigskin, cabretta, garment-weight cowhide, snakeskin and sueded-pigskin remnants.

Discounts are available to qualified wholesale accounts; write for more information.

Send a SASE for a current price list; leather swatches are $4.00.

Route 2, Box 159
West Branch, IA 52358
(319) 643-2568

Mail order, retail, manufacturer
Established in 1987

What is Mercerized Cotton?

Dull, twisted cotton threads and yarns are put under tension and immersed in a caustic-soda solution. The solution is then washed out, leaving the thread or yarn lustrous, strong and better suited for dyeing. The process is called mercerization, and was discovered in 1844 by John Mercer, one of England's most brilliant chemists and a textile worker.

Dauer Leather Company, Inc.

Dauer Leather Company has been family owned and operated since 1954. The current president, John A. Dauer, says that his company is (unfortunately) the "world's best kept secret." Dauer supplies curly-wool lambskins in natural and brownish-tan colors for making toy animals, gloves, garments, slippers, hats, personal leather goods and dolls. The skins vary in size, shape, color and curl of the wool.

Write for a free price list. Four small swatches of skins are $2.50.

P.O. Box 987
Keene, NH 03431
(603) 357-4413

Mail order
Established in 1954

Deva Natural Clothes

P.O. Box NFX 8
Burkittsville, MD 21718
(301) 663-4900

Mail order, retail, manufacturer
Established in 1978

Deva Natural Clothes offers handcrafted clothing made by home sewers who stitch their names into every garment they make. The clothing is made of 100% cotton, in white and solid colors, and is suitable for dyeing or other surface-design techniques. The garments include pants for men and women, jackets, shirts, kimonos, overalls and more. Osnaburg, crinkle cloth, denim, denim lite, corduroy, chamois cloth and Tahiti cloth are also available by the yard in various colors.

A 5% discount is given on orders over $100.00.

Send $1.00 for a current catalog (refundable with your first order).

Dharma Trading Company

P.O. Box 916
San Rafael, CA 94915
(800) 542-5227
(415) 456-7657 in California

Mail order
Established in 1969

Dharma Trading Company offers a line of ready-to-dye fabrics, including cotton print cloth, cotton poplin, cotton velveteen, rayon challis, habutai silks, pongee silk, crêpe de chine, silk satin, raw silk and others. The fabrics are available by the yard or by the bolt. (See their listing of surface-design supplies on p. 107.)

Quantity discounts are given; check the free catalog for details.

The Dharma catalog is also a good educational tool. It contains a chart on the different types of dyes and paints available on the market and offers suggestions on which to use on various fabrics.

Fab Dec

3553 Old Post Road
San Angelo, TX 76904
(915) 944-1031

Mail order
Established in 1967

Fab Dec offers both a selection of ready-to-dye fabrics and surface-design supplies (see the listing on p. 109). The fabrics include mercerized cotton organdy, bleached cotton muslin, cotton batiste, velveteen, duck and rayon challis.

Quantity discounts are given; check price list for details.

Send for a free price list.

Fabrications Fabric Club

P.O. Box 2162
South Vineland, NJ 08360

Mail order
Established in 1987

The Fabrications Fabric Club carries high-quality fabrics at reasonable prices. Many are from couture designers and ready-to-wear manufacturers. All fabrics are coordinated by color and season.

Membership dues are $10.00 per year and include four mailings with fabric swatches and prices.

G Street Fabrics

11854 Rockville Pike
Rockville, MD 20852
(800) 333-9191
(301) 231-8998 in Maryland

Mail order, retail
Established in 1940

G Street Fabrics offers a selection of basic and designer fabrics, including many imported one-of-a-kind pieces. The company carries a full selection of patterns, an inventory of notions and more than 1,000 textile books. Mail-order services include fabric sample charts; a sample club, which mails subscribers more than 700 samples a year; and a specialized custom-sampling service.

Send $4.00 for a notions catalog. Write for information on fabric samples and mail-order services.

Garden Fairies Trading Company, owned by Beth-Katherine Kaiman, offers a variety of fabrics, as well as smocking and heirloom sewing patterns. The fabrics include 100% cotton prints, pinwale corduroys, pima cotton broadcloths, 100% rayons, cotton plaid flannels, Swiss wool challis, 100% silk illusion, China silks and raw silk noils.

Discounts are given to qualified buyers; write for information.

Send $4.00 for a current catalog and fabric swatches.

Garden Fairies Trading Company

P.O. Box 5770
Santa Rosa, CA 95402
(707) 526-5907

Mail order, retail
Established in 1985

Gladstone Fabrics, owned by Robin Gladstone, is a source for theatrical, imported and display fabrics, as well as for novelty and costume fabrics, antique trims and beading.

Send $15.00 for a current catalog and fabric swatches.

Gladstone Fabrics

16 W. 56th Street, 2nd Floor
New York, NY 10019
(212) 765-0760

Mail order, retail
Established in 1929

Gohn Brothers has been supplying clothing and general supplies to the Amish people since 1904. In addition to simple, serviceable garments, they carry a line of yard goods that includes 100% cotton cheesecloth, terry toweling, outing flannel, batiste, denims and natural-fiber fabrics and blends. They also offer a number of dress materials, such as organdies, lawns, huck towelings, muslins, duck cloths and chambrays. For the surface designer, Gohn Brothers carries white 100% cotton bed and quilt sheetings in 90-in. widths for dyeing.

Send $.50 for a current price list and catalog.

Gohn Brothers

Box 111
Middlebury, IN 46540
(219) 825-2400

Mail order, retail
Established in 1904

From The Green Pepper catalog

The Green Pepper, owned by Arlene Haislip, offers a variety of fabrics suitable for active sportswear and outerwear. These include a selection of waterproof fabrics in various nylons, water-repellent fabrics, lycras, knits (such as athletic mesh and sweatshirt fabrics), 100% cotton chamois flannels, insulated fabrics, no-see-um netting, neoprene and others. A full line of patterns, hardware and notions is also included in the extensive catalog.

Send $2.00 for a current catalog.

The Green Pepper, Inc.

941 Olive Street
Eugene, OR 97401
(503) 345-6665

Mail order, retail, manufacturer
Established in 1973

Gutcheon Patchworks, Inc.

P.O. Box 57, Prince Street Station
New York, NY 10012
(212) 219-9021

Mail order, retail
Established in 1975

Gutcheon Patchworks offers a large selection of 100% cotton fabrics for quilting, including prints from the American Classic line, 55 solid colors in plain or polished finishes and an assortment of prints from other manufacturers such as Hoffman, Alexander Henry and Marcus Brothers. Gutcheon also offers "scrap packs" of fabrics in various colors and prints, JP Coats & Clark quilting threads and ecology-cloth muslin.

Various discounts are given; check catalog for information. For those interested in buying large quantities, check the catalog for information on Gutcheon's American Classic fabric club.

Send $3.00 for fabric swatches and a current price list.

The Gutcheon Patchworks logo

Homespun Fabrics and Draperies

P.O. Box 3223, Dept. FSB
Ventura, CA 93006
(805) 642-8111

Mail order
Established in 1948

Homespun Fabrics and Draperies offers 100% cotton fabrics in seamless 10-ft. widths. These include homespuns in natural or white, monk's cloth, tow cloth and others. Most fabrics are available in raw or preshrunk naturals or whites. A selection of sheers and linings in large widths and some remnants are also available.

Send $2.00 for a current catalog and swatches.

Inverness Fabrics

1142 Quarry Road
Caledonia, NY 14423
(716) 538-6284

Mail order
Established in 1982

Inverness Fabrics offers a selection of 100% cotton fabrics in calicoes and Amish solids at reasonable prices. Inverness also carries natural-colored muslin, solid white fabrics, stuffings, batts and quilting thread.

Send $1.00 for fabric sample and a price list.

J. C. Best Company

Best Cottons and Calicoes
10 Marshfield Street
Gloucester, MA 01930
(508) 281-3150

Mail order
Established in 1978

J. C. Best Company is an ideal source of cotton fabrics for professional quilters who don't want to buy all their yardage by the full bolt, but want to enjoy below-retail prices. The company currently offers over 1,000 fabrics in small prints and solids, and close to 200 larger prints.

Send $7.50 for swatches of small prints and solids (1,000 1-in. by 2-in. pieces), $3.50 for swatches of larger prints (170 3-in. by 3-in. and 2-in. by 6-in. pieces) or $10.00 for both sets, postage paid. Outside the U.S. add $3.00.

Jeanne Benjamin specializes in hand-dyed 100% wool fabrics for traditional rug hooking. She offers a selection of varied and useful swatches at reasonable prices and is "always happy to assist in color planning or shading." Ms. Benjamin teaches weekly classes in rug hooking and will color plan through the mail and dye to order.

Teacher and store discounts are available; write for details.

Send $.50 for prices and sample swatches.

Jeanne Benjamin

P.O. Box 754
West Brookfield, MA 01585
(413) 436-5980

Mail order, manufacturer
Established in 1977

Jehlor Fantasy Fabrics offers a large selection of metallic and sequined fabrics and trims, hand-beaded and sequined laces, taffetas, brocades, nylon organzas, metallic sheers, sparkle knits, lamés, lycra, spandex, stretch satin and more than 80 colors of polyester chiffons and satins.

Some discounts are given to individuals; write for information.

Send $2.50 for a current catalog (refundable with your first order).

Jehlor Fantasy Fabrics

730 Andover Park W.
Seattle, WA 98188
(206) 575-8250

Mail order, retail
Established in 1976

Joseph's Coat is a natural-fiber fabric store that specializes in patchwork and ethnic clothing design. A large line of natural fabrics is available by mail (including VIP, Concord, Ameritex and Wamsutta), as well as 100% cotton velveteens, flannels and corduroys.

Send for a free brochure and price list.

Joseph's Coat

26 Main Street
Peterborough, NH 03458
(603) 924-6683

Mail order, retail
Established in 1980

Kieffer's offers an extensive line of lingerie fabrics and supplies.

Write for more details and a free brochure.

**Kieffer's Lingerie Fabrics
and Supplies**

1625 Hennepin Avenue
Minneapolis, MN 55403
(612) 332-3395

Mail order, retail
Established in 1968

The M. Siegel Company, owned by Wayne Siegel, carries a variety of leathers and leather-making tools and trims. The various luxury leathers offered include cowhide suede splits, vicuña grey, English chamois, deerskin, elkskin, goatskin, lambskin, shearlings, latigo leathers, belt and sandal leathers, lizardskin pieces, and much more.

Quantity discounts are given to individuals; check the catalog for details.

Send $2.00 for a current catalog; specific leather samples are sent free on request.

M. Siegel Company, Inc.

120 Pond Street
Ashland, MA 01721
(508) 881-5200

Mail order
Established in 1918

Mekong River Textiles

8424 Queen Annes Drive
Silver Spring, MD 20910
(301) 589-1432

Mail order
Established in 1986

Mekong River Textiles, owned by Susan L. McCauley, is a source for the beautiful Southeast Asian textiles known as "mudmees," the blue and white cotton Ikats from Thailand. Ms. McCauley is also available for lectures on Southeast Asian textiles and Hmong needlework.

Quantity discounts are given; write for details.

Send $1.00 for a current catalog and more information.

Mini-Magic

3675 Reed Road
Columbus, OH 43220
(614) 457-3687

Mail order
Established in 1973

Mini-Magic's extensive catalog of supplies for fine handsewing and doll dressing includes a large number of fabrics such as silks, cottons, woolens, sheers, nets, knits, transparent fabrics, velvet, velveteen, pile fabrics, linens and novelties. The silks include sheers in 45 colors, silk taffeta, silk broadcloth, pongee and honan silks, silk satin, peau de soie, silk jacquard, crêpe and silk chiffon. Among the cottons are batiste, lawn, pima cotton broadcloth, crinoline, oxford cloth, chambray, cotton sateen, swiss organdy, dotted swiss, indigo blue denim, Liberty of London cotton prints, shirtings and jacquards. Available in wool are gabardine, flannel suiting, cashmere, challis, jacquard and Harris tweed. Novelties include ultrasuede, crushed metallic and sequined chiffon.

Some quantity discounts are given; check the catalog for information.

Send a check for $5.00 (or $3.00 in cash) for current catalog.

Monterey Mills

P.O. Box 271
Janesville, WI 53545
(608) 754-8309

Mail order, retail, manufacturer
Established in 1965

Monterey Mills carries a selection of deep-pile synthetic fabrics in 58-in. to 60-in. widths, including plush short piles, shag novelty piles and shearling fabrics. Also available are fun furs such as rabbit, seal, fox, mink and teddy bear. Fabrics are sold by the yard or by the bolt. Remnants and scraps are also available by the pound.

Quantity discounts are given; check the price list for details.

Send $4.00 for a price list and sample package.

Needlearts International

P.O. Box 6447
Glendale, CA 91205
(213) 227-1535

Mail order
Established in 1985

Needlearts International, owned by Bonnie Benjamin, offers imported fabrics such as Japanese yukata, Malaysian batik and Indonesian batik sarongs. Ms. Benjamin, the author of *Sashiko—The Quilting of Japan from Traditional to Today* (Needlearts International, 1986), also offers a large number of supplies for sashiko embroidery and quilt making.

Send $2.00 for a current catalog and two to three annual updates. Fabric samples are $1.00.

Fabrics available from Needlearts International

Fabric designs from New World
Fabric Supply

New World Fabric Supply offers a selection of one-of-a-kind 100% cotton prints imported directly from Africa. The current collection includes tie-dye, batik, fancy and wax prints from such countries as Cameroon, Ivory Coast, Ghana, The Gambia and Senegal. Designs range from abstract and geometric to the traditional.

Discounts are given on minimum orders of $500.00; write for details.

Send $5.00 for a full-color catalog and fabric swatches.

New World Fabric Supply

P.O. Box 401377
Brooklyn, NY 11240-1377
(718) 953-2067

Mail order, retail, wholesaler
Established in 1988

Patches, owned by Anita Butler, offers a set of 50 precut, 100% cotton quilting squares in three different sizes (4-in., 6-in and 8-in. squares) in calicoes, solids, minidots and Christmas calicoes. Ms. Butler also welcomes special color requests and will custom-cut fabric into squares or other shapes, which may require a minimum order.

Send a legal-size SASE for a current brochure.

Patches

Box 140
Dalton, MA 01226
(413) 499-3043

Mail order
Established in 1978

Stuart and Ellen Quay, owners of Qualin International, carry a number of natural white silk fabrics and scarf blanks in different weights and weaves for dyeing or painting. Also available are exclusive Chinese double-sided silk embroidery pieces from top Chinese artisans. The Quays offer classes in double-sided embroidery methods.

Volume discounts are given; write for details.

Send for a free catalog and price list. A sample set of three or four different silk scarves is $11.95, postpaid.

Qualin International

P.O. Box 31145
San Francisco, CA 94131
(415) 647-1329

Mail order, retail
Established in 1986

The Quilt Patch offers a variety of 100% cotton fabrics, including prints, calicoes and solids (both pastels and Amish shades). Lines of fabric currently stocked are VIP, Concord, Peter Pan, Springmaid, Wamsutta, Ameritex, RJR, American Classic and more. Precut fabric squares are available, as well as scrap quilt-packs, quilting supplies and patterns.

Quantity discounts are given with a minimum order of $300.00; write for details.

Send $1.00 for a current catalog.

The Quilt Patch

208 Brigham Street
Marlboro, MA 01752
(508) 480-0194

Mail order, retail
Established in 1981

Quilts & Other Comforts offers color-coordinated assortments of 100% cotton quilting fabrics in theme prints (Victorian, nouveau, hearts, etc.). The company carries over 400 cotton prints and solids in their basic stock line, as well as natural muslin and precut quilt patches.

Send $2.50 for a full-color catalog of fabrics, quilting supplies and patterns.

Quilts & Other Comforts

P.O. Box 394
Wheatridge, CO 80034-0394
(303) 420-4272

Mail order, manufacturer
Established in 1968

Rupert, Gibbon & Spider, Inc.

718 College Street
Healdsburg, CA 95448
(707) 433-9577

Mail order, manufacturer
Established in 1980

Rupert, Gibbon and Spider offers over 70 different types of silk fabrics, 23 styles of silk scarves and a large selection of 100% cotton fabrics, all of which are ready to dye. (See their listing for surface-design supplies on p. 115.)

Send for a free price list.

Seminole Sampler

Savage Mill
Savage, MD 20763
(301) 792-8240

Mail order, retail
Established in 1981

Seminole Sampler maintains a collection of over 200 solid-color fabrics in 100% cotton that can be ordered by the yard. The company is best known for their "fabric parfaits"—preselected bundles of coordinated solids and/or prints in a wide variety of color selections. Seminole Sampler also carries some notions and supplies for quilt making.

Send $5.00 ($8.00 for noncontinental U.S. and foreign addresses) for a catalog and more than 220 swatches of solid-color cottons.

Southern Fabrics

1210 Galleria Mall
Houston, TX 77056
(713) 626-5511

Mail order, retail
Established in 1939

Southern Fabrics offers an exceptional selection of couture, designer and better fabrics at competitive prices. Currently available are 100% cotton velvets from West Germany in solids or prints, 100% cashmere, printed silk crêpe de chine, wool/mohair suiting fabrics, 100% silk jacquards, 100% wool flannels, handwoven Indian silks, boiled wools, 100% camel hair, brushed herringbone, 100% wool crêpes, 100% silk charmeuse and 100% merino wool jerseys. Southern Fabrics also carries the Viyella™ line of fabrics from *Vogue Patterns*® magazine.

A sample swatch series, mailed four times a year, is $15.00. Write for more information.

Summer Leather

121 E. Tarpon Avenue
Tarpon Springs, FL 34689
(813) 934-9396

Mail order, retail, manufacturer
Established in 1984

Summer Leather is a distributor for special leathers and has "unlimited access to leather items of all kinds."

Summer Leather does not currently have a brochure; write to Colleen Allcorn with specific requests.

Sureway Trading Enterprises

826 Pine Avenue, #5
Niagara Falls, NY 14301
(716) 282-4887

Mail order
Established in 1978

Sureway Trading Enterprises specializes in silk fabrics and scarves and currently has over 200 different silk fabrics in stock.

Quantity discounts are given; write for details.

Send for a free price list.

The Tandy Leather Company offers a wide variety of leathers and leather-making supplies, including natural cowhide strips, garment leathers (deerskins, elkskins, sheepskins, rabbitskins, suedes), snakeskins and more. The company also carries a complete line of dyes, tools and books on leather making.

Some discounts are given; write for information.

Send $2.00 for a complete, full-color catalog.

Tandy Leather Company

P.O. Box 791
Fort Worth, TX 76101
(817) 551-9629

Mail order, retail, manufacturer
Established in 1919

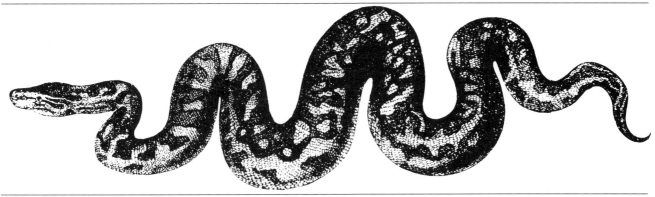

Testfabrics, under the technical direction of Thomas A. Klaas, offers a large assortment of fabrics that are scoured and prepared for dyeing, printing and painting. These fabrics include 100% cotton print cloths, sheetings, terry cloths, flannels, twills, broadcloths, sateens, T-shirt fabrics, organdies, velveteens, sailcloths and many more. Also available are 100% wools (gabardine, flannel, jersey knit), silks (crêpe, shantung, habutai, georgette, charmeuse, twill, noil) and linens (oyster, burlap, natural, suiting, handkerchief, cotton/linen blends). Testfabrics also offers an assortment of other items such as quilting fabrics, natural cotton tapes, place mats, napkins, scarves, huck towels, bib aprons, tablecloths and T-shirts that are ready to dye or print.

Quantity discounts are given; check catalog for further information.

Send for a free price list. Send $7.00 for a cotton and rayon swatch booklet; $7.00 for a linen, silk and wool swatch booklet.

Testfabrics, Inc.

P.O. Box 420
Middlesex, NJ 08846
(201) 469-6446

Mail order, manufacturer
Established in 1952

Thai Silks offers a large selection of printed and solid silk fabrics, as well as finished silk scarves and garments that are ready for dyeing. The fabrics include jacquard, crêpes de chine, blouse-weight and dress-weight silks, raw silks from India and China, shantung, brocades, broadcloths, organzas and many more.

Discounts are given to qualified buyers; write for details.

Send for a free price list and information on Thai Silks' fabric club. For $10.00 per year, you'll receive three mailings, swatches of new fabrics and closeout sale fabrics.

Thai Silks

242 State Street
Los Altos, CA 94022
(415) 948-8611

Mail order, retail
Established in 1968

Tumbleweed

99 Mount Auburn Street
Cambridge, MA 02138
(617) 492-3279

Mail order, retail
Established in 1976

Tumbleweed, owned by Deborah Greenberg, offers a large line of 100% cotton calico fabrics, as well as other prints, solids, quilteds and unbleached muslins for quilt making.

A 10% professional discount is given to qualified buyers; write for details.

Send $1.95 for a current catalog and set of swatches.

Fireproofing Fabric

You can make a fireproofing solution for fabrics or yarns easily at home. You'll need 7 oz. of borax, 3 oz. of boric acid and 2 qt. of hot water. Dissolve the boric acid by making a paste with a little of the hot water. Add the borax and remaining water and stir until the solution is clear. Dip, spray or sprinkle fabric or yarns with the solution. Be sure to test on a small sample before treating the entire garment or skein of yarn.

UTEX Trading Enterprises

710 9th Street, #6
Niagara Falls, NY 14301
(716) 282-8211

Mail order
Established in 1980

UTEX Trading Enterprises claims to carry the largest stock of silk fabrics and silk scarves. These include over 100 haute-couture silk prints, silk crêpes de chines, China silks, Thai silks, Fuji silks, silk doupioni, organzas and many more in dress and suit weights.

Send a SASE for a current brochure and price list. Refundable sample deposits are $35.00 for a complete set; $20.00 for silk prints; $8.00 for white silks; $12.00 for colored silks. Write for details.

Veteran Leather Company, Inc.

204 25th Street
Brooklyn, NY 11237
(800) 221-7565
(718) 768-0300 in New York

Mail order, retail, manufacturer
Established in 1949

Veteran Leather Company offers hard-to-find leathers, cordings, lacings, tools and books on leather working.

Quantity discounts are given with a minimum order of $25.00.

Send $2.00 for a current catalog.

W. Cushing Company

P.O. Box 351
Kennebunkport, ME 04046-0351
(207) 967-3520

Mail order, retail, manufacturer
Established in 1968

W. Cushing Company carries a variety of rug-hooking fabrics, including plain burlaps, monk's cloth and hand-dyed wool, as well as their line of Cushing dyes and rug-binding tapes. (See their listing for surface-design supplies on p. 116.)

Send $2.00 for a current catalog and dye color chart.

Sewing and Quilting Supplies

3

In this chapter you'll find a wide variety of supplies for sewing garments and quilts. Included for the garment-maker are sources for specialty patterns, marking devices, hard-to-find notions, dress forms and tailoring supplies. For the quilter, there are sources for quilt frames, quilting stencils, batting and various other quilting supplies. For sources of fabrics for garments and quilts, see Chapter 2. Letters identifying each supplier in this chapter are as follows:

S   sewing supplies and equipment
Q   quilting supplies and equipment

Aardvark Adventures

P.O. Box 2449
Livermore, CA 94551-0241
(415) 443-2687

Mail order
Established in 1976
s

Aardvark Adventures, founded and owned by the late Jerry Zarbaugh and now owned by her daughter, Deb Casteel, carries an amazing assortment of sewing and needlecraft supplies and notions. The Aardvark Adventures catalog/newsletter includes such items as needles, general sewing notions, beads, buttons, threads, books, trims (including shisha mirrors) and much more. Ms. Zarbaugh approached the field of needlework with humor, once asking "Where else can you buy belly dancer's cymbals and embroidery floss at the same place?" (See their listing for surface-design supplies on p. 117.)

Send $1.00 for a sample copy of "The Aardvark Territorial Enterprise."

Alfa Sales

P.O. Box 296
Vails Gate, NY 12584
(914) 565-2213

Mail order
Established in 1983
s

Alfa Sales manufactures Bonfit Patterners—a set of professional master pattern blocks for the home sewer. The patterns are made from sturdy plastic and include fingertip-controlled knobs that change the size of the basic pattern to fit your measurements. The patterners are available in skirt, pants or bodice versions, and include many different designs.

Write for a free brochure.

The American Quilter

P.O. Box 7455
Menlo Park, CA 94026
(415) 854-2694

Mail order, manufacturer
Established in 1982
Q

Nona Haydon, owner of The American Quilter, carries the only "stencil-cutting hot pen" on the market for cutting Mylar quilting stencils. The pen has interchangeable tips so that it can be used to cut stencils for quilts or for painting stencils. Ms. Haydon also offers the Mylar needed for the stencils.

Send a SASE for a brochure.

A quilt-stencil cutting tool, available from The American Quilter

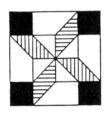

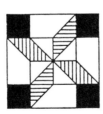

Stamp designs courtesy of Quarter Moon Rubber Stamps (see p. 114)

Atlanta Thread and Supply Company offers a wide variety of general sewing supplies, as well as more specialized supplies for tailoring. These include threads on cones or spools, zippers and zipper parts for clothing or upholstery, Velcro®, fasteners and fastening tools, hooks, eyes, snaps, chalks, pins, custom-tailoring items, linings, elastics, seam binding and hemfacings, buttons, rulers, pressing boards and pads, dress forms, scissors, cleaning fluids, store display items, pressing units, steamers and irons, rotary cutting machines, sergers and overlock machines, needles, drapery tapes, piping cords, crinolines, miscellaneous tools and specialty supplies.

Send for a current catalog.

Atlanta Thread and Supply Company

695 Red Oak Road
Stockbridge, GA 30281
(800) 847-1001

Mail order
Established in 1948
s

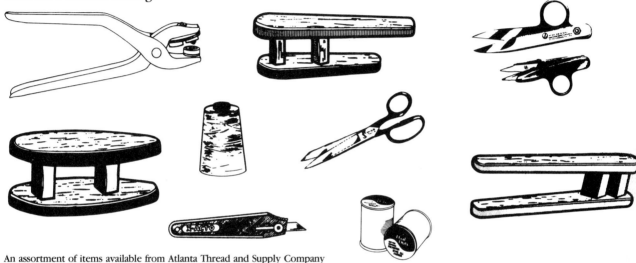

An assortment of items available from Atlanta Thread and Supply Company

The Bee Lee Company carries a full line of sewing supplies for the professional and the home sewer, with a special emphasis on products for western wear. The company carries a selection of snap fasteners unavailable elsewhere, as well as snap-setting tools, buckles, buttons, sequins and western trims. Bee Lee also offers threads, interfacings, fusing materials, elastics, zippers, miscellaneous sewing notions and scissors.

Send for a free catalog.

The Bee Lee Company

P.O. Box 36108
Dallas, TX 75235
(214) 351-2091

Mail order
Established in 1956
s

Campbell's, owned by Deborah Campbell, carries many unusual clothing pattern lines, including Past Patterns, Old World Sewing Pattern Company, Fashion Blueprints and Jenny Wren, Ltd. Campbell's also carries sewing accessories, including buttons from Fresh Water Pearl Button Company.

Send $4.00 for a current catalog of all patterns offered.

Campbell's

R.D. 1, Box 1444
Herndon, PA 17830
(717) 425-2045

Mail order
Established in 1984
s

Clotilde, Inc.

1909 S.W. 1st Avenue
Ft. Lauderdale, FL 33315
(305) 761-8655

Mail order
Established in 1972
S, Q

Clotilde offers a line of hard-to-find notions for sewing. The company sells rotary cutters and mats, interfacings, patterns and books, measuring implements, pressing aids, smocking supplies, needles and pins, marking devices, quilting supplies and much more. Clotilde also carries several exclusive items such as Sticky Stuff, the One-Step Needle Threader and the Perfect Pleater.

Send $1.00 for a current catalog.

The Fabric Carr

Sewing Tools
P.O. Box 1083
Los Altos, CA 94023
(415) 948-7373

Mail order, retail, school
Established in 1980
S

The Fabric Carr, owned by Bobbie Carr, carries a line of unique sewing items, including tailoring supplies, pressing tools, hard-to-find notions and resource books and videotapes.

Ms. Carr teaches couture sewing classes and sponsors an annual couture summer sewing camp.

Send a SASE for a catalog or write for more information on the sewing camp.

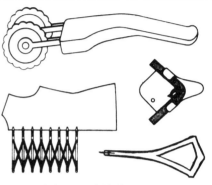

Sewing helpers, available from
The Fabric Carr

Fashion Blueprints

2191 Blossom Valley Drive
San Jose, CA 95124
(408) 356-5291

Mail order
Established in 1981
S

Fashion Blueprints, owned by Sylvia Muzzio, offers a line of creative clothing patterns based on classic, simple-to-sew ethnic designs. The patterns are available in many different styles and include Chinese jackets, Japanese robes and hippari, Thai wrap dresses and tops and more. Accessory patterns are included free with every order.

Send $1.00 for a current catalog.

Clothing patterns available from Fashion Blueprints

The Friends Pattern Company, owned by Janice and Hal Moore, offers a full line of traditional patterns for Amish clothing, including dresses, aprons, headcoverings and bonnets, underwear and nightclothes, shirts, vests, capes, overcoats, and children's clothing. Two Amish doll patterns are also available from the catalog.

Send $1.00 for a current catalog, refundable with your first order. Write for information on an active-wear clothing catalog.

Friends Pattern Company

50305 State Road 145
Woodsfield, OH 43793
(614) 472-0444

Mail order
Established in 1988
s

Home-Sew offers an extensive line of sewing and craft supplies, including threads on cones or spools, zippers and fasteners, quilting and needlecraft items, interfacings, trims and laces, elastics, sewing-machine accessories, scissors, Velcro®, seam bindings, piping cords, buttons, snaps, hooks, pins and needles and general sewing notions.

Send $.50 for a current catalog.

Home-Sew

1825 W. Market Street
Bethlehem, PA 18018
(215) 867-3833

Mail order
Established in 1959
S, Q

Manny's Millinery offers a variety of hard-to-find materials and supplies for making hats.

Send $2.00 for a current catalog.

**Manny's Millinery
Supply Company**

63 W. 38th Street
New York, NY 10018
(212) 840-2235

Mail order, retail, manufacturer
Established in 1940
s

Mary McGregor, owned by Barbara Patterson, carries a wide variety of needlework and sewing supplies, including threads, needles, yarns, magnifier lamps, general sewing notions and more.

Write for a current catalog and price list.

Mary McGregor

P.O. Box 2555
Salisbury, MD 21801
(301) 546-2390

Mail order
s

Mini-Magic

3675 Reed Road
Columbus, OH 43220
(614) 457-3687

Mail order
Established in 1973
S

Mini-Magic carries a wide variety of hard-to-locate items for fine hand sewing. The current catalog lists ribbons, threads, fabrics, laces, sewing notions (markers, scissors, pins, fusibles, snaps and other fasteners, marking pens and more), hand-sewing needles, hat-making supplies, buttons, books and much more. (See their listing for surface embellishments on p. 120 and for books on p. 198.)

Some quantity discounts are given; check catalog for details.

Send a check for $5.00 (or $3.00 in cash) for a current catalog.

Nancy's Notions

P.O. Box 683
Beaver Dam, WI 53916
(414) 887-0690

Mail order
S, Q

The current catalog for Nancy's Notions includes over 100 pages of general and specialized sewing and tailoring supplies. These include scissors, rotary cutters and mats, threads, pattern weights, marking tools, measuring notions, pins and needles, elastics, specialty presser feet and other accessories for sewing machines, quilting notions, pressing tools, machine embroidery supplies, books and patterns, notions and threads for sergers, specialty threads, knitting frames, videotapes and sewing tables.

Send for a current catalog.

Fiber Fact

Mauve, one of the most popular colors today, was actually the first color to be produced from a synthetic dye. William Henry Perkin accidently discovered the coal-tar-derivative dye in 1856 while trying to synthesize quinine, an important drug.

—Courtesy of *Shepherd's Friend Magazine*, 1985

Newark Dressmaker Supply

6473 Ruch Road
Bethlehem, PA 18017
(215) 837-7500

Mail order
Established in 1976
S, Q

Newark Dressmaker Supply carries a variety of supplies for home sewers, craftspeople and needlecrafters. These include a large line of threads (including overlock threads and accessories), zippers, buckles, ribbons and trims, pins and needles, fasteners and bindings, elastics, decorative buttons, fabrics, interfacings, appliqués, sewing machine accessories, scissors, French sewing supplies, quilting supplies, drapery and upholstery materials, measuring tools, pressing accessories, tracing and tailoring tools, labels, machine and hand-embroidery supplies, fabric paints and much more.

Send for a free catalog.

Norton House

P.O. Box 578
Wilmington, VT 05363
(802) 464-7213

Mail order, retail
Established in 1966
S, Q

Sue Wurzberger, owner of Norton House, carries over 2,500 different 100% cotton calico and cotton fabrics, as well as a large number of quilt-making notions such as threads, needles, thimbles, scissors, rulers, marking supplies, rotary cutters, frames, batts and stencils; general sewing-machine supplies (needles, bulbs, brushes); and books.

Send $1.00 for a current catalog.

Past Patterns manufactures and sells multi-sized, authentic historical clothing patterns for men, women and children from the period 1830-1949.

Send for a free brochure or $5.00 for a full Victorian and Edwardian pattern catalog.

P.O. Box 7587
Grand Rapids, MI 49510
(616) 245-9456

Mail order, manufacturer
Established in 1979
s

Patterns for a mid-1860s skirt and gathered bodice (above) and a skirt and fitted bodice with pagoda sleeves (right), from Past Patterns

---

The Perfect Notion

Ann Kennedy, owner of The Perfect Notion, carries an extensive line of hard-to-find sewing notions.

Send $1.00 for a current catalog.

566 Hoyt Street
Darien, CT 06820
(203) 329-1192

Mail order
s

Sew Craft

Gail Kibiger, owner of Sew Craft, offers hard-to-find supplies for creative machine stitchery. Gail carries Natesh® embroidery threads in an extensive array of colors, as well as a line of metallic threads by other manufacturers. Shisha mirrors are available, as are sewing-machine supplies and accessories, rotary cutters and mats, markers, books and patterns.

Send $1.00 for a current newsletter/catalog, which also contains book reviews, hints, articles and patterns.

P.O. Box 1869
Warsaw, IN 46580
(219) 269-4046

Mail order
s

Sewing Emporium

1079 3rd Avenue
Chula Vista, CA 92010
(619) 420-3490

Mail order, retail, manufacturer
Established in 1975

S

The Sewing Emporium manufactures custom attachments for overlock machines and the Big Mat cutting board for sewing.

Send $2.00 for a current catalog.

Taylor Bedding Mfg. Co.

P.O. Box 979
Taylor, TX 76574
(512) 352-6311

Manufacturer
Established in 1903

Q

The Taylor Bedding Mfg. Co. manufactures quilt batting products in various sizes and materials.

Quantity discounts are given on orders of four cases or more; write for details.

Send for a current price list.

The Vermont Patchworks

P.O. Box 229
Shrewsbury, VT 05738
(802) 492-3590

Mail order
Established in 1980

Q

The Vermont Patchworks, owned by Jan Snelling, carries a collection of hard-to-find notions and an extensive list of books on quilt making. Some of the supplies offered include quilting frames, drafting supplies, machine quilting aids and imported needles.

Send $2.00 (refundable with your first order) for a current catalog.

William Wawak Company

2235 Hammond Drive
Schaumburg, IL 60173
(312) 397-4850

Mail order
Established in 1974

S

The William Wawak Company specializes in tailoring and sewing supplies, including hard-to-find commercial tailoring equipment. Wawak's 40-page catalog offers a variety of threads, linings, zippers, buttons and other items.

Send $3.00 for a current catalog, refundable with your first order.

Wolf Form Company, Inc.

39 W. 19th Street
New York, NY 10011
(212) 255-4508

Mail order, manufacturer
Established in the early 1900s

S

The Wolf Form Company manufactures an extensive line of dress forms. The company will also make forms to a specific manufacturer's, designer's or individual's measurements.

Write for a current brochure and price list.

Supplies for Surface Design

4

The Surface Design Association defines surface design as "the coloring or patterning of fabric and fiber with dyes, pigments or manipulation." Surface design covers a diverse spectrum of techniques from batik and tie-dye to hand painting, silkscreening, blueprinting, marbling, rubber stamping, stenciling, beading, embroidering and otherwise decorating fabric.

Part I of this chapter lists sources of supplies for printing, dyeing and painting on fabric. Part II lists suppliers for other surface embellishments—laces, trims, beads, buckles, buttons and rhinestones.

Printing, Dyeing and Painting

A. I. Root Company

P.O. Box 706
Medina, OH 44258-0706
(800) BUY-ROOT
(216) 725-6677

Mail order, retail, manufacturer
Established in 1859

The A. I. Root Company specializes in supplies for beekeeping, but they also offer a selection of waxes for surface-design techniques such as batik. The company's craft-wax supply list includes pure refined beeswax sheets, bulk beeswax cylinders and craft wax in various colors.

Dealer and quantity discounts are given; write for details.

Send for a free price list.

Aljo Manufacturing Company

83 Franklin Street
New York, NY 10013
(212) 226-2878 or 966-4046

Mail order, retail, manufacturer
Established in 1917

Aljo Manufacturing Company, operated by Robin Hull and Herb Schriffrin, carries an assortment of dyes, including acid dyes for silk and wool, basic dyes for painting on silk, direct dyes for cotton and rayon, disperse dyes, and fiber-reactive cold-water dyes. All the dyes are packaged in four sizes and come in a range of colors. Aljo also carries waxes, tjantings, and washing soda.

Some quantity discounts are given; call or write for details.

Send for a free price list.

All Night Media

P.O. Box 2666
San Anselmo, CA 94960
(415) 459-3013

Mail order, manufacturer
Established in 1975

All Night Media carries over 300 rubber stamps, all made from original art designs. Stamps include animal, fantasy, food, music, romantic and holiday designs, as well as stamps personalized with your name or message. Accessories include mahogany cases, colored papers, brush-tip markers, roll-on inks in 16 colors, embossing powders, inkpads and custom stamps. Gift certificates are available.

Send $2.00 for a catalog (refundable with your first order).

All-World Scientific

5515 186th Place, S.W.
Lynnwood, WA 90837
(206) 672-4228

Distributor
Established in 1972

All-World Scientific is a laboratory chemical and supply distributor. For more information, contact Trish Mainard.

Send $5.00 for a current catalog.

Alliance Import Company

1021 R Street
Sacramento, CA 95814
(916) 920-8658

Importer, wholesaler
Established in 1970

Alliance Import Company offers a selection of natural dyes to wholesalers only.

Qualified resellers should contact Roger Wolfe for more information.

The Batik and Weaving Supplier, owned by Beth Cederberg Guertin, carries a number of supplies for both surface design and weaving. Surface design supplies include natural dyestuffs (indigo, fustic, alkanet root, logwood powder, madder, cochineal, brazilwood chips and sawdust) and mordants (alum, blue vitriol, chrome, copperas and tin).

Synthetic dyes include Pro washfast acid colors in 15 shades, Deka permanent colors, Createx pure pigments, Deka Series L textile dye, Cushing all-fabric dyes, Procion MX dyes, Setaskrib textile pens and dyeing accessories (waxes, tjantings, shinshi and brushes). The catalog also contains ready-to-dye fabrics and a book list. The Batik and Weaving Supplier sponsors a large number of workshops throughout the year. (See the listing on p. 10 for weaving supplies.)

Quantity discounts are given to individuals; write for details.

Send $2.00 for a mail-order catalog; a class schedule is free.

The Batik and Weaving Supplier

393 Massachusetts Avenue
Arlington, MA 02174
(617) 646-4453

Mail order, retail
Established in 1982

With over 450 creative rubber stamp images (airplanes to zebras) and more than 60 different subjects to choose from, the Bizzaro Rubber Stamp catalog has something to please everyone. A do-it-yourself rubber stamp kit is also included in the current catalog.

Send $1.00 for a current catalog (refundable with first order).

Bizzaro Rubber Stamps

P.O. Box 16160
Rumford, RI 02916
(401) 728-9560

Mail order
Established in 1969

Stamp design from Bizzaro Rubber Stamps

Brooks & Flynn, owned by Michael W. Flynn, manufactures their own brand of fiber-reactive cotton dyes, which can be used for dyeing rayon and linens. These dyes are offered in 50 shades and packaged in various sizes. Other supplies include soda ash, fabric softener, fixatives, color remover and thickener mix, as well as individual ingredients for making your own thickeners. The company also supplies a Color Easy all-purpose hot-water dye, which dyes nylon, wool, silk, cotton, linen and rayon in three easy steps. Deka permanent fabric paints and Deka print silkscreen inks are also available.

Quantity discounts are given to individuals; check the price list.

Send for a free catalog.

Brooks & Flynn

P.O. Box 2639
Rohnert Park, CA 94928
(800) 822-2372
(800) 345-2026 in California

Mail order, manufacturer
Established in 1980

Cerulean Blue, Ltd.

P.O. Box 21168
Seattle, WA 98111
(206) 443-7744

Mail order
Established in 1972

Cerulean Blue, owned by Ann Marie Patterson, is probably the country's most popular supplier for textile and fiber artists. They have the most comprehensive catalog of surface-design supplies available anywhere. Their inventory includes Telana dyes, Fibracron dyes, inkodyes, indigo, liquid Procion H dyes, Procion MX dyes and a number of fabric paints, including Euro-tex fabric paint and Primal Glow fabric paint. Resist supplies and tools are listed in Cerulean Blue's extensive catalog, as are a line of Japanese art supplies. Brushes, tools, safety equipment and a list of books are available, as is expert technical advice on all products.

Send $4.50 for an in-depth 56-page educational catalog, which includes a color chart and safety tips.

Colophon Hand Bookbindery

1902 N. 44th Street
Seattle, WA 98103
(206) 633-1759

Mail order, retail, manufacturer
Established in 1975

Colophon Hand Bookbindery, owned by Don Guyot, offers supplies for traditional marbling (ebru) or Oriental marbling (suminagashi) on both fabrics or papers. These include ethyl alcohol, alum, carrageenan, Colophon marbling colors, marbling combs, Colophon marbling tanks, ox gall, brushes, fabric stretchers and more. Mr. Guyot also offers a number of workshops on fabric and paper marbling at his retail location.

Quantity discounts are given to individuals; check catalog for details.

Send $1.00 for a current catalog.

Coupeville Spinning and Weaving Shop

P.O. Box 520
Coupeville, WA 98239
(206) 678-4447

Mail order, retail
Established in 1974

Coupeville Spinning and Weaving Shop carries a number of dyes and dyeing supplies, including Lanaset dyes, Ciba Kiton acid dyes, Deka Series L dyes and Euro-tex fabric paints, as well as natural dyes such as cutch, logwood sawdust, brazilwood sawdust, madder, osage orange, cochineal, natural indigo and synthetic indigo. Mordants and miscellaneous dye supplies include alum, ferrous sulfate, cream of tartar, chrome, spectralite, soda ash, synthrapol and various cylinders and storage bottles. (See the listing for spinning and weaving supplies on p. 18.)

Quantity discounts are given with minimum orders; check the catalog for details.

Send $2.00 for a current catalog (refundable with your first purchase).

Createx Colors

14 Airport Park Road
East Granby, CT 06026
(800) 243-2712
(203) 653-5505 in Connecticut

Mail order, manufacturer
Established in 1980

Createx Colors manufactures a complete line of high-quality, non-toxic dyes and art materials.

Send for a current catalog and price list.

Creek Water Wool Works

Creek Water Wool Works offers a large number of dyes, both natural and synthetic. The natural dyes include alkanet root, chamomile, juniper berries, madder root, marigold, Persian berries, sandalwood, weld and yew. Natural wood dyes include purpleheart, bloodwood, koa, ebony, padauk and Honduras mahogany. Natural dye extracts include cutch, fustic, sumac, osage orange, brazilwood, logwood, cochineal and natural indigo patties. A number of dye assistants and mordants are listed: synthrapol, washing soda, glauber's salts, spectralite, acetic acid, hydrochloric acid, natural beeswax, alum, chrome, copper, iron and tin. Synthetic dyes include Kiton wool dyes for wool, mohair or nylon; Procion MX Series dyes and Cushing Perfection dyes. The company also carries a line of supplies and equipment for weaving and spinning (see the listing on p. 19).

Send $3.00 for a full catalog and price list.

P.O. Box 716
Salem, OR 97308
(503) 585-3302

Mail order, retail
Established in 1978

DBP Unlimited

DBP Unlimited specializes in supplies for natural dyers. Their extensive listing of natural dyestuffs includes alkanet root, annatto seeds, black walnut hulls, brazilwood (chips, extract and sawdust), cochineal, cutch, eucalyptus leaves, fustic extract, henna, indigo (ground or in patties), kamala powder, logwood, madder root, osage orange and safflower. DBP carries several natural dye kits, including a natural-dye mordant set, an indigo dye kit and a historical dye kit for modern dyers. Miscellaneous supplies for dyeing are also available.

Quantity discounts are given to qualified buyers; write for details.

Write for more information.

P.O. Box 1344
Duarte, CA 91010
(818) 357-8677

Mail order

Decart, Inc.

Decart manufactures the entire line of Deka paints and dyes for fabrics.

The company does not sell directly to individuals. Qualified retailers should write for more information; others should write for the name of their nearest dealer.

Lamoille Industrial Park
Box 309
Morrisville, VT 05661

Manufacturer

Dharma Trading Company

Dharma Trading Company prides itself on its large variety of products and friendly, helpful staff. Roland Locks, contact person at Dharma, offers supplies for surface design, including Dyehouse Procion® dyes in 26 colors, Deka silk paints, Jacquard silk dyes, Peintex silk inks, Seidicolor silk dyes, Super Tinfix dyes, Deka metallic fabric paints, Texticolor irridescent fabric paints and Versatex textile paints. Gutta and gutta-like resists in clear, black, gold and silver are offered, as well as sticky wax, paraffin, beeswax and inkodye resists. Other supplies include tjantings, brushes, silk scarves, ready-to-dye fabrics (see p. 86), chemicals (soda ash, thickener, urea, synthrapol) and safety supplies.

Quantity discounts are given with a $15.00 minimum order.

Send for a free catalog. It's a good educational tool and contains a chart on the different types of dyes and paints available on the market and offers suggestions on which to use on various fabrics. It also lists the supplies needed for certain types of surface-design techniques.

P.O. Box 916
San Rafael, CA 94915
(800) 542-5227
(415) 456-7657 in California

Mail order
Established in 1969

Diana's Designs

7011 Spieth Road
Medina, OH 44256
(216) 722-2021

Mail order
Established in 1986

Diana Sammataro specializes in a dye plants and carries seeds for such plants as bouncing bet, coreopsis, marigold, teasel and thyme. Her extensive price list also gives information on the mordants needed with various plants and the colors that can be made from them.

Quantity discounts are given; write for details.

Send a SASE for a free price list.

Dyes & Wool

19902 Panther Drive
Pflugerville, TX 78660
(512) 251-3502

Mail order
Established in 1987

Gayle Bingham, owner of Dyes & Wool, says that her specialty is "giving her customers individual attention, answering questions and helping with any dye problems they may have." Ms. Bingham is a distributor for the Gaywool dyes for wool, mohair, silk, fur, nylon, angora and cashmere. These dyes are easy to use, nontoxic and safe for the environment. They are available in 18 colors, which can be mixed to make additional colors and shades. Ms. Bingham also distributes pure Gaywool sliver, premium Corriedale wool and Nooramunga spinning wools (see the listing on p. 23).

Send $1.50 for a brochure, color card, helpful hints and price list.

What is Cochineal?

Cochineal is a red dyestuff made from the bodies of female *Dactylopius coccus*, a cactus-eating insect native to tropical and subtropical America.

The insects are carefully brushed from the cactus into bags and then killed by immersing them in hot water or exposing them to steam or heat. The bodies are then dried and pulverized.

It takes 70,000 insects to make one pound of cochineal dye!

Earth Guild

One Tingle Alley
Asheville, NC 28801
(800) 327-8448

Mail order, retail
Established in 1970

Earth Guild, owned by Bud Crawford, offers a huge inventory of supplies for the fiber arts. Surface-design supplies include Deka Series L dyes, Lanaset dyes, Deka permanent fabric paints, Deka silk paints, acid wool dyes, Procion fiber-reactive dyes and natural dyestuffs (brazilwood chips, cutch extract, red henna, madder root, logwood sawdust, cochineal, natural indigo, synthetic indigo, osage orange and alkanet). A number of dye accessories and mordants are also sold, including alum, blue vitriol, cream of tartar, chrome, copperas, tin, washing soda, urea, sodium acetate, Keltex™ and marbling size. (See their listing for yarn and fiber supplies on p. 23.)

Quantity discounts are given; check the catalog for details.

Send $2.00 for a current catalog (refundable with your first order).

Fab Dec was founded in 1967 by the late Meda Parker Johnson, co-author of *Design on Fabrics* (Van Nostrand Reinhold, 1981). Her daughter, Dickie Ferro, took over the business in 1973, and takes an interest in her customers' success as dyers and fiber artists. The Fab Dec catalog includes such supplies as a Procion fiber-reactive dye and chemicals kit, Procion M and H series dye colors, thickeners, urea, tjantings, beeswax, fabrics (see the listing on p. 86) and more. Ms. Johnson's book is also available from Fab Dec.

Quantity discounts are given with a $150.00 minimum order; write for details.

Send for a free price list.

Fab Dec

3553 Old Post Road
San Angelo, TX 76904
(915) 944-1031

Mail order
Established in 1967

Working with Dyes—ICI Safety Precautions

❖ Although Procion dyes and the chemicals associated with their use are not highly toxic, these materials are industrial chemicals and should be handled with care. As a general practice, chemical products should not be allowed to get into the eyes, but if they do, wash the eyes thoroughly with clean water and then obtain medical treatment.

❖ Prolonged or repeated contact with the skin should be avoided. Wear rubber gloves and use an implement to stir solutions and dyebaths.

❖ Obviously, chemicals should not be taken internally and food, drink and smoking materials should be prohibited where chemicals are used.

❖ The utensils used for dyeing should not be used for other domestic purposes.

❖ Avoid inhaling dusts by working in a well-ventilated area and handling dye powders carefully.

❖ Reactive dyes (e.g., Procion dyes) are reactive chemicals, and occasional cases of respiratory allergy have occurred among those who have inhaled dust under industrial conditions over a prolonged period of time. Procion dyes are manufactured to minimize the formation of dust, but inhaling this dust should be avoided. If dyes are used in circumstances where particles may become airborne, a dust respirator should be worn.
—Courtesy of Fab Dec

G & K Craft Industries is the wholesale division of PRO Chemical & Dye, Inc. (see the listing on p. 114) and deals only with retail outlets. The company offers prompt and efficient service, provides technical assistance when needed and carries all dyes and supplies for surface design on fabric, including the fabrics and tools.

Interested retail store owners must send proper identification (state tax number and Federal I.D. number) to obtain a price list and further information.

G & K Craft Industries, Inc.

P.O. Box 14
Somerset, MA 02726
(617) 676-3838

Wholesale only
Established in 1971

Gramma's Graphics, Inc.

20 Birling Gap, NFSB-P9
Fairport, NY 14450
(716) 223-4309

Mail order
Established in 1980

Gramma's Graphics, owned by Susan Johnson, supplies Sun Print kits for cyanotype (blueprinting) on fabric. The process is simple: images are made by contact-printing photo negatives on fabric treated with a light-sensitive solution. Exposing the fabric to the sun or any source of ultra-violet light and washing in tap water produces a print in the characteristic colors of blueprints. The prints are permanent and can be washed or dry cleaned. The unconditionally guaranteed Sun Print kit contains directions and enough solution to print 20 9-in. by 12-in. squares or two yards of fabric. Ms. Johnson also offers cotton print cloth by the yard and color-toning instructions to alter the blue colors to brown, charcoal, wheat, green or amethyst.

Discounts are given to individuals with a 25-kit minimum order.

Send $1.00 and a long SASE for a current catalog and price list.

Susan Johnson of Gramma's Graphics (left), stitches her Centennial Quilt made from family photos and Sun Prints. The Centennial Quilt with pillow (above), made from Sun Prints from Gramma's Graphics.

The Story of Gramma's Graphics

Nine years ago, seeking a special 100th-birthday gift for her grandmother, Susan Johnson combined her quilting talents with the traditional art of blueprinting. The resulting "centennial quilt," made from squares depicting family members and homes from different generations, caused an immediate sensation among her friends and neighbors, who wanted to preserve their own family photos in the same way.

Printing a photographic negative onto fabric, while simple, requires ingredients not commonly available in convenient quantities. Ms. Johnson had to buy 10 lb. of each ingredient, although her quilt required only several ounces. Realizing that there might be a need for someone to supply smaller amounts of the chemicals, she began the mail-order distribution of her Sun Print kits. With the support and encouragement of her grand-mother, her business, Gramma's Graphics, was born.

Graphistamp

Graphistamp carries a full line of original rubber-stamp designs, which are checked for good line quality and reproducibility with ink on paper as well as with dyes and paints on fabric. Images fall under such categories as fanciful, love, communications, celestial, floral, celebrations, holidays, alphabets, food, decorative borders, farm and domestic animals, birds and marine life, wild animals and insects. Other supplies offered include stamp pads and inks in 14 colors, three rainbow-ink pads, metallics and glitters. Embossing powder, storage boxes and trays are also available.

Discounts are given to qualified retailers; write for more information.

Send $3.00 for a 24-page catalog.

225G Cannery Row
Monterey, CA 93940
(408) 373-1565

Mail order, manufacturer
Established in 1976

Fiber Fact

Wicker, reed, wood and other natural fibers can be stained with natural or synthetic dyes. Small articles can simply be dipped into a dye solution in a tub. To color larger objects, the dye can be applied with a sponge or a brush. —Courtesy of *Shepherd's Friend Magazine*, 1985

Grateful Dyes

Steven Lee, owner of Grateful Dyes, claims to be the only dye supplier in the country that caters specifically to tie-dyers. Individual supplies and complete kits are available.

Quantity discounts are given to individuals; write for information.

Send a SASE for a free price list.

4664 S. Yosemite Street
Englewood, CO 80111
(303) 721-6032

Established in 1987
Mail order

Gumbo Graphics

Gumbo Graphics, owned by David Wites, specializes in unmounted, inexpensive rubber stamps. Prices are currently $30.00 per pound (usually about 125 stamps). Mr. Wites collects original artwork from artists all over the world to use on his stamps, and says that he "enjoys talking with high-spirited people who create works of art." The Gumbo catalog contains over 1,500 different images, including humorous stamps, bugs and birds, animals, dragons, borders and lettering stamps. Custom stamps can be ordered, as well as stamps from photos or any image with halftones. Gumbo also carries a line of accessories, including stamp pads and inks.

Discounts are given with minimum orders; check catalog for details.

Send $2.00 for a current catalog.

90 North Lawrence
Eugene, OR 97405
(503) 485-4138

Mail order, manufacturer
Established in 1965

Inkadinkado, Inc.

Karen Foote Richards started her company when she began using rubber-stamped images in her batik pieces. Eventually she began specializing in the rubber stamps, and Inkadinkado was born. The company carries almost 1,000 rubber stamps in all. The images include animals, birds, insects and holiday designs. Accessories include stamp pads, embossing powder, special fabric inks in seven colors, glitter inks and rainbow inks. Custom-made stamps are also available.

Wholesale discounts are given to qualified shops only; contact Nancy Shepard for information.

Retail and mail-order customers can receive a free Inkadinkado catalog (regularly $2.00, refundable) by writing to Monica Schulze and mentioning this book.

105 South Street, Dept. FW
Boston, MA 02111
(617) 426-3458

Mail order
Established in 1979

Ivy Crafts Imports

5410 Annapolis Road
Bladensburg, MD 20710
(301) 779-7079

Mail order, manufacturer
Established in 1978

Ivy Crafts Imports, owned by Diane Tuckman, is one of the few companies that supply the Sennelier French colors for painting on silk. In addition to the Tinfix and Super Tinfix colors, the company also carries Tincoton colors, which can be used on cotton, linen and vegetable fibers. Other dyes include Tinsilk colors, Polydyes and Pearlized Texticolor dyes. A complete line of kits and sets, resists, fabrics, applicators and steamers is available. Ivy Crafts Imports also offers instructional videotapes on the art of painting on silk (see the listing on p. 188).

Various discounts are given to schools, groups and individuals. Write for details.

Send for a free catalog.

Leavenworth Jackson Rubber Stamps

P.O. Box 9988
Berkeley, CA 94709

Mail order
Established in 1979

Leavenworth Jackson Rubber Stamps, owned by Ms. Leavenworth Jackson, currently offers over 400 rubber stamps, including images of people, animals, insects, food, flowers and transportation, as well as message stamps and a large assortment of Alice in Wonderland stamps. Custom-made stamps can also be made from your camera-ready artwork.

Quantity discounts are given with a minimum order of $100.00.

Send $1.00 for a current catalog.

Mark Enterprises, Inc.

Layton, NJ 07851
(201) 948-4157

Mail order, manufacturer
Established in 1957

Mark Enterprises manufactures and distributes the Silkwerm fabric steamer, a stainless-steel fabric steamer for use by amateur and professional fiber artists for setting dyes on wool or silk. The steaming chamber on the Silkwerm is 36 in. long and 12 in. in diameter, and will easily steam a full 50-yd. bolt of silk.

Send for a free price list.

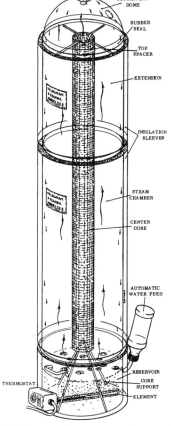

The Silkwerm fabric steamer, from Mark Enterprises

Betty Harris, owner of 100 Proof Press, prides herself on the large number of rubber-stamp images she carries in her catalog. The current 74-page catalog contains over 2,500 stamp designs, including many animal, plant, people and architectural images and 32 different alphabets. Ms. Harris can also provide custom rubber stamps from original artwork.

Send $2.00 for a current catalog (refundable on orders of $10.00 or more).

100 Proof Press

R.R. #1, Box 136
Eaton, NY 13334
(315) 684-3547

Mail order
Established in 1981

Fiber Fact

Leftovers from common Easter-egg dyes can be put to good use on prewashed wools. Put the remaining dye made from the tablets and vinegar into ovenproof dishes. Add a handful of fleece so that it soaks up most of the solution. Put the fleece in a 250° oven, occasionally turning the fleece until all of the dye is absorbed. Easter-egg dyes are acid dyes and have a strong affinity for wools. The colors will be very bright and useful for blending with other wools.

—Courtesy of *Shepherd's Friend Magazine*, 1985

Photographers' Formulary states that no order is too small—photographic kits and chemicals are available in any quantity. The company carries a large assortment of photographic chemicals, supplies (over 400 in all) and labware, including thermometers, graduated cylinders, beakers and storage bottles. For surface designers, the company sells kits for alternative photographic processes, such as palladium printing, kallitype printing, brownprinting and blueprinting. Weavers and dyers will be interested in the number of chemicals and storage supplies that this company carries as well.

Send $1.00 for a detailed 24-page catalog.

Photographers' Formulary, Inc.

P.O. Box 5105
Missoula, MT 59806
(800) 922-5255
(406) 543-4534 in Montana

Mail order, retail, manufacturer
Established in 1978

Bonnie Halfpenny, owner of Photos to Fabric, supplies reproduction papers that can be used at home to iron black-and-white photocopy machine images onto blends and synthetic fabrics with a regular iron. The papers are currently $3.00 each and can be re-used many times. They are available in six colors and can be mixed to obtain more shades. The resulting image is soft, permanent and washable.

Quantity discounts are available to individuals; write for more information.

Send $1.00 for a sample and detailed instructions.

Photos to Fabric

14413 S. 40th Place
Phoenix, AZ 85044
(602) 759-1686

Mail order
Established in 1986

Prince Street Designs, under the direction of owner Joan Kissell, offers a commission cotton-fabric dyeing service to artisans, small vendors, large manufacturers and retail stores. Prince Street Designs is known for the 24 vibrant stock colors they use and for their ability to match custom colors. Any finished cotton garment or length of material less than 6 yd. can be dyed. Cotton blends can be dyed, but consistency of color is not guaranteed. Custom colors can (in most cases) be matched, and require a 10-lb. minimum. Stock colors require no minimum order. Turnaround time is usually two to three weeks.

Send for more information and current prices.

Prince Street Designs

242 Lafayette Street
New York, NY 10012
(212) 431-6775

Mail order
Established in 1977

PRO Chemical & Dye, Inc.

P.O. Box 14
Somerset, MA 02726
(617) 676-3838

Mail order, manufacturer
Established in 1971

Don and Adelle Weiner, owners of PRO Chemical & Dye, pride themselves in having what they term as "the highest-quality dyes at the lowest prices." PRO is also said to be the primary supply source for anyone who works in surface design and other fiber arts. The company offers a number of dyes, including the Procion MX cold-water reactive dye in 34 shades, Cibacron F reactive dyes, liquid reactive dyes, PROcion H dyes in powder or liquid, Ciba Kiton acid dyes, washfast acid dyes, Lanaset dyes, PROsperse disperse dyes, PROfab textile and opaque inks, PRObrite pearlescent inks, PRO Puff three-dimensional inks, PROfab concentrates and Diazol direct dyes. A full line of chemicals, workroom supplies and accessories is available, including acetic acid, ammonium sulfate, glauber's salts, metaphos, muriatic acid, print paste mixes, synthrapol SP, PRO thickeners, urea and wool assistants. Wholesale buyers should see the listing for G & K Craft Industries on p. 109.

Send for a free catalog and price list.

Quarter Moon Rubber Stamps

P.O. Box 883
Campbell, CA 95009
(408) 296-0459

Mail order, manufacturer
Established in 1983

Quarter Moon Rubber Stamps, owned by Donnie Broadhurst, offers many original stamp designs and more than 400 images suitable for printing on fabric. Some of the images include Oriental designs, quilt blocks, holiday designs, animals, borders, people, ethnic designs and alphabets. A separate catalog includes special rubber stamps for school teachers.

Wholesale discounts are given with a $100.00 initial order and a $50.00 reorder.

Send $2.00 for current catalogs.

Quilt block rubber-stamp designs, available from Quarter Moon Rubber Stamps

Rockland Colloid Corporation

P.O. Box 376
Piermont, NY 10968
(800) 832-6606

Mail order, manufacturer
Established in 1968

Rockland Colloid Corporation manufactures Liquid Light® and Fabric Sensitizer® photographic emulsions for sensitizing fabrics. These can be used to make photo-silkscreens or to produce photographic images directly on fabric. The Fabric Sensitizer® is made for clothing and other fabrics and leaves the fabrics soft.

Send for a free brochure and price list.

Rubber Stamps of America, owned by Laurie Indenbaum, carries a large line of exclusive, unique and high-quality rubber stamps, which can be used to print on fabrics. Some of the designs in this company's extensive catalog include travel, leaves, insects, dinosaurs, birds, jungle animals, fish, holiday images and various messages. A separate catalog features images by Ken Brown.

Send for a free catalog.

Rubber Stamps of America

P.O. Box 567-F
Saxtons River, VT 05154
(802) 869-2622

Mail order, retail, manufacturer
Established in 1979

Rupert, Gibbon & Spider manufactures Jacquard Silk Colors, which are nontoxic, self-setting silk dyes that can be used on all natural fibers but are especially beautiful when applied to silk. The company also manufactures the Jacquard textile pen, a versatile pigment-paint pen that is nontoxic, permanent, washable and never fades. Also offered is a full line of silk dyes, paints and silk-painting accessories. Seventy different types of silk fabrics, 23 styles of silk scarves, and a good selection of cottons are available from this company (see the listing on p. 92).

Rupert, Gibbon & Spider has silk-painting demonstrators and teachers in most states. Contact Michael Katz, owner, for information on classes in a particular area.

Send for a free catalog.

Rupert, Gibbon & Spider, Inc.

718 College Street
Healdsburg, CA 95448
(707) 433-9577

Mail order, manufacturer
Established in 1980

Alan E. Wulzen, owner of Siphon Art Products, manufactures and offers Versatex textile paints, air-brush and stamp-pad inks in over 20 colors and Dorland's wax medium and batik wax.

Discounts are given to individuals with a $35.00 minimum order.

Write for a current price list.

Siphon Art Products

P.O. Box 710
San Rafael, CA 94915-0710
(415) 236-0949

Mail order, manufacturer
Established in 1972

Melody Hope Stein, owner of Stampberry Farms, designs and makes her own rubber stamps and claims that "most of them are as weird as I am." She also claims to be a "wacky rubber stamper who appreciates whimsy and weirdness and practices both in everyday life." Ms. Stein's delightful collection includes an assortment of trees, animals, people, holiday designs, and several fiber-related stamps such as a sewing machine, balls of thread, lace and a yarn basket.

Discounts are given to qualified businesses; write for information.

Send $1.50 (refundable with first order) for a current catalog.

Stampberry Farms

1952 Everett Street
North Valley Stream, NY 11580
(516) 285-5587

Mail order, manufacturer
Established in 1982

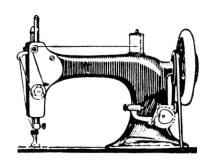

Stamp designs available from Stampberry Farms

Sureway Trading Enterprises

826 Pine Avenue, #5
Niagara Falls, NY 14301
(716) 282-4887

Mail order
Established in 1978

Sureway Trading Enterprises specializes in silk fabrics, silk scarves and French dyes for surface design.

Quantity discounts are available to individuals.

Contact Jeanne Aydelotte for more information and a current price list.

Talas

213 W. 35th Street
New York, NY 10001-1996
(212) 736-7744

Mail order, retail
Established in 1962

Talas is known for its large inventory of supplies for art conservation and archival treatment. The company also carries tools and supplies for marbling on fabrics or paper, papermaking and bookbinding. Marbling supplies that are suitable for use on fabrics include carrageen moss, carrageenan (powdered extract of carrageen moss), gum tragacanth, methyl cellulose (used as a size), marbling inks, ox gall, preserving liquid, alum and marbling combs. Several books on the art of marbling are also available.

Some quantity discounts are given; check the catalog for details.

Send $5.00 for a 114-page catalog.

W. Cushing Company

P.O. Box 351
Kennebunkport, ME 04046-0351
(207) 967-3520

Mail order, retail, manufacturer
Established in 1968

W. Cushing Company manufactures the regular Cushing Perfection dyes in 83 shades for use on cottons, silks, and wools, as well as all-fiber dyes in 38 shades. The company even packages and privately labels some of its dyes for the Navajo Indians to use in their rug weaving. Cushing also designs and sells patterns and supplies for rug hooking (see the listing on p. 94).

Various discounts are given; write for information.

Send $2.00 for a brochure and dye color card (refundable with a $10.00 minimum order.)

The alkanet plant

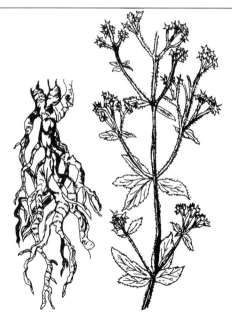

The madder plant and root

Other Surface Embellishments

The delightful Aardvark Territorial Enterprise combination catalog/newsletter was begun by the late Aardvark founder, Ms. Jerry Zarbaugh ("The Aardvark Lady") and continues to be published by her daughter, Deb Casteel. The newsletter contains many strange and wonderful things and focuses on fiber artists who work with machine or hand embroidery and stitchery. It "tries to inspire, encourage and enthuse readers to experiment with threads, fabrics, bangles and beads, clay, and whatever else strikes their fancy." This amusing publication contains information on new products, books, artists, classes, events and more. Ms. Casteel also carries supplies for embroidery—Natesh® embroidery thread in 336 shades, shisha mirrors in various sizes, beads, tools and other embellishments. (See their listing for sewing and quilting supplies on p. 82.)

Special sales on supplies are offered periodically. Discounts are given to those with resale tax numbers.

Send $1.00 for a sample newsletter/catalog.

Aardvark Territorial Enterprise

P.O. Box 2449
Livermore, CA 94551-0241
(415) 443-ANTS

Mail order
Established in 1976

Baltazor Fabrics & Laces specializes in bridal fabrics and other fine fabrics and laces. Its retail location has the largest selection of imported laces in the area. Baltazor's mail-order catalog includes a large number of trims such as French laces by the bolt, Battenberg laces, horsehair braid, ribbon rosebuds, buttons, loops, veiling and nets, pearl beads and Austrian crystals. (See their listing for fabric on p. 82.)

Quantity discounts are given to qualified businesses; write for details.

Send $2.00 for a current catalog.

Baltazor Fabrics & Laces

3262 Severn Avenue
Metairie, LA 70002
(504) 889-0333

Mail order, retail
Established in 1929

A Bridal Tip

Traditionally, pearl beads are sewn onto bridal gowns or other garments by hand. Many dressmakers and bridal shops have found that gluing the beads achieves the desired look without the time-consuming labor of hand sewing. SOBO glue is recommended for this purpose, since it will dry clear and not yellow with age, dry cleaning or preservation methods.

—From Baltazor Fabrics & Laces

Melanie Alter, owner of The Bead Room, offers a large collection of new, old and ancient ethnic beads and ornaments from all over the world. These include beads of glass, silver, wood, porcelain, ivory and brass.

Quantity discounts are given with a $50.00 minimum order.

Send $2.00 for a current catalog.

The Bead Room

12105 Bermuda, N.E.
Albuquerque, NM 87111
(505) 298-7036

Mail order, retail, wholesale
Established in 1984

Berger Specialty Company, Inc.

413 E. 8th Street
Los Angeles, CA 90014
(213) 627-8783

Mail order, retail
Established in 1925

Berger Specialty Company carries a wide selection of unique and unusual beads.

Quantity discounts are given to individuals with a $30.00 minimum order.

Send for a current price list or call for further information.

Button Creations

3801 Stump Road
Doylestown, PA 18901
(800) 346-0233

Mail order, retail, manufacturer
Established in 1979

Button Creations, owned by Larry and Janice Kutney, offers 400 different styles of buttons (including many collectibles) in a wide range of prices to individuals and wholesalers. Among the many styles and types of buttons offered are 18th-century military, Civil War, Confederate and Union reproduction buttons, pewter, wood, mother-of-pearl and crystal buttons, and custom-dyed polyester and pearl-style buttons. Custom buttons are also available in hand-painted, fired porcelain; enameled metal or cloisonné styles. Buttons are sold loose or carded, and samples can be purchased individually.

Quantity discounts are given; write for details.

Send $2.00 for a 36-page catalog (free to wholesalers).

The Cord Company

5611 Virginia
Kansas City, MO 64110
(816) 333-6851

Mail order, manufacturer
Established in 1982

Carol Koebbeman, owner of The Cord Company, supplies 100% silk cords in many colors and sizes and will custom-make silk cords to your specifications. The cords are made from a beautiful lustrous silk, dyed with commercial dyes and bound at the ends in either a matching or contrasting color. Heavier cords and silk ropes are also available. Ms. Koebbeman will also create a cord in your choice of colors or dye the cord in a progression of colors.

Quantity discounts are given with a $25.00 minimum order.

Send $3.50 for a current price list with samples.

Craft Gallery

P.O. Box 8319
Salem, MA 01971-8319
(508) 744-2334

Mail order
Established in 1971

Naomi Appleman's Craft Gallery carries a full line of needlework supplies, including glass beads, DMC machine embroidery and quilting threads in 52 colors, Balger, La Lamé and Schurers metallic threads, DMC metallics, threads made from genuine precious metals, silk embroidery threads, DMC perle cotton threads and embroidery flosses.

Discounts are given to individuals with a $25.00 minimum order.

Send $2.00 for a current catalog.

Crazy Crow Trading Post

Crazy Crow Trading Post carries a large line of beads and other decorative elements in its extensive 64-page catalog. The beads include Czechoslovakian seed beads in 27 opaque colors and 13 transparent colors, Italian seed beads, pony beads, bugle beads, French and old-style brass beads, tile beads, round glass beads, shell beads, stone beads and nuggets (tiger eye, malachite, amethyst, sodalite, jade) and antique trade beads. Other items include beading and jewelry-making supplies, beading looms and books on beading, leather working and other Indian crafts. The company also offers skins, tails, quills, leathers and hides, bells, brass tacks and nails, tin cones, brass sequins, feathers, solid brass buckles, buttons and conchas.

Quantity discounts are given with a $50.00 minimum order.

Send $3.00 for a current catalog.

P.O. Box 314
Denison, TX 75020
(214) 463-1366

Mail order, retail, manufacturer
Established in 1970

Freed Company

The Freed Company, owned by Leba Freed, is a worldwide importer of a number of fascinating items. Ms. Freed currently carries python skins, tanned cowhides, Icelandic sheepskins, sequined and beaded appliqués, semiprecious stone beads, clay and wood beads, genuine handmade Indian-wampum strands, pearls, abalone strands, scarabs, rare beads, glass seed beads in strands, hand-painted clay beads from Greece, cloisonné beads, faceted crystal beads and coral strands.

Send for a free brochure and price list.

415 Central, N.W.
Albuquerque, NM 87103
(505) 247-9311

Mail order, retail, manufacturer, importer
Established in 1920

Garden of Beadin'

Garden of Beadin' carries a large selection of beads, including many rare and antique items. The current 60-page catalog offers glass seed beads in opaque and transparent styles, bugle beads, many types of crystals, ethnic beads, large glass beads, finished and unfinished wooden beads, metal beads and spacers, sea urchin spines and mother-of-pearl beads. Semiprecious stone beads are available in rose quartz, black onyx, tiger eye, sodalite, jasper and aventurine. Supplies, books and jewelry findings are also offered.

Quantity discounts are given with a minimum order; contact Charlotte Silverstein or Alan Goodman for details.

Send $1.00 for a current catalog. Bead sample cards are available; check the catalog for prices.

P.O. Box 1535
Redway, CA 95560
(707) 943-3829

Mail order, retail
Established in 1985

Gettinger Feather Corporation

Gettinger Feather Corporation has been in the same family for four generations and is now owned and operated by Dan Gettinger. The company offers raw and colored feathers in loose or strung forms. These include guinea-hen feathers, pheasant plumage, marabou down, peacock feathers, pheasant skins and tails, ostrich plumes, feather boas, turkey quills, feather fans and bedding feathers.

Discounts are given to individuals with a $20.00 minimum order.

Send $2.00 for a generous sample package and price list.

16 W. 36th Street
New York, NY 10018
(212) 695-9470

Mail order, manufacturer
Established in 1916

JHB International

1955 S. Quince
Denver, CO 80231
(303) 751-8100

Mail order, importer, wholesaler

JHB International offers a variety of regular and fashion buttons.

Discounts are given to wholesalers only; write for details.

Send for a current catalog and price list.

Maiden Vermont-Danforth Pewterers, Ltd.

R.D. 1, Box 292
Bristol, VT 05443
(802) 453-3191

Mail order, manufacturer
Established in 1974

Maiden Vermont offers a variety of buttons, pins, earrings and ornaments designed by Judi Danforth and handcrafted of solid, lead-free pewter. The small company takes each piece from idea to finished product. Current button designs include quilt blocks, flowers, large and small hammered round and smooth square shapes, jungle animals and a series that includes a sheep, lamb, basket and heart.

Quantity discounts are given to qualified buyers; write for information.

Send $1.00 for a current catalog.

Mini-Magic

3675 Reed Road
Columbus, OH 43220
(614) 457-3687

Mail order
Established in 1973

Mini-Magic, owned by Donna Korb, carries a huge supply of fabrics, threads, trims and embellishments for fashion clothing, wearable art, costumes and doll dressing. Trims include imported French, English and Swiss laces and embroideries, Italian silk laces and cotton Valenciennes laces and French ribbons. Threads available include Belding Lily® silk in 57 colors, Japanese silk in 23 colors, cotton, silk perle, metallic embroidery flosses, silk handsewing threads and embroidery flosses and cotton chenilles. Hat-making supplies include feathers, marabou by the yard, ostrich plumes and pieces, and milliner's velvet ribbon. Ms. Korb also carries a large assortment of books on fashion, costume and sewing (see the listing on p. 198). (Also see p. 90 and p. 100 for sewing supplies.)

Quantity discounts are given to individuals; check catalog for details.

Send a check for $5.00 (or $3.00 in cash) for a current 50-page catalog.

Ornamental Resources, Inc.

P.O. Box 3010
Idaho Springs, CO 80452
(303) 567-4987

Mail order
Established in 1969

Without a doubt, Ornamental Resources carries the largest variety of beads, buckles, embellishments and ornaments available anywhere. Their extensive line includes Chinese lattice-carved hollow bone beads, Bedouin silver beads, faience Egyptian figures, costume jewelry from the 1930s, faceted crystal ball beads, brass beads and drops, metal bell caps, abalone shell pieces, old Chinese metal tube beads, old French sequin drops, brass cones, flat-backed rhinestones, glass-based pearls, metallic finish glass beads, mirror buttons, stones and semiprecious gems (garnet, jade, agate, onyx, quartz), Chinese porcelains, shell, woods, corals, feathers, horn and thousands more. A large line of instructional books on beadwork, jewelry, macramé and other crafts is also offered.

The company gives occasional hands-on workshops in various techniques. Contact Irma Fleming for more information.

A current 200-page catalog in a three-ring binder is $15.00. This includes UPS delivery and all updates and supplements, which are sent out every 10 to 12 weeks.

Quintessence '84

Debra Gordon-Hannah, owner of Quintessence '84, offers one-on-one service to her customers and provides fashion designers and other fiber artists with products usually available only in large quantities. She carries a variety of intriguing, unique items such as eelskin panels, frog skins, lambskin suedes, snakeskins (whipsnake, baby python, adult python and king cobra), scrap goods (suede, leathers, lizard and snakeskins), an exotics testing kit (includes lambskin suede, leather and snakeskin), fishskin, embossed and smooth leathers and belt strips. Quintessence '84 also offers ready-to-paint silk clothing, silk painting kits, dressmaker accessories and labels. Oriental rice pearls, abalone buttons, mother-of-pearl tusks and semiprecious stone nuggets are also available.

Below-retail prices are offered to all; check catalog for details.

Send $5.00 for a one-year subscription to the catalog, which includes several updates each year.

3166 Maple Drive, Suite 231
Atlanta, GA 30305
(404) 264-1759

Mail order, retail
Established in 1981

Shipwreck Beads

Shipwreck Beads, owned by Glenn Vincent and managed by Buck Boling, was the first North American company in over 50 years to import beads from Czechoslovakia. The company carries an amazing assortment of Austrian, Czechoslovakian, West German, Italian and Indian beads in stock.

Quantity discounts are given; write for details.

Send $3.00 for a current catalog.

5021 Mud Bay Road
Olympia, WA 98502
(206) 866-4061

Mail order, retail, wholesale, distributor
Established in 1968

Sposabella Lace Company/La Sposa Veil

Sposabella Lace Company/La Sposa Veil offers a complete line of bridal fabrics, laces, trims and veils.

Quantity discounts are given to individuals; contact Frank Sena for information.

Send for a current price list.

252 W. 40th Street
New York, NY 10018
(212) 391-4208

Mail order, retail
Established in 1974

Susan of Newport

Susan of Newport, owned by Susan Ziegler, specializes in a wide range of quality laces and ribbons at low prices. Some of Ms. Ziegler's current items include ½-in. silk roses in 21 colors, Offray double-faced satin ribbons on mini spools, white and natural pearls by the yard, 6-in. wide nylon tulle, ruffled eyelets, lace appliqués, Venetian laces, rhinestones, sequins, metallic braids, rickrack and fancy eyelet beadings.

Wholesale discounts are given on quantity orders; write for details.

Send $5.00 for a folder of catalog sheets complete with actual samples of laces (refundable on first order).

P.O. Box 3107
Newport Beach, CA 92663
(714) 673-5445

Mail order
Established in 1980

Tekison Button Company

Tekison Button Company, owned by Scott and Linda Schnebly, offers a line of beautiful buttons—most are handmade in their own workshop. All of the buttons are made of natural materials, including horn, wood, antler and walnut shells. The Schneblys also do custom work in ivory and antler.

Quantity discounts are given with a $25.00 minimum order.

Send $5.00 for a complete set of samples and a current price list.

P.O. Box 442
Hailey, ID 83333
(208) 788-3107

Mail order, manufacturer
Established in 1977

Tinsel Trading Company

47 W. 38th Street
New York, NY 10018
(212) 730-1030

Mail order, retail, wholesale
Established in 1933

Tinsel Trading Company carries authentic metallic threads from the 1920s and 1930s, in addition to modern Lurex® threads, braids, fringes, cords, tassels, gimps, medallions, edging, bullions, soutache and many other types of trim.

Quantity discounts are given to individuals; write for details.

Send for a free brochure.

Universal Synergetics, Inc.

16510 S.W. Edminston Road
Wilsonville, OR 97070
(503) 625-7168

Mail order
Established in 1977

Universal Synergetics is owned by Virginia Blakelock (author of the self-published *Those Bad, Bad Beads*, 1988) and Carol Perrenoud, both of whom are nationally known experts on the use of beads and beading. They offer a selection of opaque and transparent beads in several sizes and many colors, as well as a selection of pre-World War I Italian and Czechoslovakian beads.

Send a SASE for a current price list.

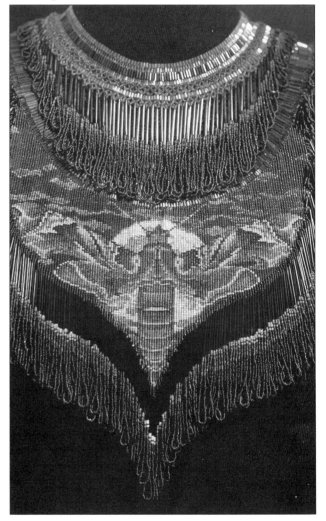

Cleopatra Collar (above), made by Virginia Blakelock of Universal Synergetics from a variety of beads. Oleander Hawk Moth necklace (right), made from size-16 vintage beads.

Papermaking Supplies 5

If you make paper by hand, this chapter contains sources for everything you need—raw fibers (including cotton linters, abaca, kozo, flax, mitsumata and other exotics), instruction books, basic tools, beaters and presses, molds and deckles and colorants. You'll also find conservation supplies for restoring or preserving finely made paper, prints and drawings, and sources of supplies for Japanese-style papermaking.

Carriage House Handmade Paper Works

1 Fitchburg Street #C207
Somerville, MA 02143
(617) 629-2337

Mail order, retail
Established in 1975

Carriage House Handmade Paper Works is owned by the mother-and-daughter team of Elaine and Donna Koretsky, both nationally recognized artists working in handmade paper. The studio was first established to research and experiment with handmade paper as an art form, which it continues to do, and now provides information, technical assistance and a full line of papermaking supplies. Papermaking kits and prepared pulps, such as manila hemp (abaca), cotton linters, sisal and Indian hemp, are available. Also available are bark fibers used in Asian papermaking, including kozo, mitsumata and daphne. Other supplies include additives such as retention agents, formation aids, soda ash, calcium carbonate and colorants. Elaine Koretsky's useful book, *Color for the Hand Papermaker* (Carriage House Press, 1983), is available from this source. The studio sponsors various workshops and other programs and sells handmade papers.

Quantity discounts are given on some items; the check catalog for details.

Send $1.00 for a current catalog and price list.

Colophon Hand Bookbindery

1902 N. 44th Street
Seattle, WA 98103
(206) 633-1759

Mail order, retail, manufacturer
Established in 1975

Colophon Hand Bookbindery, owned by Don Guyot, offers a variety of supplies and equipment for traditional and Oriental paper marbling and hand bookbinding. Papermakers will find many useful items in Colophon's extensive list of supplies. Mr. Guyot also offers instruction and workshops on paper and fabric marbling.

Quantity discounts are given to individuals with a $15.00 minimum order.

Send $1.00 for a current catalog and price list.

David Reina Designs makes high-quality, studio-sized paper-pulping equipment (Hollanders) for private, business and school use. Mr. Reina will also make papermaking equipment and equipment parts on a custom basis.

Send for a current price list or call for information on custom orders.

David Reina Designs, Inc.

24 Harvard Avenue
Maplewood, NJ 07040
(201) 762-5371

Mail order, manufacturer
Established in 1975

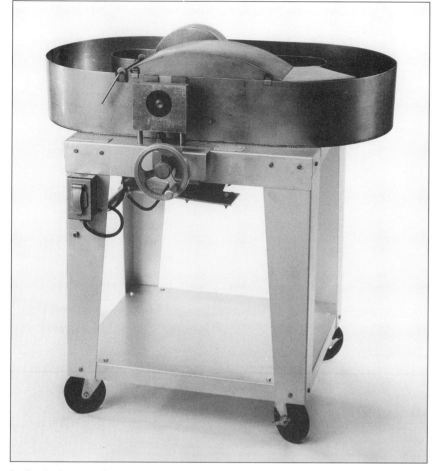

Studio-sized paper pulping equipment with a Hollander-style beater and stainless-steel tub, from David Reina Designs

Dieu Donné Press and Paper, owned by Paul Wong, supplies 100% cotton and linen beaten pulps (wet and dry) in white or custom-dyed shades, raw sheet linters, abaca half-stock and custom paper pulps. The company also offers 100% rag handmade papers, in stock or on a custom basis.

Discounts are offered to retailers only; write for information.

Send for a free price list.

Dieu Donné Press and Paper

3 Crosby Street
New York, NY 10013
(212) 226-0573

Mail order, manufacturer
Established in 1976

The Famport Company

476 A Merrick Road Rear
Lynbrook, NY 11563
(516) 887-4231

Mail order, manufacturer
Established in 1976

The Famport Company, owned by Elliott M. Ruben, manufactures Paperkits, a papermaking kit that includes all the tools and materials necessary for making paper: mold and deckle, felts, pulp and clearly written instructions. Mr. Ruben started out as a hobby papermaker, then realized that other artists and craftspeople might be interested in his procedures. Paperkits were designed as an easy source of supply for beginning papermakers. Also offered by Famport are additional cotton linters, abaca sheets and extra felts.

Send a SASE for a current catalog.

Paperkit supplies, from The Famport Company

What are Cotton Linters?

After cotton is harvested, the long fibers are removed for use in textiles. The shorter, coarser fibers that remain attached to the cotton seed are known as cotton linters. These are then cut from the seed, cooked, and used to make paper. The linters produce a pulp with low-shrinkage, which is good for paper casting. The fibers are too short, however, for making durable papers for books, prints or drawings.

Fiberplus Company

2716 Riverside Lane
Cayce, SC 29033
(803) 796-7133

Mail order
Established in 1982

Fiberplus offers a wide variety of pulps and raw fibers for papermaking at reasonable prices. These include abaca in bleached or semibleached forms, three grades of cottons, esparto, hemp and sisal. Fibers include abaca, flax, flax waste, kapok, kenaf, Thai kozo, ramie tops and sisal.

Quantity discounts are given to individuals; check the price list for details.

Send for a free price list.

Gold's Artworks, Inc.

2100 N. Pine Street
Lumberton, NC 28358
(800) 356-2306
(919) 739-9650 in North Carolina

Mail order, retail shop
Established in 1979

Joe and Frances Gold, owners of Gold's Artworks, sell papermaking supplies to leading paper artists all over the U.S., as well as to large retail art stores, small paper mills and studio workshops. The catalog includes cotton linter pulps in five different grades (sold by the sheet or by the pound) as well as raffia, sea grass and abaca pulps. Coloring materials include Perma Color dry pigments in 11 colors, retention agents, dust masks, vinyl gloves and Texticolor pearlized pigments in 12 shades. Other supplies include methyl-cellulose paste powder, sizing, calcium carbonate, acid test strips, Sculpta mold, Marblex, hydrated pulp, papermaking kits, molds and deckles, nylon and spun rayon felts, a vacuum table and an assortment of books on papermaking.

Quantity discounts are given to individuals; check the catalog for details.

Send for a free catalog.

ICOSA is the papermaking studio of Margaret Ahrens Sahlstrand. The facility can be rented and includes access to a Hollander beater, hydropulper, vacuum table and press. The fee includes three Hollander loads of pulp, beaten in advance and ready for use. In-studio workshops are available for beginners and include topics such as an introduction to fibers for sheet forming and casting, use of the Hollander beater and hydropulper, and relief and flat forms constructed on a vacuum table. Linen, cotton and oriental paper fibers are also available.

Ms. Sahlstrand will travel to present workshops in papermaking and to lecture on Japanese and Korean papermaking techniques.

Discounts are given on studio rentals of three days or more.

Send for a free brochure.

ICOSA Studio and Papermill

Route 4, Box 279
Ellensburg, WA 98926
(509) 964-2341

Mail order, manufacturer, rental facility
Established in 1975

The ICOSA logo

What is Abaca?

Abaca is a fiber obtained from the leafstalk of a banana plant *(Musa textilis)* native to the Philippines. It is sometimes called Manila hemp.

James F. Gormely, Sr., buys and sells new and used equipment for papermaking, such as beaters, vacuum pumps, motors, pulpers, fourdriniers, dryers, laminators, presses and other tools.

Write for more information.

James F. Gormely, Sr.

97 Spier Falls Road
Gansevoort, NY 12831-9631
(518) 792-2772

Mail order

What are Kenaf and Esparto?

Kenaf (pronounced "kuh-NAHF") is a fiber from the Bombay hemp plant of the East Indies. Its botanical name is *Hibiscus cannabinus,* and it is also called Java jute, bastard jute, Deccan hemp and ambari.

Esparto is a fiber from the esparto grass plant. Its botanical name is *Lygeum spartam.* The fiber has historically been used in the manufacture of cordage, shoes (espadrilles, which got their name from the fiber), baskets and paper. It is a moderately long fiber that is very tough and strong. The fiber itself can be compared to hemp, jute and sisal.

—Courtesy of Twinrocker Handmade Paper

Lee S. McDonald, Inc., Fine Hand Papermaking and Equipment

P.O. Box 264
Charlestown, MA 02129
(617) 242-2505

Mail order, manufacturer
Established in 1978

Lee S. McDonald offers all the equipment and supplies needed to make handmade paper. Easy-to-use kits are offered for beginners, as well as pulp-processing equipment for professionals. Other supplies included in the extensive catalog are molds and deckles, custom molds, mold-making supplies, mixers and beaters, pattern pistols and vacuum tables. For coloring handmade paper, aqueous-dispersed and pearlescent pigments are also offered. Pulps and fibers include cotton linters, cotton rag, abaca, Spanish flax, kozo, gampi, mitsumata and Thai kozo. Sample kits of both pulps and fibers are available. Other supplies and equipment include felts, vats, presses, drying machines, Oriental papermaking molds, stampers, Nagashizuki molds, presses and vats. A selection of books on papermaking is also listed.

Send for a free catalog.

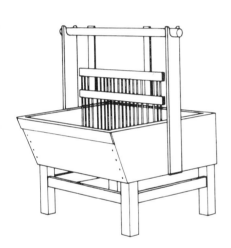

A Nagashizuki papermaking vat, available from Lee S. McDonald

From the Lee S. McDonald catalog

Paper Source, owned by Wallace Dawes, supplies pulps, fibers and additives to hand papermakers. Also available are materials for the care and preservation of handmade papers and textiles. Paper Source also houses a paper museum, which is devoted to the history and technology of paper, and sponsors a variety of workshops and seminars on paper and papermaking.

Quantity discounts are given on orders of $25.00 or more.

Send $4.00 for a current catalog.

Paper Source, Ltd.

1506 W. 12th Street
Los Angeles, CA 90015
(213) 387-5820

Mail order, retail
Established in 1977

Rod Garrett manufactures the Garrett hydropulper and mixer, the first real alternative to the kitchen blender or the Hollander beater. This safe, convenient, compact, quiet and efficient unit rehydrates cotton linter, sheet abaca and other processed fibers in a few minutes. The mixer evenly disperses pigments, dyed pulp and additives, and mixes solutions. The hydropulper is available in two sizes: the portable unit and the studio model. Also available from Mr. Garrett is a pulp sprayer assembly, which sprays up to one gallon of pulp per minute.

Discounts are given to qualified dealers only.

Send for a current brochure and price list.

Rod Garrett: Design

P.O. Box 2996
San Rafael, CA 94912
(415) 232-0949

Mail order, manufacturer
Established in 1987

Sea Pen Press and Paper Mill, owned by Suzanne Ferris and Neal Bonham, offers custom-made pulps for hand papermakers. The company also specializes in custom watermarks in handmade papers.

Discounts are given to individuals with a $50.00 minimum order; write for information.

Send $6.00 for a current catalog and paper samples.

Sea Pen Press and Paper Mill

2228 N.E. 46th Street
Seattle, WA 98105
(206) 522-3879

Manufacturer
Established in 1976

Talas specializes in products for paper-art conservation and archival treatment, although they do supply general papermaking, marbling and bookbinding supplies. Cotton pulps, linter fibers, Dr. Martin's dyes and rag half-stuff fibers are offered, as well as sizing agents (alum, Aquapel 380, methyl cellulose and calcium carbonate). A selection of books on papermaking are also listed in the extensive catalog.

For those papermakers who also use bookbinding or marbling techniques in their work, Talas offers book presses, binding supplies and tools, leathers and preservatives, machine-cut type, bookcloths, papers and boards and adhesives. Marbling supplies include carrageen moss, carrageenan, gum tragacanth, marbling inks, ox gall, preserving liquid and a marbling comb.

Quantity discounts are given to individuals; check the catalog for details.

Send $5.00 for the current 115-page catalog.

Talas

213 W. 35th Street
New York, NY 10001-1996
(212) 736-7744

Mail order, retail
Established in 1962

Twinrocker Handmade Paper

P.O. Box 413
Brookston, IN 47923
(317) 563-3119

Mail order, retail, manufacturer
Established in 1971

The Twinrocker logo

Twinrocker, owned by Kathryn and Howard Clark, offers a full range of papermaking supplies for the beginner and advanced papermaker. The owners believe (and many agree) that Twinrocker has played a major role in the revival of hand papermaking in the U.S. and has aided the development of many artistic techniques. In addition to specializing in custom handmade paper, Twinrocker also offers a wide range of supplies for papermaking. Ready-to-use pulps and dry fibers include cotton linters and linter pulp, 100% cotton rag and rag pulp, unbeaten cotton rag half-stuff, raw cotton pulp and unbeaten raw cotton fiber. Raw flax, raw line flax, ready-to-use cooked flax pulp, Spanish flax pulp, ready-to-use linen pulp and unbeaten linen fibers are also offered. Other fibers available in raw, unbeaten or ready-to-use forms include Russian hemp, abaca, coir, kapok, sisal and wheat straw. Japanese fibers include kozo, mitsumata, gampi, esparto and kenaf.

Papermaking molds and deckles are available in a variety of sizes, and include deckles for making envelopes. Studio equipment includes the Howard Clark hand papermaker's press and a Hollander beater. Additional supplies for papermaking include a classroom-sized papermaking kit, individual papermaking kits, sizing, pigments, retention agents, kaolin, calcium carbonate, PMP formation aid (for use in Japanese-style papermaking), methyl cellulose and safety aids. Twinrocker is also a professional paper mill that makes custom and stocked handmade artist papers in all shapes and sizes up to 34 in. by 48 in. The Clarks also offer technical assistance, welcome visitors and give workshops at the studio and other locations.

Quantity discounts are given to individuals; check the catalog for details.

A papermaking-supplies catalog is free; a swatch set of handmade papers is $7.50; a sample book with studio services is $40.00.

University Products, Inc.

P. O. Box 101
Holyoke, MA 01041
(800) 628-1912
(413) 532-3372 in Massachusetts

Mail order
Established in 1968

University Products is the largest manufacturer and distributor of archivally safe materials for the preservation of documents, photos and textiles. Makers of handmade paper will especially be interested in the archival storage boxes, specimen trays, acid-free tissue papers and binders, dry mounting supplies, adhesives and albums useful for preserving works of art on paper. The company also offers a selection of handmade Japanese papers, acid-free adhesives and tapes, humidity indicators and other conservation supplies.

Quantity discounts are given with a minimum order of $25.00.

Send for a free 130-page catalog.

Basketmaking Supplies   6

This chapter contains sources for all the basic supplies needed to make baskets. You'll find sources for traditional basketry fibers, as well as "wild collectibles" like swamp-dogwood shoots and yucca leaves.

ACP Inc.

P.O. Box 1426
Salisbury, NC 28145-1426
(704) 636-3034

Mail order, retail, manufacturer
Established in 1978

ACP carries a variety of supplies and materials for basketmaking. These include flat and flat-oval reeds, basket hoops, various handles, tools and dyes, kits, birch bases and caning and seating supplies such as binder cane, sea grass and rush, as well as books.

Discounts are given to teachers and professionals; contact Pat Laughridge for details.

Send $1.00 for a current catalog.

Allen's Basketworks

P.O. Box 02648
Portland, OR 97202
(503) 238-6384

Mail order, retail
Established in 1982

Allen's Basketworks, owned by Allen and Nancy Keeney, supplies a complete line of basket materials, including first-quality natural, smoked, or ultra-bleached reeds in round, flat, flat-oval or square-cut styles; rattans; hoops and handles; wood strips; cornhusks; raffia; sea grass; pine needles; fiber rush and fiber core; wooden bases; and tools, dyes, books and kits.

Quantity discounts are given to individuals; write for details.

Send a SASE for a free catalog.

A Word about Rattan

Rattan (derived from the Malay word *rotan*) is a vining palm. Rattan palms grow from South China to Australia and from Fiji to West Africa. These commercially important plants thrive in the climates of these countries, but attempts to grow them elsewhere have failed.

Light, strong and resilient, rattan has long been used as a structural material. The material we call reed is more properly called rattan core, and is cut from poles of rattan the same way lumber is cut from logs.

Harvested in the jungles of Southeast Asia, notably in Indonesia, the raw poles are transported to factories in Singapore, Hong Kong and China for processing, which is a labor-intensive industry. Many countries treat rattan as a valuable resource and in some cases prohibit its export. If present trends continue, first-quality reed will be a difficult and expensive material to obtain.

—Courtesy of Allen's Basketworks

Alliance Trading Company

1021 R Street
Sacramento, CA 95814
(916) 442-9225

Wholesale
Established in 1986

Alliance Trading Company offers a good selection of reeds and other basketry fibers at low prices to wholesale customers only.

Qualified buyers should send for a free catalog.

Bamboo & Rattan Works is a small family-owned and operated business, which has more than 108 years of experience in the field of basket supplies and materials. The company offers different types and sizes of bamboos, rattans, flat and round reeds, chair canes, cords, mattings, rattan rings and many other items. The company will also custom-manufacture any of their raw materials to your specifications.

Quantity discounts are given; check the catalog for more information.

Send for a free catalog and price list.

Bamboo & Rattan Works, Inc.

470 Oberlin Avenue S.
Lakewood, NJ 08701
(201) 370-0220

Mail order, manufacturer, importer
Established in 1880

Basketree, Etc. offers flat, flat-oval and round reed; sea grass; cane; ash splints; ash and oak handles; oak hoops; rattan rings and much more.

Quantity discounts are given; write for details.

Basketree, Etc.

2709 Corunna Road
Flint, MI 48503
(313) 235-0079

Mail order, retail
Established in 1983

Maggie Silva offers a full line of supplies for making Nantucket baskets, including round and oval pine molds, rim molds, flat handles, hardwood bases and spring-loaded cutters. Ms. Silva also offers several instruction booklets on making Nantucket lightship baskets.

Quantity discounts are given to individuals; write for information.

Write for a current price list.

Basketry by Maggie Silva

55 Leonard Street
Raynham, MA 02767
(508) 822-9773

Mail order
Established in 1984

The Basket Works, owned by Barbara Worthington, carries a number of books on basketmaking, as well as supplies for the craft. Materials include round and flat reed, half-round reed, ash splints, sea grass, flat paper fiber, strand cane, wheat, binding cane, handles, raffia, wooden hoops and frames.

Discounts are given on retail orders over $75.00.

Send $1.00 for a current catalog.

The Basket Works

4900 Wetheredsville Road
Baltimore, MD 21207
(301) 448-0800

Mail order, retail
Established in 1977

Bill Fimpler, Jr., owner of Cane & Basket Supply Company, carries a full line of basketry and caning supplies. These include cane webbing, chair cane, fiber rush, Hong Kong sea grass, flat reed and flat-oval reed splint, ash and fiber splint, coiled round and split reeds, hoops, handles, rims, bases, raffia, bamboo, willow and buri sticks. Also offered is a selection of kits, tools, other supplies and books. Mr. Fimpler also restores cane, rush and wicker furniture.

Quantity discounts are given with a minimum order of $50.00.

Send $1.00 for a complete catalog and price list.

Cane & Basket Supply Company

1283 S. Cochran Avenue
Los Angeles, CA 90019
(213) 939-9644

Mail order, retail
Established in 1934

The Caning Shop

926 Gilman Street
Berkeley, CA 94710
(415) 527-5010

Mail order, retail
Established in 1971

The Caning Shop is owned and operated by Jim Widess, co-author of *The Caner's Handbook* (Van Nostrand Reinhold, 1983). He takes pride in his company's personal service, and states, "If your order is not what you expected, send it back for a full refund." In addition to tools and supplies for chair caning, Mr. Widess also carries many items suitable for hand-made baskets. Included are reed splines, cane webbing, hand-caning supplies, binder cane, Danish seat cord, rawhide, rubber webbing, reed splint, fiber rush, Hong Kong sea grass, ash splint, Shaker tapes, round reeds, wicker braid, handles, rattan poles, kooboo rattan and whole rattan. The Caning Shop offers a large selection of books and videotapes on caning and basketmaking (see the listing on p. 187).

The Caning Shop also offers a wide variety of basketry workshops; write for a current schedule.

Send $1.00 for a current catalog (refundable with your first order).

From The Caning Shop catalog

Carol's Canery

Route 1, Box 48
Palmyra, VA 22963
(804) 589-4001

Mail order
Established in 1984

Carol and Gary Powell, owners of Carol's Canery, offer handmade white oak hoops by special order, as well as other basketmaking supplies. They supply "good-quality materials with fast turnaround on orders."

Send $1.00 for a current catalog.

The Country Seat

The Country Seat claims to be the largest retail supplier of basketmaking supplies in the U.S. Their 21-page catalog includes such items as natural cane in seven thicknesses, binding cane in three sizes, slab and round rattan, prewoven cane, Danish seat cord and nails, round reed, fiber rush, Hong Kong sea grass, raffia, basket bases, raw wooden beads, flat kraft-paper fiber, ash splint, oak splints, ACP cold water dyes for reeds, handle fillers, basket feet, tools and a large selection of kits, as well as all types and sizes of hoops and handles. The current catalog also includes eight pages of books and pamphlets on basketmaking.

Quantity discounts are given to individuals; check the current catalog for details.

Send a large envelope with $.65 postage for a current catalog.

Box 24, R.D. 2
Kempton, PA 19529-9411
(215) 756-6124

Mail order, retail
Established in 1975

Day Basket Company

Ross and Lori Gibson, owners of Day Basket Company, offer handmade baskets and supplies for basketmaking, including top-grade, hand-drawn white oak splints, hoops and handles.

Quantity discounts are given with a minimum order of $200.00.

Send $1.00 and a SASE for a current catalog.

110 W. High Street
North East, MD 21901
(301) 287-6100

Mail order, retail, manufacturer
Established in 1982

Day Basket Company

In 1982, my husband, Ross, bought an old, run-down work-basket factory, fixed it up, and started making baskets again. We still make work baskets, but only a few since they've been replaced by plastic containers. We find that our baskets are being used to maintain the grounds around the White House, and are used to hold cotton that's picked in the South. We now sell most of our baskets for garden and yard work, laundry and decoration. Our baskets are completely handmade the same way they were in 1876. We feel that the old way is still the best way.

—Lori Gibson of Day Basket Company

Photos courtesy of Day Basket Company

English Basketry Willows

R.D. 1, Box 124A
South New Berlin, NY 13843-9649
(607) 847-8264

Mail order
Established in 1983

Bonnie Gale, owner of English Basketry Willows, states that hers is the only business devoted solely to the craft of traditional willow basketmaking. Her willows are available steamed or unsteamed, in natural brown, purple, white and buff colors. Ms. Gale also supplies specialized tools, books and classes on the subject, and offers cuttings of willow plants. The American Willow Growers Network (see the listing on p. 153) was formed by Ms. Gale to promote the growing of willows and exploration of their use.

Quantity discounts are given; check the price list for details.

Send $1.00 for six brochures with samples and information on using willows for basketmaking.

Bonnie Gale of English Basketry Willows

I see myself as a basketmaker and not as an artist. I am involved solely in the strong tradition of European willow basketry, which has centuries of technique to be honored and followed. The function of the finished basket determines the type and size of material and techniques used. Willow is such an exciting plant—it has unique rooting and growing abilities. Each rod is so intrinsically strong that it creates a powerful form of basketry. There is great potential for growing cultivated basketry willows and making traditional willow baskets in North America.

—Bonnie Gale, owner of English Basketry Willows

Frank's Cane and Rush Supply

7252 Heil Avenue
Huntington Beach, CA 92647
(714) 847-0707

Mail order, retail
Established in 1972

Frank's Cane and Rush Supply carries natural materials unavailable elsewhere, such as coir (coconut fiber), sisal cordage, Pakistan grass, sugar-palm fiber, and raffia needles. They also offer reeds, fiber rush, caning supplies, round reed, tools, implements, kits and books.

Quantity discounts are given; write for details.

Send for a free catalog.

From Frank's Cane and Rush Supply catalog

Storing Natural Materials

❖ Never store natural materials outdoors. Heat and sunlight can hurt their flexibility and usefulness.

❖ Store materials in brown paper bags (it's a good idea to label the bag with the contents). Then put the bags in a cardboard box and store it in a cool, dry place. The paper bag absorbs any excess moisture and protects the materials from sunlight (ultraviolet light changes the color of natural materials). The cardboard box protects against heat and moisture.

❖ Never store wet materials—reeds and sea grass can mildew. Make sure they are completely dry before storing.

❖ It's a good idea to coil your materials into a bundle before putting them into the paper bag. Reeds, cane webbing, stand and binder canes can be soaked again when you need them, with no change of color.

—Courtesy of *The Craftsman's Newsletter*, a publication of Frank's Cane & Rush Supply

Michael Sims, of GH Productions, carves a basket handle.

GH Productions

GH Productions, owned by Scott Gilbert and Beth Hester, offers a wide selection of supplies for basketmaking, including handcrafted white oak handles, American-made hardwood hoops, complete Nantucket basketry supplies, white oak splints and rims, books, kits and tools, first-quality reed, binding cane, chair cane, bottoms, brass ears and molds.

Discounts are given to qualified retailers.

Send $1.00 for a current catalog.

8400 Old Hartsville Road
Adolphus, KY 42120
(502) 237-4821

Mail order, manufacturer
Established in 1982

Gratiot Lake Basketry

Carole Kaeding, owner of Gratiot Lake Basketry, offers an assortment of materials for the basketmaker, including round reed, half-round reed, flat-oval reed, multi-color reed mixes, ash splint, red oak, sea grass, cane, oak and poplar rims and hoops, spline, kits and handles. Books, tools and dyes for basket materials are also offered.

Discounts are given to individuals with a $150.00 minimum order.

Send for a free price list.

S.R. 1, Box 16
Mohawk, MI 49950
(906) 337-5116

Mail order, retail
Established in 1982

What is Natural Rush?

Natural rush, a common material used in basketmaking, is simply flat cattail leaves that have to be twisted into a strand before weaving.
—Courtesy of H. H. Perkins Company

H. H. Perkins Company

The H. H. Perkins Company, in business for over 75 years, carries a huge inventory of supplies for basketmaking and chair caning. Some of these include natural strand cane, plastic cane, hardwood pegs, tools, wide binding cane, flat-oval and flat reed, round reeds, half-round and smoked reeds, ash and fiber splint, fiber and natural rush, Hong Kong sea grass, laced and unlaced Danish cord, cane webbing in a variety of sizes and mesh, reed spline, hoops and handles, stencils and dyes for coloring baskets, basket kits, bases, kooboo, rattan poles, raffia, raffia needles, wooden beads, waxed linen and macramé cord. The company also carries a large inventory of books on basketmaking, chair caning and other crafts.

Quantity discounts are given to individuals; check the catalog for details.

Send $1.00 for a current catalog and price list.

10 S. Bradley Road
Woodbridge, CT 06525
(203) 389-9501

Mail order, retail
Established in 1914

Homestyle Shop

Donna Dipzinski, owner of the Homestyle Shop, carries a variety of supplies for the basketmaker, including round and flat reeds, native American maple, black walnut, hickory, cherry and sweet gum strips, wood molds, bases, walnut hull powder for coloring, hand-pounded ash strips, handle fillers, basket legs and a large selection of handles.

Quantity discounts are given to individuals; check the price list for details.

Send for a free price list and catalog.

8400 Caine Road
Millington, MI 48746
(517) 871-3654

Mail order, retail, manufacturer
Established in 1982

Joanne's Baskets & Supplies

219 Squaw Creek Road
Marshall, MI 49068
(616) 781-4919

Mail order, manufacturer
Established in 1984

Joanne's Baskets & Supplies, owned by Joanne Jackson, is the manufacturer and distributor of Weave Rite™ tools for basketmaking. These hand-crafted tools take the place of the more common objects often used, such as ice picks, awls and knitting needles. They are safer and easier to use, and they prevent fraying and splitting of the weaving material. The five basic types of Weave Rite™ tools include small implements with walnut handles for close, accurate work; regular-sized tools for medium baskets; heavy-duty tools for large baskets; extra-long tools for a long reach; and a heavy-duty packing tool. All but the small tools come with cherry handles. The tools, developed and patented by Ms. Jackson's husband, are handmade, hand forged, ground and polished from stainless steel.

Quantity discounts are available; write for details or contact your nearest craft supplier.

Write for a free brochure and price list.

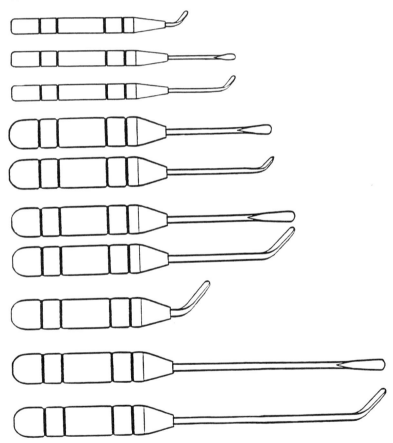

Weave Rite™ tools, available from Joanne's Baskets & Supplies

John E. McGuire, a nationally recognized authority on woodsplint basketry, carries a variety of supplies for traditional basketmaking. These include molds in assorted shapes and sizes, Nantucket bases and findings, and tools such as froes, drawknives, portable lathes and shavehorses. He also supplies pounded black ash splint in coils. Mr. McGuire is available for private classes and seminars on traditional New England splint basketry, Shaker basketry and Nantucket lightship basketry.

Quantity discounts are given to individuals; write for details.

Send a long SASE for a current price list.

**John E. McGuire
Basket Supplies**

398 S. Main Street
Geneva, NY 14456
(315) 781-1251

Mail order
Established in 1983

John McGuire, working at a shavehorse, uses a drawknife to prepare fresh hickory for basket handles.

North Star Wood Products

247 N. Ash Street
Gwinn, MI 49841
(906) 346-6195

Mail order, manufacturer
Established in 1987

North Star Wood Products, owned by Jacqui Day, offers solid-oak basket handles at low prices, along with "prompt, courteous and personal service." The handles are available in four basic styles: round, square with center grips, side-swing and round-swing. Some handles can also be made to order on a custom basis.

Wholesale price lists are available to craft stores and distributors only. Call for further details.

Send a long SASE for a current price list (specify retail or wholesale).

What is Kooboo?

Kooboo is natural rattan reed with the skin intact. This material is ideal for weaving large baskets and containers, and it possesses great strength.

—Courtesy of H. H. Perkins Company

Ozark Basketry Supply

P.O. Box 56, Highway 21 N.
Kingston, AR 72742
(501) 665-2702

Mail order, retail
Established in 1981

Pamela Janus, owner of Ozark Basketry Supply, offers "prompt, personal service with top-quality supplies at low prices." These include flat and smoked reeds, flat-oval reeds, ash and oak splints, fiber splint, chair and binding cane, slab rattan, reed spline, round reeds and rattans, ropes, cords and braids, handles, kits, dyes and tools. Ms. Janus also offers an unusual selection of "wild collectibles" including cattail leaves, yucca leaves, broom corn, palmetto leaves, willow shoots, swamp-dogwood shoots, pine needles, cornhusks, and barks from red cedar, mulberry root, basswood, paper birch, tulip poplar and hickory trees. Also available is a selection of books, including some on Japanese basketry. Ms. Janus sponsors an annual Ozark Basketry Seminar in Arkansas.

Discounts are given to individuals with a $125.00 minimum order. Check the current catalog for details.

Send $.50 for a current catalog and price list.

Pamela Janus of Ozark Basketry Supply

Pamela (Weiland) Janus has been weaving baskets using natural fibers for 17 years. She is currently researching early Indian basketry of the Northeast coast in her efforts to reproduce the few remaining examples and remnants. An instructor at restorations, art centers and museums throughout the country (including the Smithsonian's National Museum of Design and the Museum of American Folk Art), Pamela was invited to live with the Jicarilla Apaches in New Mexico to study their basketry techniques.

Plymouth Reed and Cane Supply

1200 W. Ann Arbor Road
Plymouth, MI 48170
(313) 455-2150

Mail order, retail
Established in 1982

Plymouth Reed and Cane Supply offers materials for the basketmaker, including round and flat reed, splint, ash, poplar and cherry splint, sea grass, Basketree® dyed reed, chair cane, binding cane, cane webbing, fiber rush, spline, Shaker chair tape, handles in various sizes, Shaker molds, Nantucket basket bases, Weave Rite™ tools, dyes and stains, kits and books. Plymouth Reed and Cane Supply also offers a number of classes at their retail location.

Quantity discounts are given with a $100.00 minimum order.

Send $1.00 for a current catalog.

Richard Spicer, owner of Poplin Hollow Baskets, supplies several different styles of hand-carved white oak basket handles on a stock or custom basis. Some of the stock handles include a square/closed notch handle, a swing-attachment handle and an outside wedge/closed notch handle. Mr. Spencer also teaches white oak basketry and produces his own white oak baskets.

Quantity discounts are given; write for prices.

Send for a free price list.

Poplin Hollow Baskets

Route 3, Box 146
Linden, TN 37096
(615) 589-5696

Mail order, manufacturer
Established in 1982

Richard Spicer, of Poplin Hollow Baskets, with one of his handmade laundry baskets

Sarah's Basket

Route 23, Box 22C
Fayetteville, NC 28301
(919) 483-4396

Mail order, retail
Established in 1978

Sarah O. Cain, owner of Sarah's Basket, sells high-quality basket materials, including all types of reed (flat, flat-oval and round), handles, hoops, rush, sea grass, cane, patterns and books.

Quantity discounts are given; write for details.

Send for a free price list.

Tint & Splint Basketry, Inc.

30100 Fort Road—Sheridan Square
Garden City, MI 48135
(313) 522-7760

Mail order, retail, manufacturer
Established in 1984

Tint & Splint Basketry, owned by Kathleen P. Crombie, is a company catering to the amateur and professional basketmaker. The company carries supplies and offers classes, workshops, lectures and seminars. It also hosts some of the nation's finest basketry exhibitions in its newly opened Bay Window Gallery. Supplies offered include round, half-round, flat and flat-oval reed, ash strips, sea grass, philodendron leaf sheaths, English willow bundles, dyes, hardwood hoops, handles, tools and books.

Quantity discounts are given to individuals with a $150.00 minimum order.

Send a SASE for a free catalog.

Guest instructor Char TerBeest (right) chats with a student during a two-day willow basketry workshop at Tint & Splint Basketry.

Virgin Islands Reed & Cane

P.O. Box 8478
Hot Springs Village, AR 71909
(800) 852-0025
(501) 922-3298 in Arizona

Mail order, retail, manufacturer
Established in 1982

Virgin Islands Reed & Cane is a supplier of fresh tropical rattan, reed, cane, exotic basketweaving fibers, hoops, handles and more. Basketry Studio A® instructional basketweaving kits are also available in 19 different designs.

Quantity discounts are given on orders over $100.00.

Send $2.00 for a current catalog or $5.00 for a sample card of fibers.

Miscellaneous Supplies and Services 7

This chapter includes a potpourri of miscellaneous supplies and services for fiber artists. You'll find custom photographers to help you document your work, graphic designers to help create sales materials, manufacturers of labels and tags, suppliers of packaging materials, restoration services and sources for computer software for weavers.

Aleene's

(A Division of Artis, Inc.)
85 Industrial Way
Buellton, CA 93427
(805) 688-7339

Mail order, manufacturer
Established in 1947

Aleene's offers a line of glues and adhesives that can be used with fabrics and other natural fibers. These include Aleene's fabric stiffener (a synthetic substitute for starch or sugar-water stiffeners), hot stitch glue (which permanently bonds fabrics without sewing) and several others.

Write for a current price list.

Charm Woven Labels

P.O. Box 30027
Portland, OR 97230

Mail order
Established in 1955

Charm Woven Labels, owned by Charles Henry, offers a variety of woven labels, including personalized styles, content labels, size tabs, "Made in U.S.A." labels and a variety of stock care labels for clothing and other textile items.

Send for a free price list.

Great Stuff Studio

P.O. Box 51483
Raleigh, NC 27609
(919) 846-2961

Mail order
Established in 1987

Carol Kotsher Marden, owner of Great Stuff Studio, provides business advice and graphic-arts services to small, nontraditional businesses, particularly those that are home based and craft oriented. Ms. Marden will do line drawings and logo designs, as well as provide marketing and promotion advice for craftspeople.

Send a SASE for a current brochure.

Handweaving by Lois Larson

Studio 25
25 Montcalm Avenue
Camrose, AB T4V 2K9
Canada
(403) 672-2551

Mail order, publisher

Here's a one-stop source for all computer software for weavers and other fiber artists. Lois Larson, of Handweaving by Lois Larson, has provided a much-needed service by reviewing and evaluating over 100 computer software programs. She has self-published these reviews in a book, *Software for Weavers...a resource*, which is periodically updated. The book, now in its second edition, provides information on the features, sources and costs of various programs and cites references to magazine reviews. The book includes a large appendix of sample printouts from the programs, programs written in BASIC, free and almost-free programs, as well as a complete listing of source addresses.

Write for current prices and further information.

Helmor Label Company

5143 W. Diversey Avenue
Chicago, IL 60639
(312) 237-6163

Mail order, manufacturer
Established in 1963

Helmor Label Company offers a line of fabric labels for wearing apparel and crafts. The labels can be custom printed with any wording or logo in various fabrics, sizes and ink colors.

Send a #10 SASE for a current price list.

The Kentucky Woman, otherwise known as Nancy Eversole, is a weaver and spinner who also sings and plays a mountain dulcimer, Irish harp, guitar and autoharp. Ms. Eversole says "I have always felt that music and weaving go hand in hand. In fact, I do a lot of singing while I am weaving. It establishes wonderful rhythms." To share her love of music with other weavers, Ms. Eversole has recorded and produced five record albums and tapes, including the most recent *Ballad Weaver* and *A Spinner of Songs*. The albums and tapes, currently $11.00 each (including shipping and handling), contain enchanting Appalachian folksongs from the Southern highlands.

Write or call for more information.

The Kentucky Woman

1124 E. 3rd Street
Mishawaka, IN 46544
(219) 259-0859

Mail order

Betty Smith, owner of Leafwood Studio, provides authentic restoration and maintenance of looms and spinning wheels. Ms. Smith is experienced in museum-level work and gives "individual attention to each customer."

Write or call for further information.

Leafwood Studio

3007 Leafwood Drive
Marietta, GA 30067
(404) 952-0694

Mail order, retail
Established in 1981

M. Dursin & Sons, owned by Marcel Dursin, will custom-dye wool top and blend colors to order. The company offers an exact color match with a minimum 100-lb. order. Vigoureux printing, a process where each fiber is dyed with a small bit of color and a bit of natural, is also available.

Write or call for further information.

M. Dursin & Sons, Inc.

P.O. Box 909
Woonsocket, RI 02895
(401) 767-0700

Mail order, manufacturer
Established in 1959

Mary Lorish Jahn has created a delightful line of notecards and other useful things, such as tags for yarn skeins and handmade items, specifically geared to the weaver, spinner and basketmaker.

Send for a free catalog.

Mary Lorish Jahn

P.O. Box 590
McCall, ID 83638
(208) 253-6081

Mail order
Established in 1981

Note cards available from Mary Lorish Jahn

145

Museum Quality Storage Box Company and Preservation Service

9 Laurel Lane
Pleasantville, NY 10570
(914) 769-4956

Mail order, retail
Established in 1979

Mrs. Viola M. Lappe, owner of Museum Quality Storage Box Company, offers acid-free box units for the conservation and storage of wedding gowns and other textile items, as well as a dry-cleaning and storage service for old textiles. Mrs. Lappe is a member of the Textile Conservation Group, the Costume Society of America and the American Institute for Conservation of Historical and Artistic Works.

Send for a current brochure and price list.

Polybags Plus

3602 Harbor Boulevard
Port Charlotte, FL 33952
(813) 629-6050

Mail order
Established in 1980

Polybags Plus offers a selection of high-quality zip-close polyethylene bags, which can be ordered in small quantities. The bags, available in different weights and sizes, are perfect for organizing and storing threads, buttons, fabrics, patterns and needles. Polybags Plus also carries cloth drawstring bags made of 100% unbleached cotton muslin.

Send for a free price list.

Sterling Name Tape Company

9 Willow Street
Winsted, CT 06098
(203) 379-5142

Mail order, manufacturer
Established in 1901

Sterling Name Tape Company offers custom printed labels on woven edge tapes. The company has a low minimum order and offers several type styles and stock designs to choose from.

Send $1.00 for a current catalog and samples.

Steve Meltzer, regular photography columnist for *The Crafts Report*, offers custom photography services for artists and craftspeople. His specialty is "quick, high-quality photographs of crafts." He is also the author of a comprehensive book entitled *Photographing Your Craftwork* (Madrona Publishers, Inc., 1986) for do-it-yourselfers and leads one-day and two-day seminars on the subject.

Call for more information.

Steve Meltzer Photographer

4721 W. Roberts Way
Seattle, WA 98199
(206) 284-5822

Mail order, photographic services
Established in 1977

Tom Hodge can provide high-quality photos or slides of fiber work and other craft work.

Write for a current price list.

Tom Hodge/Photographics

P.O. Box 401
Belle Mead, NJ 08502
(201) 247-8869

Mail order, photographic services
Established in 1976

Unique Ideas, owned by Marlene R. Proct, offers a number of woven care labels for clothing or fabrics. Eleven stock designs are available, as well as custom-designed labels.

Send for a free brochure.

Unique Ideas

P.O. Box 627
North Bellmore, NY 11710

Mail order
Established in 1980

Vermont Business Cards, owned by Earl and Carole Emerson, offers a line of custom-designed business cards with matching envelopes and letterhead for creative people. The Emersons use only raised print, and offer a wide selection of ink colors, card stocks and type styles. They also have almost 200 stock logos, including images of spinning wheels, sheep, looms and fabrics. These logos are printed free of charge on the business cards, or you can design your own logo to be included. The company also offers a free layout service.

Send $1.00 for a current price list, samples and ordering information.

Vermont Business Cards

R.D. 4, Box 1690-FS
Montpelier, VT 05602
(802) 229-9579

Mail order
Established in 1974

Associations, Education & Information

Associations and Organizations

8

This chapter contains information on the trade and membership associations and organizations representing various areas of the fiber arts. These groups are wonderful sources of general technical information; news of local and regional fiber guilds; and news of local, regional, national and international competitions and shows. Many also produce informative, specialized publications (see Chapter 11), and they may prove helpful in locating experts to speak at guild or chapter meetings.

Since most of these groups are nonprofit organizations with small, often volunteer, staffs, please include a self-addressed, stamped envelope when writing for information.

American Craft Council

Membership Department
P.O. Box 1308
Fort Lee, NJ 07024-9990

Nonprofit organization
Established in 1943

The American Craft Council is a national nonprofit membership organization founded to encourage craftsmen, foster appreciation of their work and provide various educational programs. The Council maintains the American Craft Museum in New York City (which is open to the public) and a research library and audiovisual service (which are available to the public at nonmembership rates). Through its subsidiary, American Craft Enterprises, craft markets are sponsored in various areas of the U.S.

Membership includes a subscription to *American Craft* magazine (see p. 204), free admission to exhibits at the American Craft Museum and more.

Write for current membership fees.

The American Minor Breeds Conservancy

P.O. Box 477
Pittsboro, NC 27312
(919) 542-5704

Nonprofit organization
Established in 1977

The American Minor Breeds Conservancy works for the conservation of rare breeds of livestock in North America. The AMBC wants to preserve endangered and minor breeds to ensure against the loss of genes that may have commercial or cultural value in the future. The group serves as a clearinghouse for information and assists breeders and breed associations.

Contact Don Bixby or Carolyn Christman for more information.

American Needlepoint Guild

P.O. Box 3525
Rock Hill, SC 29731

Nonprofit association
Established in 1972

The American Needlepoint Guild is an educational, nonprofit organization dedicated to the art of canvas embroidery. The guild sponsors a bimonthly magazine, *Needle Pointers,* as well as a national annual meeting, programs of certification in teaching and judging, correspondence courses and regional chapters.

Write for current membership fees and information.

American Quilt Study Group

833 Market Street, Suite 620
San Francisco, CA 94103
(415) 495-0163

Nonprofit association
Established in 1980

The American Quilt Study Group's major aim is to develop an accurate body of information on the history of quilt making in America. The AQSG encourages research in the history of quilts, quilt making and textiles, and sponsors a variety of publications, seminars and scholarships.

Write for current membership information.

American Quilter's Society

P.O. Box 3290
Paducah, KY 42002-3290
(502) 898-7903

Nonprofit association
Established in 1984

The American Quilter's Society sponsors a national quilt competition and contest every April and publishes *American Quilter* magazine.

Write to Meredith Schroeder for membership information.

The American Sewing Guild, sponsored by the American Home Sewing Association, is an organization for people who like to sew simply because it's a creative and rewarding activity. The purpose of the Guild is to provide up-to-date sewing information for all skill levels through expert lectures, demonstrations, classes, seminars and fashion shows. Local guild chapters function autonomously under a volunteer chairperson. All members receive a local chapter newsletter.

Write for information on your local ASG chapter.

American Sewing Guild

P.O. Box 50976
Indianapolis, IN 46250-0976
(317) 845-9128

Nonprofit organization
Established in 1978

The American Tapestry Alliance was formed to promote an awareness of and appreciation for tapestries designed and woven in the U.S.; to establish a professional network of artists; to sponsor and coordinate juried exhibits of tapestry; and to encourage the purchase of tapestries by private collectors and corporate buyers. The Alliance also works to educate the public about the art of tapestry weaving and to establish a national directory and slide archive of tapestries. Membership benefits include a quarterly newsletter, source files, news of shows and exhibits, workshops, seminars and listing in a membership directory.

An associate-level membership is currently $25.00 per year; write for more information.

American Tapestry Alliance

Route 2, Box 570-D
Chiloquin, OR 97624
(503) 783-2507

Nonprofit organization
Established in 1982

The American Willow Growers Network is a new organization formed to promote the growth and use of American willows in basketmaking. The Network provides information on growing and harvesting willows and offers willow cuttings for sale.

Contact Bonnie Gale for more information.

American Willow Growers Network

R.F.D. 1, Box 124A
South New Berlin, NY 13843
(607) 847-8264

Established in 1988

Arts, Crafts and Theater Safety, directed by Monona Rossol, provides health and safety information services to artists. ACTS answers written and telephone inquiries; refers clients to medical, legal and technical experts; provides speakers for lectures; and distributes educational materials. ACTS also provides information about specific hazards in the fiber arts and suggests suitable precautions, helps fiber businesses and schools meet new federal and state toxic substance regulations, and teaches and trains fiber-arts workers and students in the use of safety devices.

Write to Ms. Rossol for further information on ACTS.

Arts, Crafts and Theater Safety

181 Thompson Street, #23
New York, NY 10012
(212) 777-0062

Health and safety services
Established in 1987

The Center for the Study of Beadwork, directed by Alice Scherer, sponsors classes and exhibitions on beadwork. The Center offers access to research material on beads and sells a number of books on the subject.

Write for more information; a book catalog is $.50.

Center for the Study of Beadwork

P.O. Box 13719
Portland, OR 97212
(503) 249-1848

Resource center
Established in 1986

Crafts Council of Australia

100 George Street, The Rocks
Sydney, NSW 2000
Australia
(02) 241-1701

Nonprofit association
Established in 1971

The Crafts Council of Australia offers a variety of activities and services for Australian craftspeople, including national workshops, lectures and conferences; the quarterly *Craft Australia* journal; and crafts marketing and information services. The Council also maintains a National Craft Register and slide library of Australian craftsmen, operates a computer-based craft information retrieval service and maintains a library.

Write for more information.

The Crafts Council
of Australia logo

The Embroiderers' Guild of America

335 W. Broadway, Suite 100
Louisville, KY 40202
(502) 589-6956

Nonprofit association

The Embroiderers' Guild of America has over 25,000 members in 300 nationwide chapters. The Guild's main purpose is to "foster the highest standards of excellence in the practice of the art of embroidery through an active program of education and study, and to preserve the heritage of the art of embroidery." The EGA sponsors regional and national exhibits, competitions, seminars and correspondence courses. Members receive *Needle Arts* magazine, the quarterly publication featuring embroidery news, articles on technique and more. (See the listing on p. 208.)

Write for current membership fees and more information.

The Embroiderers'
Guild of America logo

Friends of the Dard Hunter Paper Museum

P.O. Box 1039
Appleton, WI 54912

Nonprofit association
Established in 1981

The Friends of the Dard Hunter Paper Museum is the world's largest organization of people interested in the art of hand papermaking. The group is comprised of leading papermakers, artists, scientists and professionals from the pulp and paper industry. Members have access to the most comprehensive library of hand-papermaking information in the world and receive newsletters containing technical and informative articles on papermaking, as well as news of conferences, meetings and educational opportunities. An annual directory of members, cross indexed to their various fields of interest and expertise, is published and sent to each member. (See the museum's listing on p. 160.)

Membership fees are currently $15.00 per year; contact Doug Stone for further information.

Handweaver's Guild of America

120 Mountain Avenue, B101
Bloomfield, CT 06002
(203) 242-3577

Nonprofit association
Established in 1969

The Handweaver's Guild of America is an international nonprofit organization dedicated to the fiber arts. The Guild sponsors Convergence, a biennial conference of fiber artists from all over the world (to be held in San Jose, California in 1990) and Small Expressions, an annual national juried show of small textile pieces. Certificates of excellence certifying proficiency in weaving or spinning and awards of merit are given to members at local or regional exhibits. The HGA also offers a number of textile and slide kits for rent to individual members and guilds, scholarships, publications and a subscription to *Shuttle, Spindle & Dyepot*, the group's official publication (see the listing on p. 209).

Current membership fees are $25.00 per year; write for more information.

The International Silk Association provides a variety of information on silk fiber and its production, history and use. Written guides on silk are available to teachers and students at a minimal charge. A cocoon box is also available for $1.00 and includes a cocoon, a pamphet entitled "The Story of Silk," samples of raw silk, silk sewing thread and a swatch of silk fabric.

Call or write for more information.

International Silk Association

1359 Broadway
Suite 1704
New York, NY 10018
(212) 967-3400

Nonprofit association
Established in 1950

The Knitting Guild of America is a national organization formed to provide educational opportunities and communication between hand and machine knitters. The KGA offers correspondence courses, a master and junior knitter program, national design competitions, sponsorship of local guilds, retail markets, regional seminars and a professional designer membership (screened by special committee). The Guild also publishes *Cast On*, a magazine that features designs and informative articles on knitting (see the listing on p. 205).

Current membership fees are $18.00 per year and include a subscription to *Cast On*.

The Knitting Guild of America

P.O. Box 1606
Knoxville, TN 37901
(615) 524-2401

For-profit association, publisher
Established in 1984

The Mohair Council of America is the promotional organization for mohair produced in the U.S. Dedicated to promoting the general welfare of the mohair industry, the council emphasizes market research and survey and development activities. The council also conducts trade-level advertising and various workshops, seminars and competitions.

Write for further information.

Mohair Council of America

516 Central National Bank Building
San Angelo, TX 76901
(915) 655-3161

Nonprofit association
Established in 1966

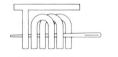

The National
Needlework
Association logo

The National Needlework Association is the trade organization for needlework store owners and retailers. The group represents manufacturers, importers, distributors and retailers from around the country, and its purpose is the "advancement of needlework quality, understanding and marketing in the U.S." through its various membership, educational and promotional programs.

Retailers interested in membership should write for a descriptive brochure.

The National Needlework Association

230 5th Avenue
New York, NY 10001
(212) 685-1646

Trade association
Established in 1974

The National Standards Council of American Embroiderers is an educational, nonprofit organization dedicated to encouraging and nurturing artistic growth through the art of embroidery and other types of needlework. The Council sponsors classes, seminars, tours, study retreats, the biennial Needle Expressions juried competition, a lending library that circulates books by mail and the NSCAE Correspondence School (see the listing on p. 180). The Council also publishes *The Flying Needle*, a quarterly magazine (see the listing on p. 206).

Current membership rates are $20.00 per year and include a subscription to *The Flying Needle*. Write for further information.

National Standards Council of American Embroiderers

P.O. Box 8578
Northfield, IL 60093-8578
(312) 256-1497

Nonprofit organization, school, publisher
Established in 1969

Natural Colored Wool Growers Association

18150 Wildflower Drive
Penn Valley, CA 95946
(916) 432-1589

Nonprofit association
Established 1977

The Natural Colored Wool Growers Association is a national organization for breeders and owners of colored sheep, as well as for people who use or have an interest in colored wools. The purpose of the group is to assist members in the development, improvement and promotion of colored sheep, colored wool and the many uses of the wools. Membership includes a subscription to *The Marker,* a listing in a national directory and affiliation with a regional group.

Current membership fees are $15.00 per year (regular member), $10.00 per year (associate member) or $5.00 per year (junior member). Contact Elaine Vogt for further information.

The Navajo Sheep Project

Animal, Dairy & Veterinary
Science Department
Utah State University
Logan, UT 84322-4815
(801) 750-2154 or 753-7950

Nonprofit organization

The Navajo Sheep Project, directed by Dr. Lyle G. McNeal at Utah State University, is responsible for rescuing the Navajo Churro sheep from extinction. The project sponsors various classes, seminars and tours, and sells raw wool from the Navajo sheep.

Write to Dr. McNeal for more information on the project or to receive a price list for the Navajo wools.

Northern Textile Association

230 Congress Street, 3rd Floor
Boston, MA 02110
(617) 542-8220

Trade association
Established in 1984

The Northern Textile Association is a trade association that aids in the promotion and protection of luxury fibers.

Contact Karl Spilhaus, President, for more information.

Surface Design Association

4111 Lincoln Boulevard, Suite 426
Marina del Rey, CA 90292
(213) 392-2274

Nonprofit association
Established in 1977

The Surface Design Association is a nonprofit, educational organization for artists, designers and teachers who work in the area of surface design, both within and beyond the textile field. The group is dedicated to the promotion of surface design, and sponsors a national conference every two years, as well as annual regional conferences. The SDA also publishes the *Surface Design Journal* (see the listing on p. 209).

Various membership categories apply; write for further information.

Textile Collections 9

This chapter introduces the many textile collections in the U.S. You'll find some museums with broad collections and others devoted to a single area of fiber. And whether the artifacts you find in these collections are examples of Egyptian linens from the early Christian period or 20th-century designer fashions, a visit is sure to delight and inspire.

Many of these museums have small staffs, low budgets and little time, and you should take this into account when corresponding with them. Because many of the collections have seasonal hours, it's a good idea to call or write before visiting. Arrangements can also be made at most of the museums for in-depth study and research by calling or writing the curator.

Also note that the only collections included in this listing are those whose curators responded to our questionnaire. If your favorite collection is missing, suggest to the curators that they send information for inclusion in the next edition of this sourcebook. Meanwhile, for additional information on U.S. textile collections, consult *Quilt Collections: A Directory for the United States and Canada* by Lisa Turner Oshins (Acropolis, 1987) and *United States and Canada: An Illustrated Guide to Textile Collections in United States and Canadian Museums*, edited by Cecil Lubell (Van Nostrand Reinhold, 1976).

Abby Aldrich Rockefeller Folk Art Center

307 S. England Street
P.O. Box C
Williamsburg, VA 23187

Contact persons: Barbara R. Luck, Curator; Richard Miller, Associate Curator

The Abby Aldrich Rockefeller Folk Art Center textile collection currently consists of 110 bedcovers of various sorts: woven coverlets, appliqué quilts, pieced quilts, stuffed-work whole cloth covers, embroidered blankets and more. In addition, the museum has a few miscellaneous items such as pieces of woven carpeting, hooked rugs, show towels, purses and belts. The museum also has a sizable collection of embroidered pictures, including mourning pictures, family records and a few samplers.

Note: The Folk Art Center will be closed for building and remodeling for at least two years. Most of the collection will not be accessible during this time, although some of the pieces may be shown in other museums within the Colonial Williamsburg Foundation. In the meantime, the curators of the museum will be glad to respond to mail queries about the collection.

Art Institute of Chicago Department of Textiles

Michigan Avenue at Adams Street
Chicago, IL 60603
(312) 443-3600

Contact person: Christa C. Meyer Thurman, Curator of the Department of Textiles

The Art Institute of Chicago Department of Textiles contains the most comprehensive collections of Western textiles in the Midwest. Included are fabrics, costume and clothing accessories dating from A.D. 100 to the present. Among the textile holdings are woven, embroidered and printed fabrics; a large lace collection; and a growing contemporary collection.

Interested researchers and visitors should contact the Department of Textiles for more information.

Bernice Pauahi Bishop Museum

P.O. Box 19000-A
Honolulu, HI 96817-0916
(808) 848-4135

The Bernice Pauahi Bishop Museum, one of the world's leading scientific institutions, is the principal museum of the Pacific in research, collection and publication. The museum is dedicated to preserving the cultural heritage of Hawaii and collects examples of barkcloth, featherwork, ceremonial costumes, lauhala plaitings and Hawaiian quilts, among other things.

Call or write for a current exhibit schedule.

Burlington County Historical Society

457 High Street
Burlington, NJ 08016
(609) 386-4773

Contact person: Rhett Pernot

The Burlington County Historical Society textile collection consists of a number of samplers, quilts and costumes. The samplers include several Burlington County pictorial samplers and examples of the more ordinary darning and alphabet samplers. The quilt collection contains pieced and appliqué quilts in a variety of fabrics and patterns, as well as a few handwoven coverlets. The costume collection includes Quaker attire and Victorian dresses.

Write or call for further information.

The Busch-Reisinger Museum is a small university museum with an important collection of Bauhaus textiles. These include samples and larger weavings by Anni Albers as well as samples by Otti Berger, Gunda Stadler-Stolzl, Marli Ehrmann and Florence Knoll Associates. Other Bauhaus artists represented include Josef Albers, Benita Otte and Margarete Bittkow-Koehler.

Interested persons should contact the museum in advance for permission to visit.

Busch-Reisinger Museum

Harvard University
32 Quincy Street
Cambridge, MA 02138
(617) 495-2317
(617) 495-2338 (for recorded information about exhibitions and other programs)

Contact person: Emilie Norris, Curatorial Associate

The Center for the History of American Needlework (CHAN) began in 1974 when five women from the University of Pittsburgh saw the need to document and preserve the work of the American needleworker. Today CHAN publishes a quarterly newsletter that contains articles about contemporary needlework as well as reprints of pertinent articles from the past. The textile collection of CHAN contains examples of various needlework techniques, unfinished work that shows work in progress, ethnic pieces and more.

CHAN also holds classes and seminars on various aspects of historical needlework. A series of reworked Victorian patterns is also available from the center.

Send $2.00 for a sample newsletter and more information.

Center for the History of American Needlework

P.O. Box 359
Valencia, PA 16059

Contact person: Mary Ann Geiger

The textile collection of the Cleveland Museum of Art consists of nearly 3,800 pieces from all parts of the world, dating from 2000 B.C. to the present. Pieces of major significance can be found in the areas of medieval Spanish, Italian and German textiles, including an extremely rare 14th-century Spanish carpet, a German 14th-century lenten cloth, a large Nasrid curtain, and three Florentine embroideries. Also significant are medieval Iranian and Iraqi textiles, with three complete garments; and Egyptian/Syrian textiles from the early Christian period through the Mamluk period.

The collection also includes European printed, woven, and embroidered textiles of the 16th century to the 19th century; Chinese textiles of the 8th century to the 20th century, including fragments from the Shosoin and Horiuji collection, a rare embroidered priest's robe (circa 1400) and a 15th-century embroidery from Chinese Turkestan; Indian textiles from the 12th century to the 20th century; late 19th century and 20th century Indonesian textiles; and distinguished Peruvian textiles from the Chavin, Paracas, Nazca, Huari-Tiahuanaco and Chimu cultures.

Write or call for further information.

Cleveland Museum of Art

11150 E. Boulevard
Cleveland, OH 44106
(216) 421-7340, ext. 256

Contact person: Anne E. Wardwell, Curator, Department of Textiles

Cooper-Hewitt Museum

The Smithsonian Institution's
National Museum of Design
2 E. 9th Street
New York, NY 10128-9990
(212) 860-6868

Contact persons: Milton Sonday,
Curator of Textiles; Gillian Moss,
Assistant Curator of Textiles

The Cooper-Hewitt Museum textile collection includes more than 30,000 pieces, ranging from the Han Dynasty of third-century B.C. China to the present day. Among this impressive array of textiles are ancient and modern woven fabrics; embroidered, resist-dyed and printed textiles; and many nonwoven fabrics such as lace, crochet, knitting and macramé. Comprised mostly of textiles, with few costumes or rugs, the collection is drawn from all corners of the world and includes many artifacts from Western Europe.

Call or write for more information.

Dard Hunter Paper Museum

P.O. Box 1039
Appleton, WI 54912
(414) 738-3455

Contact person: George Boeck or
Doug Stone

The Dard Hunter Paper Museum includes a fascinating and important collection of historical papers, literature and equipment on the art of hand papermaking. Among the most intriguing artifacts in the collection are a number of watermark portraits and "drawings." The collection is in storage until 1991 or 1992, when it will be moved to and associated with Georgia Tech University. Activities of the Friends of the Dard Hunter Paper Museum membership organization (see the listing on p. 154) will continue throughout this transition period. Dues are $15.00 per year.

Write or call for more information.

Denison University Art Gallery

Granville, OH 43023
(614) 587-0810

Contact person: Letha Schetzsle,
Registrar

The Denison University Art Gallery textile collection has a large number of Burmese items among its diverse holdings, including 400 silk and non-silk longyis, tameins, shoulder bags, head scarfs, coats, robes, shirts, jackets and fabrics, cataloged by tribe. The gallery also has 75 Chinese dragon robes and 100 hangings, Cuna Indian molas, 16th-century and 17th-century French tapestries, Indian rugs, Mexican serapes and textiles from Java and Sumatra.

Write or call for further information.

DeWitt Wallace Decorative Arts Gallery

The Colonial
Williamsburg Foundation
P.O. Box C
Williamsburg, VA 23187
(804) 229-1000

Contact person: Linda Baumgarten,
Curator of Textiles

The DeWitt Wallace Decorative Arts Gallery displays a broad range of English and American decorative arts—furniture, metals, prints, maps and textiles—dating from about 1600 through 1830.

Write or call for more information.

Dumbarton Oaks is a private research center with three main textile collections open to the public: the House collection, the Byzantine collection and the Pre-Columbian collection.

The House collection includes approximately 75 medieval, Islamic and Oriental textiles, the majority of which are 16th-century and 17th-century carpets from Persia and Asia Minor. Most of these are currently in storage. Medieval Flemish and German tapestries are generally on display in the music room of Dumbarton Oaks. Several of these works have been published in catalogs, and a bibliography of individual works is available upon written request. Textiles not on exhibition are made available to scholars engaged in projects requiring direct study upon receipt of written request.

The Byzantine collection includes approximately 220 Coptic, medieval and Islamic textiles. A textile gallery exhibits representative works of the collection on a rotating basis. Direct study of the collection is limited to scholars, and a request for permission for access should be directed to the curator.

The Pre-Columbian collection includes 37 textiles from ancient Peru. Among these artifacts are examples from the Chavin, Chancay, Chimu, Inca, Nazca, Paracas and Wari cultures. The textiles are available for study by serious scholars upon written request to the Curator, Pre-Columbian Collection. Space and facilities are extremely limited, so advance arangements are required.

Dumbarton Oaks

1703 32nd Street N.W.
Washington, D.C. 20007
(202) 342-3200

The combined collections of the New York State Historical Association and the Farmers' Museum present an extensive survey of New York State personal, household, functional and ornamental textiles from the 18th, 19th and 20th centuries. Quilts, coverlets, linens, lace and clothing are stored and exhibited at the museums.

Equally extensive is the museum's collection of hand-powered textile tools and equipment from the 18th and 19th centuries. Spinning wheels, looms, sewing machines and small hand tools, as well as a rare vertical spinner and its functional reproduction, provide an in-depth view of home and professional textile production in New York State. An active spinning and weaving loft exhibit and a reproduction textile-production area demonstrates these processes to museum visitors and produces reproductions for special orders and public sale.

Researchers are welcome at the museum and in the storage area by prior appointment. Call or write for more information.

The Farmers' Museum, Inc.

New York State
Historical Association
P.O. Box 800, Lake Street
Cooperstown, NY 13326
(607) 547-2593

Contact person: Kathryn Boardman, Associate Curator

Fashion Institute of Technology
The Edward C. Blum Design Laboratory

227 W. 27th Street
New York, NY 10001
(212) 760-7772

The Fashion Institute of Technology (FIT) Edward C. Blum Design Laboratory is the combined project of The Brooklyn Museum and FIT. It contains one of the world's largest collections of textile swatches, costumes and dress accessories dating from the 14th century to the 20th century. Among FIT's holdings are more than four million indexed swatches, most of them American and European textile, apparel and furnishing fabrics. Also of note are more than 300 swatch books of mid-19th-century and 20th-century European fabrics, jacquard point paper, quilts, croquis, rug samples, laces, embroideries and color swatch cards.

FIT's costume collection contains more than one million articles of dress dating from the 17th century to the present. Included in this collection are men's, women's and children's clothes; furs; foundation garments; lingerie; an outstanding selection of 19th-century and 20th-century designer clothing; and accessories such as hats, bags, gloves, hosiery, shoes and costume jewelry.

The two collections are used mainly on a membership basis by developers and designers of textiles for apparel, home furnishings and accessories. Members may research the collections and have access to the slides, files, sketch books, clippings and manuscripts that make up the FIT library. Members may also use private study rooms on the premises of the Design Laboratory and borrow from the collection for study in their own workrooms. With various restrictions and by prior arrangement, the collections can also be used by museum curators and serious scholars on a nonmembership basis.

The current annual membership fee is $500.00. Use of the collections is by appointment only. Write or call for more information.

Fine Art Museums of San Francisco

Textile Department
M. H. de Young
Memorial Museum
Golden Gate Park
San Francisco, CA 94118
(415) 750-7609

One of the Fine Art Museums of San Francisco, the M. H. de Young Memorial Museum has a broad range of textiles from different cultures and periods. The textiles are on view to the public on a rotating basis.

A catalog of selected works is $8.95. Write or call for further information.

Harris County Heritage Society

1100 Bagby
Houston, TX 77002
(713) 655-1912

Contact person: Brenda R. Jordan, Registrar/Curator

The Harris County Heritage Society has a costume collection that contains approximately 2,500 artifacts, with another 1,500 miscellaneous textile items. Some of this material is always on exhibit in one of the seven historic structures in Sam Houston Park, and special exhibits are shown in the Museum of Texas History.

Write or call for further information.

The Henry Art Gallery of the University of Washington textile collection emphasizes handwoven and hand-decorated costumes and textiles, both functional and decorative, dating from 1500 B.C. to the present. The collection currently totals 14,800 objects and includes a number of ethnic costumes and textiles from South and Central America, India, East and Southeast Asia, Eastern Europe, the Middle East and Central Asia. Among the pieces of Western clothing and textiles are costumes from the late 18th century to the present and 20th-century designer fashions. The collection also includes 16th-century to 19th-century ecclesiastical vestments and altar cloths from France, Italy, Spain, England and Russia; handmade and machine-made laces from France, Belgium, England, Italy and the U.S.; a number of 16th-century to 19th-century brocades, velvets, damasks and embroideries from Belgium, France, Italy, Spain, England and Russia; and 17th-century and 18th-century Belgian tapestries.

Access to the entire collection is by appointment; call or write for information.

Henry Art Gallery

University of Washington
Seattle, WA 98195
(206) 543-2280

Contact person: Judy Sourakli,
Curator of Collections

A woman's Chichicastenango Tzute from Guatemala, possibly 1930s (courtesy of the University of Washington, gift of the Seattle Weavers' Guild)

A late 19th-century, early 20th-century woman's dress from Palestine (courtesy of the Henry Art Gallery, John Dutton Wright Collection, gift of Thomas and Anna Drumheller)

The Hunter Museum of Art

10 Bluff View
Chattanooga, TN 37403
(615) 267-0968

Contact person: Jacquelyn Casey,
Registrar

Although The Hunter Museum of Art houses a collection of American paintings, drawings, prints and sculpture, it also has a small but growing collection of textiles, including several good examples of Southern quilts dating from 1830 to 1976. The museum also sponsors an annual quilt exhibition, curated by Bets Ramsey.

Since the textiles are not on permanent display, arrangements should be made with the registrar before visiting. Call or write for more information.

Indianapolis Museum of Art

1200 W. 38th Street
Indianapolis, IN 46208
(317) 923-1331

Contact person: Peggy S. Gilfoy,
Curator of Textiles and Costumes

The Indianapolis Museum of Art textile collection contains a number of textiles (including many quilts) representing a wide range of dates. The museum sponsors the newly formed Textile Society of America, a membership association for those interested in the historic, cultural, socio-economic, artistic and technical aspects of textiles.

Write or call for further information.

Kansas City Museum

3218 Gladstone Boulevard
Kansas City, MO 64123
(816) 483-8300

Contact person: Julie Mattsson,
Registrar

The Kansas City Museum clothing and textile collection represents one of the largest collections in the Midwest. Spanning the period from 1750 to the present, the collection contains an assortment of men's, women's and children's clothing and accessories. Central to the collection are special-occasion garments: presidential-inauguration gowns, tuxedos, and bridal and debutante dresses. The strengths of the collection are women's clothing of the 1920s and children's everyday clothing from the late 19th century and 20th century. Shoes, hats, fans, underwear, handwoven coverlets, more than 85 quilts and other household textiles are also included in this considerable collection.

Write or call for further information.

Landis Valley Museum

2451 Kissel Hill Road
Lancaster, PA 17601
(717) 569-0401

Contact person: Vernon S.
Gunnion, Curator of Collections

The Landis Valley Museum has an extensive collection of quilts and coverlets, in addition to a small collection of samplers and "show towels."

Most of the textile objects are currently in storage. Write or call for further information.

The Looms

Far End, Shake Rag Street
Mineral Point, WI 53565
(608) 987-2277

Contact person: Ken Colwell

The Looms is a weaving school that attracts students from around the world to study a variety of complex handweaving equipment. The school has a major collection of old looms and pieces of textile equipment, many of them operable. A large number of 19th-century woven coverlets are also displayed. Visitors are given demonstrations of the process of turning raw materials into finished fabric, including spinning and weaving. The Looms is one of only two or three museums in the country that provide a demonstration of a jacquard loom, one of the first uses of the binary system of memory and control as used by the modern computer.

The museum is currently open seven days a week from May through October. Special rates are given to large groups if arrangements are made in advance. Call for current hours and more information.

The vast holdings of the Metropolitan Museum of Art are divided into ten departments: American decorative art, ancient Near Eastern art, Asian art, Costume Institute, Egyptian art, European sculpture and decorative art, Islamic art, medieval art, primitive art and 20th-century art. Each of these departmental collections contains textiles, with some textile holdings more substantial than others. If you are interested in visiting or studying a particular textile collection, contact the individual department for more information.

The Costume Institute is entirely devoted to textiles. This collection includes a broad range of fashionable Western urban clothing, as well as non-Western and regional traditional costumes. The collection includes more than 40,000 pieces and contains the earliest complete fashionable costume in this hemisphere, an elaborately embroidered dress from around 1695. The fragile nature of costumes prevents any type of permanent exhibition, so most examples in the collection remain in storage, except for special exhibitions of short duration. Scholars and researchers interested in studying the collection should contact the curator.

Metropolitan Museum of Art

5th Avenue at 82nd Street
Ne York, NY 10028
(212) 570-3908

Contact person: Jean L. Druesedow, Curator of the Costume Institute

Museum of Appalachia

P.O. Box 359
Norris, TN 37828
(615) 494-7680

Contact person: John Rice Irwin,
Owner-Operator

The Museum of Appalachia is part of a 60-acre, 30-building "living southern Appalachian mountain village." The museum has an extensive display on the pioneer-frontier method of processing, spinning and weaving textiles. This exhibit includes tools, articles and artifacts connected with the growing and processing of flax and cotton, as well as those related to the processing of wool. Many cabins in the village have tools and relics displayed in an in-use manner. There are also examples of coverlets, quilts and clothing throughout the village.

Write or call for operation hours and further information.

A scene from the textile display at
the Museum of Appalachia

Museum of Early Southern Decorative Arts

P.O. Box 10310
Winston-Salem, NC 27108
(919) 721-7360

Contact person: Sally Gant

The Museum of Early Southern Decorative Arts, located within the restored village of Old Salem, includes a collection of textile objects made or used in the South from 1600 to 1850. Among these artifacts are furniture, samplers, quilts, curtains and floor coverings. The museum also holds the only regional collection of decorative arts produced by artisans working throughout the Southeast from 1650 through 1820.

Specialized studies may be arranged by advance request. Educational events take place throughout the year and a graduate Summer Institute in Southern history and decorative arts is offered annually.

The museum publishes the *Journal of Early Southern Decorative Arts* and a newsletter, *The Luminary*. A sample copy of the *Journal* is currently available for $7.88 (including tax).

The National Museum of American History textile collection consists of an amazing array of over 50,000 items that fall into three main categories: raw fibers, yarns and fabrics made in the U.S., or made elsewhere and used here; machines, tools, implements and patent models related to the production of textiles in the U.S.; and artifacts in these two categories that are also related to the history of textile technology.

The collection is unique because it has five to ten of the earliest and most important extant American textile machines, the largest known group of significant American sewing and textile machinery patent models and a well-balanced and extensive collection of American household and costume fabrics of all categories, dating mainly from the 18th and 19th centuries. The museum also holds some excellent separate collections, such as linen damasks and 18th-century and 19th-century laces, and an extensive collection of natural fibers gathered throughout the world, including some from now extinct or rare plants and animals.

Write or call for further information and visiting hours.

National Museum of American History

Science, Technology and Culture
Smithsonian Institution
Washington, D.C. 20560
(202) 357-1300

The New England Quilt Museum collection consists of both antique and contemporary quilts and a large number of quilt books and patterns.

Write or call for further information and visiting hours.

New England Quilt Museum

256 Market Street
Lowell, MA 01852
(617) 452-4207

Contact person: Doreen C. Burbank, 16 W. Shore Road
Windham, NH 03087
(603) 893-3029

The New Hampshire Historical Society textile collection consists of over 2,000 items, ranging from quilts to baby bonnets. Most of the textiles date from the 19th century, although there are significant pieces dating from the 18th century. A small number of 20th-century pieces round out the collection. Most items have a history of use or manufacture in the state, and document changes in style and production in clothing and household textiles.

Researchers who wish to examine the complete collections are required to make a written request at least two weeks prior to their visit, describing the nature of their study, any publication involved and the dates and times of the visit.

New Hampshire Historical Society

30 Park Street
Concord, NH 03301
(603) 225-3381

Contact person: Barbara E. Austen, Curator/Assistant Director, Collections Management

---

The Oakland Museum has a number of fiber pieces in their permanent collection and has sponsored several exhibitions on the fiber arts. The museum has guided art tours to visit galleries and artists' studios, and gives occasional lectures and seminars on fibers. The museum exhibits the work of California artists only, except when that work is included in an exhibition of wider scope, such as the recent Eloquent Object and Tangents exhibits.

The Oakland Museum

1000 Oak Street
Oakland, CA 94607-4892
(415) 273-3005

Contact person: Kenneth R. Trapp, Curator, Crafts and Decorative Arts

Oklahoma Historical Society State Museum of History

2100 N. Lincoln Boulevard
Oklahoma City, OK 73105
(405) 521-2491

Contact person: Nina Jacobson,
Curator of Costumes and Textiles

The State Museum of History has a large collection of textiles and costumes, including over 60 pieced and appliqué quilts; overshot and jacquard coverlets; and American Indian ribbonwork, quillwork, basketry and horsehair bridles. Examples of these are exhibited on a rotating basis.

Call or write for further information.

Old Sturbridge Village

1 Old Sturbridge Village Road
Sturbridge, MA 01566
(508) 347-3362

Contact person: Jessica F. Nicoll,
Curator of Textiles and Household
Furnishings

The textile collections of Old Sturbridge Village document the role of textiles in rural New England from 1790 through 1840. The collection includes four general areas: clothing and accessories, embroidery, samples of fabrics and household textiles. The latter category includes quilts, coverlets, blankets and other bed coverings; bed and window curtains; bed and table linens; and floor coverings. There are more than 5,000 objects in the current collections.

The objects in the textile collection are study pieces. Occasionally displayed in a formal exhibit context, they are seldom shown in the residential exhibits of Old Sturbridge Village. Rather, the collection pieces are carefully copied for demonstrations and exhibits. Qualified students may make special appointments to study individual pieces. Appointments for textile study should be requested in writing, at least three weeks in advance of the desired date.

Write or call for more information.

Rhode Island School of Design Museum of Art

224 Benefit Street
Providence, RI 02903
(401) 331-3511

Contact person: Susan Anderson
Hay, Curator of Costume and
Textiles

The Rhode Island School of Design Museum of Art textile and costume collection contains approximately 14,000 textiles and 6,000 examples of costumes. These range from ancient Egyptian linens to contemporary Japanese artists' textiles, and include significant Coptic textiles, African weavings and a small but choice collection of tapestries and fine European and Asian silks. The museum's textiles from ancient Peru, printed textiles from India and the West, and 20th-century American textiles and costume are particularly important. A collection of 18th-century and 19th-century robes from Japan used in the performance of the Noh drama is one of the best in this country. The collection also incorporates the Lucy Truman Aldrich collection of Asian textiles.

A World of Costume and Textiles: A Handbook of the Collection, written by Susan Anderson Hay, Curator of Costume and Textiles, and Pamela Parmal, Assistant Curator, with the assistance of 11 other specialist authors, illustrates and describes 113 of the most important textiles and costumes in this large collection. The book includes a history of the collection and an extensive bibliography. The handbook is available from the Museum Shop for $25.00 plus $1.50 postage and handling.

The collection of the Saint Louis Art Museum contains examples of American, European, Asian, African, Oceanic and Near Eastern textiles. Highlights include collections of English 18th-century and 19th-century needlework, Chinese costumes, American quilts, Middle Eastern rugs and Greek Island textiles.

Write or call for further information.

Saint Louis Art Museum

Forest Park
St. Louis, MO 63110
(314) 721-0067

Contact person: Kristan H. McKinsey, Acting Assistant Curator, Decorative Arts

The State Museum of Pennsylvania has a good quilt and coverlet collection, as well as a fairly extensive costume collection. Among approximately 200 pieced and appliqué quilts in the collection are 20 cradle quilts and many autograph and album quilts. The costume collection includes a number of accessories, Civil War uniforms, civilian uniforms and athletic uniforms.

Except for the Civil War uniforms on display in the military history gallery, most of the textile collection is not on permanent exhibit.

State Museum of Pennsylvania

William Penn Memorial Museum and Archives Building
P.O. Box 1026
Harrisburg, PA 17108-1026
(717) 783-2641

Contact person: Gail M. Getz, Associate Curator, Decorative Arts and History

The Textile Museum

2320 S Street, N.W.
Washington, D.C. 20008
(202) 667-0441

Contact person: Rebecca Caldwell,
Public Relations Manager

The Textile Museum's collection represents approximately 13,000 textiles and 1,500 carpets ranging from antiquity to the present from both the Old and New Worlds, and is known nationally and internationally for its individual masterpieces and for its depth in selected areas. Special strengths of the collections include pre-Columbian objects from Peru, Oriental carpets, and Egyptian and Islamic textiles. The museum also has significant holdings representing the textile arts of India, Indonesia, China, parts of the African continent and indigenous traditions of the Americas. Collections from the recent past are represented in the textiles of Mexico, Guatemala, Panama, Ecuador, Peru, Bolivia and the American Southwest. (See the listing on p. 210 for the *Textile Museum Journal.*)

Write or call for an exhibition schedule and further information.

An Eastern Caucasus prayer rug, late 19th century, early 20th century (courtesy of The Textile Museum, gift of Arthur D. Jenkins)

The Thousand Islands Textile Museum has a collection of 20th-century handwoven textile samples, as well as weaving and spinning tools of North America.

Write for a current brochure.

Thousand Islands Craft School & Textile Museum

314 John Street
Clayton, NY 13624
(315) 686-4123

Contact person: Margaret J. Rood, Director

The Valentine Museum has been collecting costumes and textiles since the late 1890s and now holds the largest collection (nearly 40,000 items) of this kind in the South. All types of women's, men's and children's costumes and accessories from the 18th century to the present are found in quantity and in impressive quality. Some notable examples include the entire wardrobe of an 18th-century Virginia gentleman, designer gowns worn by well-known Virginia women, and a number of slave garments. The collection is also known for its excellent examples of flat textiles such as coverlets, samplers, laces and 200 examples of quilts from every corner of Virginia. Other research materials in the collection include period fashion magazines and fashion plates, as well as a small library of costume and textile histories.

The museum holds periodic exhibitions featuring items from the collections. The collection is also available for research by appointment. Contact the curator for more information.

The Valentine Museum of the Life and History of Richmond

1015 E. Clay Street
Richmond, VA 23219
(804) 649-0711

Contact person: Colleen Callahan, Curator of Costumes and Textiles

From the 1987 exhibition Elegant Attire, Genteel Entertainments, Leisure and the Elite, 1787-1830 (courtesy of The Valentine Museum)

Vesterheim, the Norwegian-American Museum

502 W. Water Street
Decorah, IA 52101
(319) 382-9681

Contact person: Lila Nelson,
Curator of Textiles

Vesterheim, the oldest and most comprehensive immigrant museum in the country, is dedicated to preserving the Norwegian and Norwegian-American heritage through care and display of various artifacts including weavings, rosemaling and woodcarving. The Vesterheim textile collection includes many pieces of traditional Norwegian weavings and needlework. The museum offers workshops in traditional Norwegian crafts (such as rosemaling, weaving, embroidery and woodcarving), conducts educational tours to Norway and consults on the identification and care of early Norwegian and immigrant materials.

Write to the curator for more information.

Wheelwright Museum of the American Indian

P.O. Box 5153
Santa Fe, NM 87502
(505) 982-4636

Contact person: Steve Rogers

The Wheelwright Museum of the American Indian contains a collection of textiles from the pre-1900s to the present, including a number of weavings and pieces of clothing from the Navajo, Hopi, Zuñi, Pueblo, Apache, Mescalero, Jicarilla, Comanche, Northern Plains, Plateau, Crow, Cree, Chimayo, Mohave, Kiowa, Seri, Northwest Coast and Seminole Indians.

Regular rotating exhibits are open to the public. The entire collection is open to interested persons by appointment.

Call or write for further information.

Witte Museum

3801 Broadway
P.O. Box 2601
San Antonio, TX 78299-2601
(512) 226-5544

Contact person: Mrs. Eric Steinfeldt,
Senior Curator

The Witte Museum textile and costume collection, established in 1926, is the largest in the Southwest. The collection is very strong in certain areas, primarily historical costumes from 1800 to the present. Also included in the collection are many regional textiles, including artifacts from Europe, the Mideast, Mexico, Central America, South America, the Philippines and China. The Witte also has Native American textiles, laces, samplers and whitework, as well as a collection of furnishing fabric samples and early laces.

Call or write for museum hours and more information.

Educational Opportunities   *10*

The sources listed in this chapter can teach you how to spin, weave, knit, crochet, sew, paint on silk, resist-dye fabric, produce dyes from natural materials, and make felt, paper and baskets—in short, almost any fiber techique you could ever want to learn. Part I lists colleges and schools offering undergraduate and graduate degrees, as well as nonprofit arts organizations sponsoring workshops and classes. Part II presents opportunities for widening your horizons in fiber through travel. Part III gives sources for instructional videotapes on the fiber arts.

If a school near you is not listed, it's because it didn't respond to our request for information. Contact the school's admission office or registrar for information on its fiber programs.

"The lyf so short, the craft so long to learn...."
—Chaucer

Colleges and Schools

Appalachian Center for Crafts

Box 347, Route 3
Smithville, TN 37166
(615) 597-6801

The Appalachian Center for Crafts offers a BFA degree and a certificate program in fibers, loom and off-loom weaving and surface design.

Send for a free catalog.

Arizona State University

Fiber Arts Program, School of Art
Tempe, AZ 85282
(602) 965-7177

Arizona State University offers undergraduate and graduate degrees in fine arts with a concentration in fibers.

Write to Ms. Janet Taylor, Professor of Art, for more information.

Arrowmont School of Arts and Crafts

P.O. Box 567
Gatlinburg, TN 37738
(615) 436-5860

Arrowmont School of Arts and Crafts offers one-week and two-week workshops for students of all ability levels. The school also hosts media conferences, seminars and community classes. Students may receive credit from the University of Tennessee or audit courses in photography, paper-making, fiber and other subjects. Arrowmont also houses a gallery, a resource center and a bookstore.

Send for a current course brochure.

An Arrowmont student (above) applies a paste resist on fabric using a traditional katazome tool known as a *tsutsu* before she adds another layer of dye. Another student (right) threads a loom during a weaving workshop.

Auburn University

Auburn University offers undergraduate and graduate programs with courses in surface design, dyeing and weaving.

Write for more information.

Consumer Affairs Division
Spidle Hall
Auburn, AL 36849
(205) 844-4048

Augustana College

Augustana College offers undergraduate degrees with courses in weaving, fabric design, fiber sculpture and advanced fibers.

Write for a current course catalog.

Art and Art History Department
Rock Island, IL 61201
(309) 794-7490

The Basketry School

Connie and Tom McColley, owners of The Basketry School, claim to have established the first craft school in the country devoted exclusively to basketry. Past workshops have included instruction on white oak and honeysuckle baskets, and on white oak and hickory bark baskets. In the workshops, students learn the entire process of making a basket.

Send for a current brochure.

Route 3, Box 325
Chloe, WV 25235
(304) 655-7429

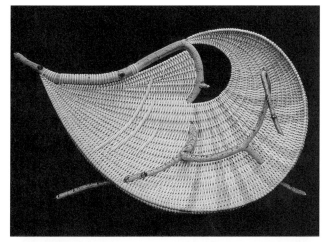

Baskets by Connie and Tom McColley of The Basketry School

175

Brookfield Craft Center

P.O. Box 122
Route 25
Brookfield, CT 06804
(203) 775-4526

Brookfield Craft Center claims to have the "widest educational curriculum in America" and offers a variety of workshops, seminars, symposia and conferences throughout the year. A sampling of past workshops includes native splint basketry, banner and flag making, airbrush on fabrics, handspinning luxury fibers, knitting and papermaking with exotic fibers. (See the listing for instructional videotapes on p. 187.)

Send for a current course catalog.

A Brookfield Craft Center student in a basketmaking class

California State University at Long Beach

1250 Bellflower Boulevard
Long Beach, CA 90840
(213) 985-4380 or 985-4376

California State University at Long Beach offers a BA degree in general art and BFA, MA and MFA degrees in textiles. The undergraduate program in textiles/fiber arts includes courses in weaving, surface design, dyeing, fiber structures, papermaking and special studies. Graduate courses are also offered in all of these areas.

Contact Mary Jane Leland or Carol Shaw-Sutton for more information. A course catalog is free.

California State University at Northridge

Art 3-D Media
Northridge, CA 91330
(818) 885-2784

California State University at Northridge offers a design program that combines computer technology with creativity and excellent lab facilities.

Write to Professor Mary Ann Danin for more information. A current course catalog is $5.50; a brochure is free.

Center for Creative Studies

College of Art and Design
245 E. Kirby
Detroit, MI 48202
(313) 872-3118

The Center for Creative Studies offers both undergraduate and graduate degrees in fine arts, and includes a summer program featuring courses in the fiber arts.

Write for a current course schedule.

Central Michigan University offers an undergraduate BAA and BFA degree and a graduate MA and MFA degree, with classes in weaving, surface design (silkscreening, batik, etc.) and off-loom techniques (basketry, felting and papermaking).

Contact Sally Rose for more information or send for a course schedule.

Central Michigan University

Art Department—Pearce Hall
Mt. Pleasant, MI 48859
(517) 774-3025

Colophon Hand Bookbindery, under the direction of Don Guyot, offers a number of workshops on paper and fabric marbling and Japanese marbling (suminagashi) methods.

Send $1.00 contribution for a current catalog.

Colophon Hand Bookbindery

1902 N. 44th
Seattle, WA 98103
(206) 633-1759

Colorado State University offers BA, BFA, and MFA degrees with a concentration in fibers.

Contact Tom Lundberg for more information, or send $3.00 for a course catalog.

Colorado State University

Department of Art
Fort Collins, CO 80523
(303) 491-6774

The Coupeville Arts and Crafts Center sponsors an annual series of fiber workshops each September.

Write for a current workshop schedule.

Coupeville Arts and Crafts Center

P.O. Box 171
Coupeville, WA 98239
(206) 678-3396

Elkhorn Mountains Weaving School, owned by Joanne Hall, offers all levels of weaving instruction to a limited number of students so that they can receive individual instruction. Ms. Hall, author of the self-published *Mexican Tapestry Weaving* (1976), offers beginning, intermediate and advanced classes at the school each summer in tapestry, traditional and pictorial 4-harness weaving, Scandinavian weaves, fabric and rug weaves, color and design, and spinning and dyeing. (See the listing for weaving supplies on p. 24.)

Send for more information.

Elkhorn Mountains Weaving School

S.R. Box 165
Clancy, MT 59634
(406) 442-0354

The Fashion Institute of Technology offers various degree programs in all areas of textile and fashion design, from fashion buying and merchandising to fashion illustration and pattern making. Also offered are certificate programs in ladies' tailoring and millinery.

Call or write for a current course bulletin.

Fashion Institute of Technology

7th Avenue at 27th Street
New York, NY 10001-5992
(212) 760-7650

Georgia State University offers both undergraduate and graduate degrees in art and an assortment of beginning, intermediate and advanced courses in weaving.

Send for a current school catalog, or write to Zenaide Reiss for more information.

Georgia State University

University Plaza
Atlanta, GA 30324
(404) 651-2257

Guilford Handcrafts, Inc.

P.O. Box 589
Guilford, CT 06437
(203) 453-5947

Guilford Handcrafts is a nonprofit school that actively promotes hand-crafts and fine art. The Weaving and Fibers department offers classes in floor-loom weaving, basketry, tapestry weaving, basic quilting, surface de-sign on silk, spinning, natural dyeing, advanced weaving and stenciling. Other areas of instruction include children's classes, jewelry and metals, sculpture and graphics.

Send for a free course catalog.

Harrisville Designs

Weaving Center
Harrisville, NH 03450
(603) 827-3996

Harrisville Designs Weaving Center offers various workshops in weaving and fibers, including courses such as drafting for weavers, introduction to rag-rug weaving, Early American coverlets and tapestry weaving. (See the listing for weaving supplies on p. 32.)

Write for a current workshop schedule.

Haywood Technical College

Production Crafts Department
Clyde, NC 28721
(704) 627-2821

Haywood Technical College offers a production-crafts-in-fibers program, which includes courses in weaving, clothing and costume, production weaving and the textile industry. The schools's emphasis is on technique, business and marketing.

Write for a current course schedule.

Hill Country Weavers

918 W. 12th Street
Austin, TX 78703
(512) 474-6773

Hill Country Weavers, owned by Suzanne Middlebrooks, offers a variety of classes and workshops throughout the year on such subjects as rigid-heddle weaving, beginning floor-loom weaving, basic knitting, natural dyeing, tapestry and natural-fiber basketry. The store also stocks a large supply of yarns, looms, fibers and books.

Write for a current course schedule.

Illinois State University

Department of Art—Fiber Program
Normal, IL 61761-6901
(309) 438-5621

Illinois State University offers undergraduate and graduate degrees and courses in fibers, weaving, surface design and papermaking.

Write for a current class schedule.

Kansas City Art Institute

4415 Warwick Boulevard
Kansas City, MO 64111
(816) 931-5224

Kansas City Art Institute is a four-year college of art and design, which offers a concentration in fiber. Associate Professors Jane Lackey and Jason Pollen lead the department, along with nationally recognized visiting art-ists whose classes include tapestry techniques, painting or printing on fabric, photo processes, computer-generated weaving design, dyeing, silk-screening and papermaking.

Write for a current course schedule and more information.

Kent State University

School of Art
Kent, OH 44242
(216) 672-2192 or 672-2158

Kent State University sponsors the Blossom Festival School, which in-cludes a series of summer credit workshops offering students the oppor-tunity to work intensively with visiting artists in one area or discipline.

Write for a free catalog.

The Kirmeyer School of Basket and Fiber Studies, owned by Maxine Kirmeyer, offers a variety of courses on handmade basketry and basketry fibers.

Write for a current course schedule.

Kirmeyer School of Basket and Fiber Studies

P.O. Box 24815
San Jose, CA 95154
(408) 269-4513

The Looms offers an annual Colloquy conference and workshops specializing in complex weaving techniques. The school's looms include dobby, draw and jacquard. (See the listing for weaving supplies on p. 41.)

Write for a current schedule.

The Looms

Far End, Shake Rag Street
Mineral Point, WI 53565
(608) 987-2277

The Machine Knitters Cooperative offers annual workshops for machine knitters taught by American and international instructors.

Write or call Reasha Nelson for more information.

Machine Knitters Cooperative

612 Sagamore Avenue
Teaneck, NJ 07666
(201) 836-9364

The Mannings offers weaving and spinning classes on a year-round basis, as well as a three-day spinning workshop and annual spinning seminar in June, a three-day weaving seminar in October and a handweavers' show and exhibit for three weeks in April through the beginning of May. (See the listing for spinning and weaving supplies on p. 42.)

Write for additional information.

The Mannings Creative Crafts

P.O. Box 687
East Berlin, PA 17316
(717) 624-2223

The Marshfield School of Weaving, owned by Norman Kennedy, offers weaving courses "as practiced by rural, professional weavers in the early 19th century, using looms and wheels from that era."

Write to Mr. Kennedy for further information.

Marshfield School of Weaving

Plainfield, VT 05667
(802) 426-3577

The Mendocino Art Center offers a certificate program in weaving and surface design, and sponsors classes in basketry, weaving, dyeing, knitting, quilting and papermaking.

Write for a current course schedule.

Mendocino Art Center

Box 765
Mendocino, CA 95460
(707) 937-0228

Montclair State College offers a BA, BFA and MFA degree in fiber arts. Special workshops are also offered on computer design for weaving, papermaking, Navajo weaving and Papago basketry.

Write for a current course catalog, or contact Carol Westfall for more information.

Montclair State College

Fine Arts Department
Upper Montclair, NJ 07043
(201) 893-7293

National Standards Council of American Embroiderers

Correspondence School
600 Bell Avenue
Carnegie Office Park, Building #1
Carnegie, PA 15106
(412) 279-0299

The National Standards Council of American Embroiderers offers comprehensive home-study courses in the art of embroidery. The courses provide independent-study guidelines and enable the student to develop skills at the beginning, intermediate or advanced level. Among the courses offered are needlepoint and canvas work, creative surface stitchery, basic appliqué, quilting and crewel embroidery. Teacher-training courses are also offered. (See the listings on p. 155 and p. 206.)

Write for a current list of courses offered.

North Georgia College

Fine Arts Department
Dahlonega, GA 30597
(404) 864-3391, ext. 351

North Georgia College is a small four-year liberal-arts college that offers undergraduate degrees in art, art education, crafts marketing and music. A graduate degree in art education is also granted.

Contact Tommye Scanlin for more information.

Northern Illinois University

School of Art
DeKalb, IL 60115
(815) 753-1473

In addition to BA, BFA, MA and MFA degrees in studio art, Northern Illinois University offers a variety of courses in weaving, off-loom techniques and fabric printing and dyeing.

Write to the Admissions Office for a current catalog.

Oregon School of Arts and Crafts

8245 S.W. Barnes Road
Portland, OR 97225
(503) 297-5544

The Oregon School of Arts and Crafts offers a BFA degree or a three-year certificate program in book arts, ceramics, drawing, fibers and textiles, metal and woodworking.

Summer workshops and short courses are also taught by national artists.

Contact Becky Banyas, Director of Public Relations, for more information.

Parsons School of Design

Department of Textile Design
66 5th Avenue
New York, NY 10011
(212) 741-8668

Parsons School of Design offers a certificate program in textile design and an AAS degree in clay/glass/metal/textile design.

Write for further information.

Pendleton Fabric Craft School

465 Jordan Road
Sedona, AZ 86336
(602) 282-3671

The Pendleton Fabric Craft School, owned by Mary Pendleton, offers a series of workshops and classes on beginning handweaving, intermediate weaving, Navajo and Hopi weaving, crocheting, spinning and knitting. (See the listing for spinning and weaving supplies on p. 53.)

Write for a current class schedule.

Penland School

Penland, NC 28765
(704) 765-2359

The Penland School offers one-week, two-week and three-week sessions in fibers, weaving, surface design, jewelry, graphics, paper, printmaking, book arts and photography.

Send for a current schedule of classes.

Pennsylvania Guild of Craftsmen

P.O. Box 820
Richboro, PA 18954
(215) 860-0731

The Pennsylvania Guild of Craftsmen, a nonprofit organization, sponsors year-round workshops on various crafts. Recent workshops have addressed marbling, basketry, weave structure and continuous rug braiding.

Write for a current workshop schedule.

Peters Valley Craftsmen offers a variety of workshops in contemporary fiber techniques taught by nationally recognized professionals. These workshops include fabric marbling, rag-coil baskets, paper marbling, handmade paper, speed-quilting techniques, painting on silk, white oak basketry and spinning.

Contact Jeanie Eberhardt for more information, or write for a free catalog.

Peters Valley Craftsmen, Inc.

Route 615
Layton, NJ 07851
(201) 948-5200

Basketmaker Jeanie Eberhardt (left) discusses a project with a student during a workshop at Peters Valley.

Pyramid Atlantic, a nonprofit arts organization, offers a variety of classes on the art of papermaking, printmaking and bookmaking. Artists can use the well-equipped facilities to develop their ideas in handmade paper; photography; and offset, letterpress and intaglio printing. Throughout the year, workshops and lectures are offered at the facility.

Membership in the organization is currently $20.00 per year. Send for more information.

Pyramid Atlantic

6925 Willow Street, N.W.
Washington, D.C. 20012
(202) 291-0088

San Francisco Fiber offers year-round workshops and classes in weaving, basketry, dyeing, machine knitting, surface design and other subjects. (See the listing for spinning and weaving supplies on p. 60.)

Write for a current workshop schedule.

San Francisco Fiber

3435 Army Street, #222
San Francisco, CA 94127
(415) 821-2568

The School of the Art Institute of Chicago offers various courses in the fiber arts, including basketry, fashion design, papermaking, surface design, weaving and knitting.

Write to Park Chambers, Chairman, Fiber Department, for more information.

School of the Art Institute of Chicago

Columbus Drive and
Jackson Boulevard
Chicago, IL 60603
(312) 443-3791

School of Needle Arts

P.O. Box 1606
Knoxville, TN 37901
(615) 521-6034

The School of Needle Arts is an annual gathering of heirloom-sewing and smocking enthusiasts. Many workshops are offered during the annual meeting, such as adapting commercial patterns to heirloom sewing, smocking techniques and French sewing by machine.

Write for a free conference catalog (available in April of each year).

Sievers School of Fiber Arts

Jackson Harbor Road
Washington Island, WI 54246
(414) 847-2264

Sievers School of Fiber Arts offers year-round classes and workshops on such subjects as rag-rug weaving, felting, quilting, batik, spinning, basketry, dyeing and basic weaving fundamentals. (See the listing for spinning and weaving supplies on p. 63.)

Send for a current class schedule.

Southwest Craft Center

300 Augusta
San Antonio, TX 78205
(512) 224-1848

The Southwest Craft Center is developing a national reputation as an art center. It offers various educational programs for adults and children, and sponsors exhibitions, residencies and performances. Fiber workshops have included spinning and dyeing with Ann Matlock and paper for bookmaking with Timothy Barrett. Classes are offered in weaving, surface design and other fiber arts.

Send for a free course catalog.

Syracuse University

119 Comart
Syracuse, NY 13244-5050
(315) 443-1135

Syracuse University offers BFA and MFA degrees in fine arts.

Write for more information.

TEMARI, Center for Asian and Pacific Arts

P.O. Box 12185
Honolulu, HI 96828
(808) 735-1860

TEMARI, Center for Asian and Pacific Arts, specializes in the traditional arts and crafts of the Asian and Pacific region, such as Japanese papermaking, indigo dyeing and surface design on fabric using resist techniques like batik, shibori, tsutsugaki and katazome.

TEMARI sponsors craft fairs, lectures and demonstrations, special classes and activity programs for children.

Contact Rae C. Shiraki, Education Director, for information.

Tennessee Technological University

Joe L. Evins Appalachian
Center for Crafts
P.O. Box 5106
Cookeville, TN 38505
(615) 372-3051

Tennessee Technological University offers BS and BFA degrees in fibers. The school facilities are "among the finest and best equipped in the nation," with a 50,000-sq. ft. studio, more than 4,000 sq. ft. of exhibition and sales space, a gallery, a library, a cafeteria and student housing.

Contact Alfred Ward, Director, for more information, or write for a course schedule.

Texas Women's University offers various courses in fibers, including surface design, basketry, papermaking and weaving.

Contact Corky Stuckenbruck for more information.

Texas Women's University

Art Department
Denton, TX 76204
(817) 898-2530

Touchstone Center for Crafts is Pennsylvania's only resident arts school. Week-long classes are offered in an outdoor mountain setting during the summer, and workshops are offered in conjunction with Pennsylvania State University during the fall and spring of each year. Fiber workshops have included beginning 4-harness weaving, painting on silk, sculptural branch basketry, woven landscapes and papermaking.

Write for a current catalog and class schedule.

Touchstone Center for Crafts

Pioneer Crafts Council
P.O. Box 2141
Uniontown, PA 15401
(412) 438-2811

The University of Arizona offers a complete selection of textile and fibers courses. Gayle Wimmer, Associate Professor and head of the fiber department, states that the emphasis of her department is on "assisting each individual to develop a personal vocabulary and approach to the fibers medium."

Write to Ms. Wimmer for a complete brochure.

University of Arizona

Art Department, Room 104
Tucson, AZ 85721
(602) 621-5984

The University of California at Davis offers a BS degree in design with an emphasis in textile design or costume design.

Write for a current school catalog.

University of California at Davis

Department of Applied and
Behavioral Science
Davis, CA 95616
(916) 752-1011

The University of California at Los Angeles offers BFA and MFA degrees in textile design.

Write for a current catalog of courses.

**University of California at
Los Angeles**

Art Department
Los Angeles, CA 90024
(213) 825-9411

The University of Colorado offers undergraduate and graduate courses in marketing, basketry, dyeing, papermaking and surface design.

Write to Professor Lin Fife for further information.

University of Colorado

Fine Arts Department
Colorado Springs, CO 80933-7150
(303) 593-3563

The University of Delaware offers a BA degree in textile design.

Write for a current school catalog.

The University of Delaware

Department of Art
Newark, DE 19711
(302) 451-2351

The University of Georgia

Department of Art
Athens, GA 30602
(404) 542-1511

The University of Georgia offers BFA and MFA degrees in textile design.

Write for a current school catalog.

University of Hawaii

2535 The Mall—Art Building
Honolulu, HI 96822
(808) 948-8251

The University of Hawaii at Manoa offers BFA and MFA degrees in studio art with a major in fiber.

For more information or for a current course catalog, contact Sheri Simons, head of the fiber department.

University of Texas

Art Department
Austin, TX 78712
(512) 471-3365

The University of Texas offers BFA and MFA degrees, with various courses in weaving, fibers and surface design.

Write for more information.

University of Vermont

School of Home Economics
Burlington, VT 05401
(802) 656-3131

The University of Vermont offers a BS degree in textile design.

Write for further information.

University of Washington

School of Art DM-10
Seattle, WA 98195
(206) 543-0970

The University of Washington offers BA, BFA and MFA degrees in fiber arts with courses in weaving, surface design, nonloom and nonwoven structures, dye technology and computer-aided design for weaving and surface design.

Contact Layne Goldsmith for more information, or write for a course brochure.

The Weavers' School

Route 1
Fayette, MO 65248
(816) 248-3462

The Weavers' School, headed by Madelyn van der Hoogt, offers small, intensive courses in weaving theory, emphasizing coverlets, the use of more than four harnesses, unusual weave structures and the draw loom. Students may board at the school and spend five days learning and weaving on a variety of looms threaded with many different structures. The instruction is designed for the individual students in the class.

Send for a free brochure.

Travel and Tour Opportunities

Connoisseur Tours, owned by Rachel Skolkin, offers a number of fiber-arts tours with an emphasis on all areas of the fiber arts—embroidery, knitting, weaving and so on.

Write for more information and a current tour schedule.

Connoisseur Tours

75 East End Avenue
New York, NY 10028

Craft World Tours, owned by Professor Tom Muir Wilson and Sherry Clark Wilson, sponsors international textile tours with a special focus on meeting the craftspeople and folk artists of each country. Regular tours are offered to such places as the Himalayas, India, Morocco and Thailand. The Wilsons have backgrounds in woodworking, felting and weaving and believe that "meeting the craftspeople makes the country come alive."

Send for a free current tour schedule.

Craft World Tours

6776 Warboys Road
Byron, NY 14422
(716) 548-2667

Earthquest Travel offers an annual Peruvian textile tour.

Write for a current tour brochure.

Earthquest Travel

401 W. Aspen
Flagstaff, AZ 86001
(602) 779-5415

Folkways Institute

14600-B S.E. Aldridge
Portland, OR 97236-6518
(800) 225-4666
(503) 658-6600 in Oregon

The Folkways Institute sponsors domestic and international lecture tours and workshops, as well as foreign tours designed for the independent artist. A series of educational travel workshops with area specialists is also offered.

Send for a free brochure.

Holbrook Travel, Inc.

3540 N.W. 13th Street
Gainesville, FL 32609
(800) 451-7111
(800) 345-7111 in Florida

Holbrook Travel offers several tours of interest focusing on ancient Bolivian and Peruvian weaving, Thai weaving and Australian arts, crafts and textiles.

Write for further information.

Ishimoto Tours, Inc.

150 Powell Street, Suite 305
San Francisco, CA 94102
(415) 781-4350

Ishimoto Tours offers periodic art and textile study tours to India, as well as annual art and textile workshops in Japan.

Write for current information.

Strathaven Needlework Tours

Strathaven Tours
North Sandwich, NH 03259
(603) 284-7785

Strathaven Needlework Tours, owned by Betsy E. Leiper, offers a variety of custom needlework tours for women only. A current tour includes travel throughout England to study outstanding examples of needlework and costume in museums, stately homes and castles, with an optional side trip to London.

Write for further information.

Tamaki Tours

2016 10th Street
Boulder, CO 80302
(303) 443-2251

Tamaki Tours, owned by Yoko Tamaki, offers special-interest tours to Japan designed for crafts-oriented people. Ms. Tamaki also owns the Tamaki Gallery, which houses her collection of authentic Japanese folk crafts gathered from her travels.

Write for more information.

Instructional Videotapes

Brookfield Craft Center Video Library offers several videotapes of interest to fiber artists, including *Traditional New England Basketmaking with John McGuire.* (see the school listing on p. 176.)

Write for current prices and further information.

Brookfield Craft Center

P.O. Box 122
Route 25
Brookfield, CT 06804
(203) 775-4526

The Caning Shop, a major supplier of basketry supplies (see the listing on p. 134), also carries several videotapes on basketmaking for purchase or rental.

Send $1.00 (refundable with your first order) for a current catalog.

The Caning Shop

926 Gilman Street
Berkeley, CA 94710
(415) 527-5010

Halcyon Yarn offers a selection of videotapes available for rental or purchase, including videos by Constance LaLena on weave drafting and dressing the loom, Mabel Ross on handspinning and Donna Seitzer on machine knitting techniques. (See the listing for fiber supplies on p. 32.)

Write for a current information sheet and price list.

Halcyon Yarn

12 School Street
Bath, ME 04530
(800) 341-0282

Bonnie McCoy with one of her quilts. She shows how to make it in the HB Enterprises video series.

HB Enterprises, owned by Holly Beckley-Bailey, offers a selection of videotapes on quilt making that include *The ABC's of Quiltmaking: Pieced and Appliquéd Quilts, Step-by-Step to a Sampler Quilt, Fast Lone Star, Shadow Quilting, Stained Glass Quilting, Reversible Log Cabin,* and *Quick Machine-Piecing Techniques.* The videos feature Bonnie McCoy, founding member and current director of the Texas Heritage Quilt Society.

Write for a current price list and brochure.

HB Enterprises

P.O. Box 161
Stockdale, TX 78160
(512) 996-3841

Imagination Unlimited

1425 S. Hillcrest Avenue
Clearwater, FL 34616
(813) 443-3383

Imagination Unlimited, owned by Betty F. Kemink, offers a videotape on basketmaking entitled *How to Weave an Egg Basket and Creative Variations.*

Write for current prices.

A wall basket by Betty Kemink of Imagination Unlimited, made from palm-tree seed stems, wild grapevine roots and other natural materials

Ivy Crafts Imports

5410 Annapolis Road
Bladensburg, MD 20710
(301) 779-7079

Ivy Crafts Imports, owned by Diane Tuckman, offers instructional videos on the art of painting on silk, in addition to their regular line of supplies (see the listing on p. 112).

Write for more information.

Kaye's Artistic Stitchery

4949 Rau Road
West Branch, MI 48661
(517) 345-3028

Kaye Wood, owner of Kaye's Artistic Stitchery, offers a series of videotapes on quilting techniques, including the basic log cabin, log cabin triangles, reversible quilts and more. She also offers the *Strip Like a Pro* series of tapes on strip piecing for quilting.

Send $.50 for a current catalog.

Quilting videos available from Kaye's Artistic Stitchery

Lenore Davis has produced two useful videos on various aspects of surface design. The Surface Design Workshop I video, *Direct Application of Fiber-Reactive Dyes on Cotton,* includes information on fabrics and an introduction to dyes, including preparing the media, mixing the colors, directly applying the dyes, curing and fixing the dyes, and rinsing and finishing. The Workshop II video, *Direct Application of Textile Pigments on Fabrics and Three-Dimensional Surfaces,* includes information on fabrics and the characteristics of pigments, including mixing the pigments, preparing the surfaces, drying, setting and curing.

Ms. Davis is available for information and problem solving by phone to those who purchase her videotapes.

Write for a free brochure and price list.

Lenore Davis Surface Design Video Workshops

P.O. Box 47
Newport, KY 41072
(606) 261-4523

Lenore Davis demonstrates the application of dyes to fabrics in her surface-design video workshop.

Power Sewing

World Trade Center, Suite 275H
San Francisco, CA 94111
(415) 954-0949

Sandra Betzina, owner of Power Sewing, offers several sewing videos for rental or purchase. These include the *Power Sewing Video* (patterned after her unique sewing book, *Power Sewing: New Ways to Make Fine Clothes Fast*) and a video entitled *Pants That Fit*. Ms. Betzina's videos stress ready-to-wear methods from California designers that can be used by the home sewer to achieve a more professional look.

Write for a free brochure and price list.

Schoolhouse Press

6899 Cary Bluff
Pittsville, WI 54466
(715) 884-2799

Schoolhouse Press produces a series of knitting videos featuring Elizabeth Zimmermann, author of *Knitting Workshop* (1981). (See the listings for knitting supplies on p. 61 and books on p. 200.)

Write for a current price list and more information.

The String Slinger

P.O. Box 23272
Chattanooga, TN 37422
(615) 843-0272

The String Slinger, owned by Lynne Higgins, offers video lessons with workbooks on machine-knitting techniques.

Write for a current price list.

Theta's Videos and Seminars

2209 N.W. 46th
Oklahoma City, OK 73112
(405) 848-8449

Theta Happ, owner of Theta's Videos and Seminars, offers several booklets and videos, including *English Smocking on the Sewing Machine* and *Counted Cross-Stitch and Needlepoint on the Sewing Machine*.

Write for more information.

Victorian Video Productions, Inc.

1304 Scott Street
Petaluma, CA 94952
(707) 762-3362

Victorian Video Productions, owned by Nancy Harvey, is probably the most complete source for fiber-related how-to videotapess in the U.S. Some of the videos available for purchase or rental include *Tapestry Weaving Level I and II* by Ms. Harvey, *Card Weaving* by Candace Crockett, *Introduction to Weaving* by Deborah Chandler, *Splint Basketry I and II* by Robin Taylor-Daugherty, *Rigid-Heddle Weaving* by Betty Davenport and *Fundamentals of Handspinning* by Rachael Brown.

Send for a free video catalog.

VideoSchool House

167 Central Avenue
Pacific Grove, CA 93950
(408) 375-4474

The VideoSchool House offers over 7,000 instructional videotapes for rental or purchase on such subjects as academics, business, biography, children, commercial art, computers and home improvement. Fiber artists will appreciate the section on crafts, hobbies and home arts, especially the videotapes on basketmaking, knitting, crocheting and needlepoint, sewing, weaving, quilting and spinning.

The VideoSchool House Knowledge Collection catalog is currently $9.95. Write to Leslie T. Roschke for more information.

Wild Willow Video

P.O. Box 438
Baraboo, WI 53913
(608) 356-9048

Wild Willow Video, owned by Char TerBeest, offers a video entitled *Wild Willow—A Basketmaker's Guide*. (See p. 203 for Wild Willow books.)

Write for more information and current prices.

Publications *11*

In this chapter you'll find sources of books and periodicals on every imaginable area of textiles and fiber. Part I lists book publishers and booksellers, as well as book dealers who specialize in locating hard-to-find titles. Part II lists publishers of magazines, journals and newsletters.

Book Publishers and Booksellers

Alpel Publishing

P.O. Box 203
Chambly, PQ J3L 4B3
Canada
(514) 658-6205

Publisher
Established in 1982

Alpel Publishing, owned by Leila Albala, offers a variety of books she's written on sewing. These include *Easy Sewing for Infants* (1988), *Easy Halloween Costumes* (1988), *Easy Sewing for Adults* (1988) and *Easy Sewing for Children* (1988). These books have been immensely popular since their publication and have been featured in many national magazines.

Write for a current book brochure.

Always Knitting

P.O. Box 32566
Richmond, VA 23294
(804) 282-3644

Mail order
Established in 1973

Always Knitting, owned by Peggy Liddle, offers a comprehensive selection of books on hand knitting and crochet.

Send a long SASE for a current book list.

B. R. Artcraft Company

6701 Cherry Hill Road
Baldwin, MD 21013
(301) 592-2847

Mail order
Established in 1935

The B. R. Artcraft Company specializes in books on arts and crafts and carries an extensive selection of needlework and design books. Bernhard Rogge, company contact, says that 90% of their stock of 18,000 books consists of out-of-print and hard-to-find books.

Send $2.00 for a current book catalog.

Bark Service Company

P.O. Box 637
Troutman, NC 28166
(800) 999-2275

Mail order
Established in 1974

Bark Service Company offers a wide range of books on needlework, weaving, quilting and other fiber arts with convenient toll-free ordering. The shipping charges are paid on every order.

Discounts are given on all books; check the catalog for details.

Send for a free book list.

Bizarre Butterfly Publishing

P.O. Box 16186
Phoenix, AZ 85011
(602) 266-2426

Mail order; publisher
Established in 1981

Bizarre Butterfly Publishing, owned by Judy Green Davis, offers books written by Olive and Harry Linder such as *Techniques of Code Drafting* (1983), *Handspinning Cotton* (1985) and *Handspinning Flax* (1986). The company also publishes *Lacemaking Today* (see p. 209).

Send for a current book brochure.

Books available from Bizarre Butterfly Publishing

The Brooklyn Botanic Garden publishes several handbooks of interest to fiber artists. Two of these are *Natural Plant Dyeing* and *Dye Plants & Dyeing*. The garden also offers a film entitled *Nature's Colors—The Craft of Dyeing with Plants* for sale or rental.

Write to Susan Moran, Marketing Manager, for a current brochure and information on the handbooks. Write to the film library for information on the film.

Brooklyn Botanic Garden

1000 Washington Avenue
Brooklyn, NY 11225
(718) 622-4433

Mail order; publisher
Established in 1923

C & T Publishing is a family-owned business devoted to publishing high-quality craft-related books at the lowest possible price. A number of these books are on quilt making, and include *Fans* (1987) by Jean Wells, *Fine Feathers* (1987) by Marriane Fons and *An Amish Adventure* (1983) by Roberta Horton.

Some discounts are given on prepaid orders; write for details.

Send for a free book catalog.

C & T Publishing

5021 Blum Road #1
Martinez, CA 94553
(415) 370-9600

Mail order; publisher
Established in 1983

The Crafts Report Book Service offers several books for sale on marketing, legal aspects of small business, and crafts photography. These include *The Crafts Business Encyclopedia* (Harcourt, Brace, Jovanovich, 1973) by Michael Scott, editor of *The Crafts Report* (see p. 205), *Photographing Your Craftwork* (Madrona, 1986) by Steve Meltzer, and *The Law (in Plain English) for Craftspeople* (Madrona, 1984) and *Business Forms and Contracts (in Plain English) for Craftspeople* (Madrona, 1986) by Leonard D. DuBoff.

Write for further information.

The Crafts Report Book Service

3632 Ashworth N.
Seattle, WA 98103
(206) 632-7222

Mail order; publisher
Established in 1975

Linne Lindquist, owner of The Craftsman's Touch, offers a large variety of books on various crafts. The books cover such subjects as fashion and costume, sewing, design, textile art and needlework, weaving, lacemaking, knitting and crochet, and papermaking.

Send $3.00 for a current 50-page catalog.

The Craftsman's Touch

812 Beltrami Avenue
Bemidji, MN 56601
(218) 751-3435

Mail order; retail
Established in 1979

Diane Maurer, an artist who works with hand-marbled papers, has written and published *An Introduction to Carrageenan and Watercolor Marbling* (1984). The useful information contained in the booklet can also be applied to fabric-marbling projects.

Discounts are given to craft teachers and shops; write for details.

Write for further information and current prices.

Diane Maurer

R.D. 1, Box 11
Centre Hall, PA 16828
(814) 364-9618

Mail order; publisher
Established in 1982

Dos Tejedoras Fiber Arts Publications

757 Raymond Avenue
St. Paul, MN 55114
(612) 646-7445

Publisher
Established in 1976

Dos Tejedoras Fiber Arts Publications, owned by Suzanne Baizerman and Karen Searle, offers a number of books on ethnic and international weaving techniques, both contemporary and traditional, and other fiber arts.

Write for a current book brochure.

Dover Publications, Inc.

31 E. 2nd Street
Mineola, NY 11501
(516) 549-1815

Mail order; publishers
Established in 1940

If you haven't seen any of the current book catalogs from Dover Publications, you're missing a real treat. The company now carries over 3,000 high-quality paperback books, most of which sell for $3.00 to $5.00. The catalog includes a huge selection of books on needlework, textiles, hobbies, arts and crafts.

Send for a free general catalog, or request the craft and needlecraft catalogs only.

Dover Street Booksellers, Ltd.

P.O. Box 1563
Easton, MD 21601
(301) 822-9329

Mail order; retail
Established in 1988

Dover Street Booksellers sells over 600 quilting-book titles, and their 52-page catalog gives a description of each book.

Quantity discounts are given on orders over $100.00.

Send $2.00 for a current book catalog.

Down East Books

P.O. Box 679
Camden, ME 04843
(207) 594-9544

Mail order; publisher
Established in 1963

Down East Books publishes a line of knitting books, as well as books on other subjects. The knitting books include *Maine Woods Woolies* (1986) and *More Maine Sweaters* (1987) by Helene Rush, and Robin Hanson's popular mitten books, *Fox & Geese & Fences* and *Flying Geese & Partridge Feet* (1986, co-authored with Janetta Dexter).

Send for a free book catalog.

Embroidery Research Press

10800 Alpharetta Highway
Suite 200G4
Roswell, GA 30076
(404) 578-6544

Publisher
Established in 1987

Embroidery Research Press publishes books on topics where no book is available, or where all the books on the subject are out of print. Current books published by this company include *Lady Evelyn's Needlework Collection* by Mary-Dick Digges et al. (1988) and *Bell Pull Finishing* by Mary-Dick Digges (1988).

Send for a free book catalog.

Lady Evelyn's Needlework Collection
by
Mary-Dick Digges, Dolly Norton Fehd, Nancy Lawson & Martha Pearle Vogt

Contains an illustrated catalog of the entire collection and instructions for contemporary adaptations

One of the books available from Embroidery Research Press

Lois Ericson, owner of Eric's Press, has written and published a line of books on creative sewing and design. Among others, these include *Fabrics Reconstructed: A Collection of Surface Changes* (1985) and *Design and Sew It Yourself* (1983), co-authored with Diane Frode.

Quantity discounts are given on books; write for details.

Send for a free book brochure.

Eric's Press

P.O. Box 1680
Tahoe City, CA 95730

Mail order; publisher
Established in 1980

Fairchild Books and Visuals publishes an extensive line of books on fashion design and textiles. Some currently available titles include the *Dictionary of Fashion* (1988) by Charlotte Calasibetta, *A Survey of Historic Costume* (1988) by Phyllis Tortora and *A Guide to Fashion Sewing* (1986) by Connie A. Crawford.

Send for a free catalog.

Fairchild Books and Visuals

7 E. 12th Street
New York, NY 10003
(212) 741-5814

Mail order; publisher
Established in 1950

Fiberworks Publications, owned by Bobbi A. McRae, is the publisher of *The Fiberworks Directory of Self-Published Books on the Fiber Arts* (1988) ($11.95 postpaid) and several other books on textiles and fibers. Ms. McRae (author of *The Fabric & Fiber Sourcebook*) also offers *The Fiberworks Booklist,* an ongoing selection of new, "previously loved" or out-of-print books for sale on weaving, spinning, knitting, sewing, dyeing, design, needlework and quilting.

Discounts are given on all books; write for more information.

Send $1.00 for a current catalog and ordering information.

Fiberworks Publications

P.O. Box 49770
Austin, TX 78765
(512) 454-7160

Mail order; publisher
Established in 1984

The Ginger Press Bookstore offers a wide selection of English, American, Canadian and some foreign books on the fiber arts. These include *Flax Culture* (Ginger Press, 1989) by Mavis Atton, *Ikat Textiles of India* (Chronical, 1988) by Chelma Desai and *Contemporary Basketry* (F.A. Davis, 1978) by Sharon Robinson.

Quantity discounts are given; write for details.

Send for a free book list.

The Ginger Press Bookstore

848 2nd Avenue, E.
Owen Sound, ON N4K 2H3
Canada

Mail order; retail
Established in 1978

Owned by Bette S. Feinstein, Hard-to-Find Needlework Books buys and sells new, rare, out-of-print and imported books and magazines on the fiber arts. The catalog contains more than 600 entries, and a search service is available.

Send $1.00 for a current catalog.

Hard-to-Find Needlework Books

96 Roundwood Road
Newton, MA 02164
(617) 969-0942

Mail order
Established in 1978

Hazelcrafts Publications, owned by Hazel Lambert, offers a large number of books and patterns specializing in hand knitting. Ms. Lambert also edits and publishes *The Knitter's Newsletter* (see p. 207).

Quantity discounts are given on some items; check the catalog for details.

Send $1.00 for a current catalog.

Hazelcrafts Publications

P.O. Box 175
Woburn, MA 01801
(508) 454-8483

Mail order; publisher
Established in 1972

Interweave Press, Inc.

306 N. Washington Avenue
Loveland, CO 80537
(303) 669-7672

Mail order; publisher
Established in 1975

Interweave Press is "dedicated to good literature for fiber craftsmen," according to owner Linda Ligon. Interweave offers a number of informative and inspirational books and several magazines (see the listing on p. 206) on the textile arts of weaving, spinning, knitting and dyeing. The press also sponsors an annual handspinning retreat each fall and a forum each spring.

Discounts are given to qualified buyers; write for details.

Send for a free book catalog.

Jo Bryant Books

630 Graceland S.E.
Albuquerque, NM 87108
(505) 268-7775

Mail order
Established in 1983

Jo Bryant carries a large selection of new, used and out-of-print books on the fiber arts and needlework. She also offers a book-search service.

Discounts are given to libraries; write for details.

Send $1.50 for a current book catalog.

John Ives Antiquarian Books

5 Normanhurst Drive
St. Margarets
Twickenham, Middlesex TW1 1NA
England
011-44-1-892-6265 (from the U.S.)

Mail order

John Ives offers a large number of books on antiques and collecting, costume and needlework, including lacemaking, embroidery, weaving and textiles. The current catalog lists over 2,100 volumes of scarce and out-of-print books.

Write for a current catalog.

From the John Ives Antiquarian Books catalog

Katherine Ramus Books

2100 E. Eastman Avenue
Englewood, CO 80110
(303) 789-3115
(303) 838-5945 in the summer

Mail order
Established in 1938

Katherine Ramus offers books on all crafts, particularly weaving, spinning, dyeing, embroidery and quilting. She also acts as a book service to many guilds of weavers, embroiderers and quilters.

Discounts are given to individuals, libraries and shops; write for details.

Send a SASE and ask for specific titles or subjects.

Knitting Books, Etc.

2247 Shiawassee S.E.
Grand Rapids, MI 49508

Mail order; publisher
Established in 1984

Knitting Books, Etc. offers a selection of books on knitting, including *A Time to Knit Raglans*, *A Time to Knit Drop Yoke Sweaters*, *A Time to Knit Mittens* and more.

Quantity discounts are given on orders of six or more books; write for details.

Send a SASE for a current booklist.

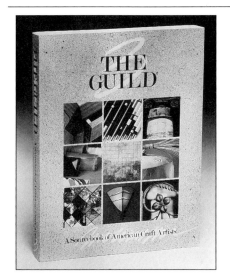

Kraus Sikes publishes *The Guild: A Sourcebook of American Craft Artists.* The full-color, beautiful book is distributed free of charge to 10,000 professionally affiliated architects and interior designers who buy and commission artwork directly from the artists advertising in the book. Kraus Sikes also promotes each of the participating artists through exhibitions and national and local publications.

Write for a current brochure or information on future listings.

The Guild, published by Kraus Sikes.

Kraus Sikes, Inc.

150 W. 25th Street
New York, NY 10001
(212) 242-3730

Mail order; publisher
Established in 1985

Liliaceae Press, owned by Lilian A. Bell, publishes books on the art of papermaking, such as *Plant Fibers for Papermaking* (1986) and *Papyrus, Tapa, Amate and Rice Paper* (1985), both by Ms. Bell.

Quantity discounts are given; write for details.

Send a SASE for a current book flyer.

Liliaceae Press

1970 S. Davis Street
McMinnville, OR 97128
(503) 472-3566

Mail order; publisher
Established in 1980

Main Street Press publishes a variety of high-quality books and calendars on quilts, quilting and other forms of needlework. Some current books include *Childhood Dreams* (1988) by Susan Bennett Gallagher, *Plain and Fancy* (1988) by Anita Schorsch, *Quilts of Illusion* (1988) by Laura Fisher and many more.

Discounts are given to qualified buyers; write for information.

Send for a free book catalog.

Main Street Press

William Case House
Pittstown, NJ 08867
(201) 735-9424

Mail order; publisher
Established in 1975

Books available from Main Street Press

Mini-Magic

3675 Reed Road
Columbus, OH 43220
(614) 457-3687

Mail order
Established in 1973

In addition to Mini-Magic's line of trims, threads and costuming supplies (see pgs. 90, 100 and 120), the company also carries a large number of books on fashion, costume and sewing.

Send a check for $5.00 (or $3.00 cash) for a current 50-page catalog.

Nine Press, Inc.

50 College Street
Asheville, NC 28801
(704) 253-0467

Mail order; publisher
Established in 1985

Nine Press publishes many books on fiber and textile arts under the imprint of Lark Books. The current book list contains titles such as *The Basketmaker's Art* (1986) by Rob Pulleyn, *Printed Textiles: A Guide to Creative Design Fundamentals* (1987) by Terry Gentille, *The Maker's Hand* (1987) by Peter Collingwood, *The Structure of Weaving* (1983) by Ann Sutton and *The Sampler Book* (1987) by Irmgard Gierl. Nine Press also publishes *Fiberarts* magazine (see p. 206).

Discounts are given to qualified buyers; write for information.

Send for a free book catalog.

Northland Press

P.O. Box N
Flagstaff, AZ 86002
(602) 774-5251

Mail order; publisher

Northland Press offers a variety of books by Noel Bennett on weaving— from basic how-to lessons on Navajo weaving to an anthology of stories about Navajo culture.

Send for a free book brochure.

Oliver Press

P.O. Box 4096
St. Paul, MN 55104
(612) 426-9681

Mail order; publisher
Established in 1975

Oliver Press, owned by Jeannie M. Spears, writes and publishes a number of small booklets that provide basic skills for careers in quilting. These include *Mastering the Basics of Quiltmaking* (1982) and *Slides: Photographing Your Work* (1987). Ms. Spears also publishes a few books by other authors, including *Shops: Start-up Steps* (1988) by Joyce Sloan, as well as *The Professional Quilter Magazine* (see p. 208).

Quantity discounts are given on books; write for details.

Send for a free brochure.

Open Chain Publishing

P.O. Box 2634
Menlo Park, CA 94026
(415) 366-4440

Mail order; publisher
Established in 1973

Open Chain Publishing, owned by Robbie Fanning, sells books on the creative use of the sewing machine, all of which are edited, written or published by Ms. Fanning.

Discounts are given to qualified buyers; write for details.

Send for a free book catalog.

The Pat Cairns Studio sells a comprehensive collection of books on the textile arts, with the main emphasis on quilting. The current catalog lists over 400 titles, including Ms. Cairns' and Jean Affleck's new book, *Putting It All Together: A Contemporary Approach to Quiltmaking* (Alexander Nicholls Press, 1987).

Quantity discounts are given to qualified buyers; write for details.

Send $3.00 for a current book catalog.

Pat Cairns Studio

1420 Old Bridge Street
Granville Island
Vancouver, BC V6H 3S6
Canada
(604) 684-6661

Mail order; publisher
Established in 1980

The Quilt Digest Press, the only full-service publisher of quilt books, specializes in the techniques, history, art and humorous aspects of quilt making.

Discounts are given to qualified buyers; write for details.

Send for a free book catalog.

The Quilt Digest Press

955 14th Street
San Francisco, CA 94114
(415) 431-1222

Mail order; publisher
Established in 1983

Books available from The Quilt Digest Press

Quilting Books Unlimited

1158 Prairie
Aurora, IL 60506
(312) 896-7331

Mail order; retail
Established in 1981

Darlene Roberts, owner of Quilting Books Unlimited, carries every quilting book in print (including many foreign titles) through her mail-order company. The book list is updated every two months. Ms. Roberts also carries related books on the fiber arts, such as stitchery and lacemaking.

A 10% discount is given on orders over $100.00.

Send $1.00 for a current catalog.

R. L. Shep, Publishers and Booksellers

P.O. Box 668
Mendocino, CA 95460
(707) 937-1436

Mail order; publisher
Established in 1963

R. L. Shep sells unusual books on textiles and costume and publishes books on Victorian costume and needlework.

Send $2.50 for a complete book catalog, or write for a free brochure.

The Rugging Room

10 Sawmill Drive
Westford, MA 01886
(508) 692-8600

Mail order; publisher
Established in 1982

Jeanne H. Fallier, owner of The Rugging Room, has written and published several books for rug hookers. Among them is *The Fallier Manual for Traditional American Hooking* (1987), which includes sections on planning, preparation, hooking the design and finishing, and *Little Critters,* a pattern book. (See *The Rugging Room Bulletin* on p. 208.)

Quantity discounts are given to teachers; write for information.

Send $1.50 for a current book brochure.

S & C Huber American Classics

82 Plants Dam Road
East Lyme, CT 06333
(203) 739-0772

Mail order; publisher
Established in 1984

S & C Huber American Classics, owned by Carol Huber, publishes knitting-pattern books with unique designs based on American folk art. The two pattern books currently available are *Countryknits* and *Countryknits for Kids.*

Quantity discounts are given on orders of ten or more books; write for details.

Send $2.50 for a complete catalog; future catalogs are free.

Schoolhouse Press

6899 Cary Bluff
Pittsville, WI 54466
(715) 884-2799

Mail order; publisher
Established in 1959

Schoolhouse Press is owned by the delightful mother-and-daughter team of Elizabeth Zimmermann and Meg Swansen, who are "attempting to liberate hand knitters from instructions; to help them think and design for themselves." Mrs. Zimmermann has written three well-known books: *Knitting Without Tears* (Scribner's, 1973), *Knitter's Almanac* (Dover, 1981) and *Knitting Workshop* (Schoolhouse Press, 1981), the last designed to accompany her latest video series of knitting classes. Schoolhouse Press also has many knitting books for sale. (See the listings for knitting supplies on p. 61 and videotapes on p. 190.)

Mrs. Zimmermann's books can be ordered wholesale with various discounts; write for more information.

Send $1.00 for a current book catalog and price list.

Shuttle-Craft Books, Inc.

Shuttle-Craft Books offers a number of volumes on weaving and specializes in the classics by Mary Atwater and Harriet Tidball. Books by Mary Atwater include *Design and the Handweaver* (1969), *The ShuttleCraft Book of American Hand-Weaving* (1986), *Byways in Handweaving* (1988) and others. Books by Harriet Tidball include *Build or Buy a Loom* (1969), *Color and Dyeing* (1969), *Contemporary Satins* (1969) and *Handweaver's Instruction Manual* (1988). Also offered are books by Virginia Harvey and other authors, as well as note cards for fiber enthusiasts.

Send for a free book catalog.

P.O. Box 550
Coupeville, WA 98239
(206) 678-4648

Mail order; publisher
Established in 1974

One of the note cards available from Shuttle-Craft Books

Sterling Publishing Company

Sterling Publishing Company is one of the largest publishers in the country featuring books on the fiber arts.

Write for a free catalog.

2 Park Avenue
New York, NY 10016
(212) 532-7160

Mail order; publisher
Established in 1949

Straw into Gold

Straw into Gold offers a large number of books and magazines on textiles and the fiber arts. (See the listing for knitting, spinning and weaving supplies on p. 67.)

All books offered are not listed in the catalog. Interested buyers should write for information on specific books.

3006 San Pablo Avenue
Berkeley, CA 94702
(415) 548-5247

Mail order
Established in 1971

The Sweater Workshop

Box 5
Hingham, MA 02043
(617) 749-3649

Mail order; publisher
Established in 1981

Jacqueline Fee's book, *The Sweater Workshop* (Interweave Press, 1983), provides an "alternative to pattern reading." It also gives full instructions for making a completely seamless sweater to your own gauge, with any yarn, in any size or style, that requires no sewing.

Send for a free brochure on the book and various knitting supplies.

The Taunton Press

63 S. Main Street
Newtown, CT 06470
(800) 888-8286
(203) 426-8171 in Connecticut

Mail order; publisher
Established in 1975

The Taunton Press, publisher of *Threads* magazine (see p. 210) and *The Fabric & Fiber Sourcebook,* has begun publishing books on needlework and textiles. Among currently available titles are *Alice Starmore's Book of Fair Isle Knitting* (1988) and *Knitting Counterpanes: Traditional Coverlet Patterns for Contemporary Knitters* (1989) by Mary Walker Phillips.

Call or write for a complete book catalog.

The Unicorn, Books for Craftsmen, Inc.

1304 Scott Street
Petaluma, CA 94952
(707) 762-3362

Mail order
Established in 1969

The Unicorn, owned by Lars Malmberg, is the largest source of weaving and other fiber-related books in the U.S. The current catalog lists books on weaving, spinning, dyeing, the business of crafts, color, basketry, costume, fabric decoration and knitting.

Send $1.00 for a current catalog with descriptions of all books listed.

University of Washington Press

P.O. Box 50096
Seattle, WA 98145-5096
(206) 543-8870

Mail order; publisher
Established in 1915

The University of Washington Press publishes a number of books on the textile arts. Among these are *The Techniques of Basketry* (1986) by Virginia Harvey, *Surface Design for Fabric* (1984) by Richard M. Proctor and Jennifer F. Lew, *Southwestern Indian Baskets* (1988) by Andrew Whiteford and *Looms and Textiles of the Copts* (1988) by Diane Lee Carroll.

Send for a free book catalog.

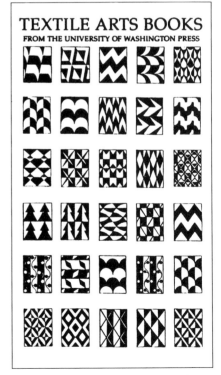

From The University of Washington Press textile-arts catalog

The University Press of New England publishes and distributes a variety of books on needlework. One of the current titles is *The Ladies' Work Table: Domestic Needlework in Nineteenth-Century America* (1988) by Margaret Vincent.

Send for a current book catalog.

University Press of New England

17½ Lebanon Street
Hanover, NH 03755
(603) 646-3054

Mail order; publisher
Established in 1970

The Westminster Trading Corporation publishes books on knitting and needlework such as *Summer & Winter Knitting* (1987) edited by Stephen Sheard, *Sasha Kagan's Big & Little Sweaters* (1987), *Designer Needlepoint* (1987) edited by Augh Ehrman, and Kaffe Fassett's *1989 Diary*.

Send for a free book list.

The Westminster Trading Corporation

5 Northern Boulevard
Amherst, NH 03031
(603) 886-5041

Mail order; publisher
Established in 1987

Wild Willow Press, owned by Char TerBeest, offers books on basketmaking as well as instructional videos on the subject (see p. 203).

Send a SASE for a current book list.

Wild Willow Press

P.O. Box 438
Baraboo, WI 53913
(608) 356-9048

Mail order; publisher
Established in 1983

Lois J. Mueller, owner of Wooden Porch Books, sells out-of-print and rare books and magazines on the fine, applied and textile arts. The current catalog contains over 360 books on such subjects as knitting, costume, needlework, quilting, spinning and weaving.

Send $2.00 for a current catalog.

Wooden Porch Books

Route 1, Box 262
Middlebourne, WV 26149
(304) 386-4434

Mail order
Established in 1975

Magazines, Journals and Newsletters

American Craft

American Craft Council
40 W. 53rd Street
New York, NY 10019
(212) 956-3535

Established in 1943

American Craft is a high-quality, full-color magazine published bimonthly by the American Craft Council (see p. 152). The magazine serves as a showcase for contemporary professional crafts (including fiber), historical movements, important exhibitions, new books and much more. The magazine also includes regular information on shows and exhibits, educational opportunities and the craft marketplace.

The magazine is included with membership dues in the American Craft Council. Write for more information.

Basketmaker

MKS Publications, Inc.
P.O. Box 340
Westland, MI 48185-0340
(313) 326-8307

Established in 1983

Basketmaker, published and edited by Sue Kurginski, is a quarterly publication for designers, weavers and collectors of basketry. The 50-page magazine contains lots of exciting information on suppliers, patterns and techniques for beginning and advanced weavers, profiles of basketry artists, book reviews, shows and exhibits, educational opportunities and views on traditional and contemporary basketry.

The current subscription price is $12.00 per year. Write for more information.

The Basketry Express

1054 Burnhamthorpe Road
R.R. #1 E.
Oakville, ON L6J 4Z2
Canada

Established in 1985

The Basketry Express is edited and published by Ankaret Dean, the well-known Canadian basketmaker, author and instructor. Ms. Dean's quarterly newsletter is devoted entirely to the craft of basketmaking in Canada and includes a variety of topics such as exhibition reviews, basketmaker profiles, historical information, book reviews and information on gathering and preparing natural materials for baskets.

The current subscription price is $7.50 per year; write for additional information.

Black Sheep Newsletter

1690 Butler Creek Road
Ashland, OR 97520
(503) 482-5901

Established in 1974

The *Black Sheep Newsletter*, edited by Dona Zimmerman and Kent Erskine, is a 32-page international publication for raisers and users of colored wool and other animal fibers. Issues contain information on producing top-quality fleeces and on diseases and health care for sheep. There are articles on various animals and historical subjects, as well as a purebred directory, a list of coming events and fair reviews.

The current subscription rate is $10.00 per year for four issues; write for additional information.

204

Cast On, the official publication of The Knitting Guild of America (see the listing on p. 155), is a full-color magazine published five times per year. A recent issue contained patterns for children's and men's sweaters, profiles of knitters, information on the various knitting stitches, a crazy-quilt sweater pattern for women, book reviews, an article on finishing cut edges of knitted pieces and a guild directory.

Cast On is sent to all members of The Knitting Guild of America; the current membership fee is $18.00 per year.

Cast On

The Knitting Guild of America
P.O. Box 1606
Knoxville, TN 37901
(615) 524-2401

Established in 1984

Color Trends, edited and published by Michele Wipplinger, is a one-of-a-kind limited journal published in the spring and fall of each year. *Color Trends* reports on the trends in fashion colors and shows textile artists how to duplicate these colors in their own work. Each issue contains actual fabric swatches and samples of dyed fibers and yarns. The journal features exciting uses of dyes in dipping, resisting, discharging and painting applications. It is packed with useful technical information on dyes, fabrics and fibers.

A one-year subscription is currently $32.00; write for further details.

Color Trends

8037 9th N.W.
Seattle, WA 98117

Established in 1985

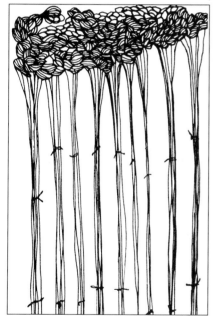

Illustrations from a recent issue of
Color Trends magazine

The Crafts Report is a professional publication for craftspeople who are serious about selling their work. It contains information on marketing, business management, pricing and the legalities of running a small business—all vital information for the working craftsperson. Regular features include protecting your health, craft photography, wholesale-show dates, new products, crafts available (listings from craftspeople), crafts wanted (listings by shop owners looking for specific crafts) and book reviews and more.

The Crafts Report is currently $17.50 per year for 11 issues. Send for more information.

The Crafts Report

3632 Ashworth N.
Seattle, WA 98103
(206) 632-7222

Established in 1975

CraftSource

7509 7th Place, S.W.
Seattle, WA 98106
(206) 767-4720

Established in 1988

CraftSource, owned by Teri Hales, offers three newsletters—the *Crafter's SourceLetter*, the *Stitcher's SourceLetter* and the *Sewer's SourceLetter*. These newsletters give unbiased information and evaluations on mail-order companies offering sewing, needlework or craft supplies.

A sample of each newsletter is $4.00; the current subscription rate for one newsletter is $15.00 per year (specify the crafts, sewing or needlework edition).

Fiberarts

50 College Street
Asheville, NC 28801
(704) 253-0467

Established in 1974

Fiberarts, published by Rob Pulleyn and edited by Carol Lawrence, provides an overview of the fiber-art field. The full-color magazine is informative and inspirational. Special issues have focused on tapestry, papermaking, quilting, surface design, wearables and rugs. Regular articles contain information on historical design, technique and contemporary fiber artists, as well as news of international fiber artists. Exhibit and book reviews are included, as well as listings of educational opportunities.

The current subscription rate is $18.00 per year (five issues); write for more information.

The Flying Needle

The National Standards Council of
American Embroiderers
P.O. Box 8578
Northfield, IL 60093-8578
(312) 256-1497

Established in 1969

The Flying Needle is the official publication of The National Standards Council of American Embroiderers (see p. 155). The full-color magazine, edited by Glennis McNeal, contains information on all types of embroidered work. A recent issue included a feature on Virginia Blakelock and her beaded neckpieces, a history of beads, guild news, an article on rozashi, exhibit and book reviews and market news.

The Flying Needle is sent to all members of the Council. Send a long SASE for current membership rates and additional information.

Hand Papermaking

P.O. Box 10571
Minneapolis, MN 55458
(612) 788-9440

Established in 1985

Hand Papermaking, edited by Amanda Degener and Michael Durgin, is a bi-annual magazine for everyone who appreciates or makes handmade paper. The publication is dedicated to advancing traditional and contemporary ideas in the art of hand papermaking, and includes information on artists, techniques, natural fibers for papermaking and equipment. Each issue of the magazine features at least one beautiful sample of handmade paper.

The current subscription price is $15.00 per year; write for further information.

Handwoven

306 N. Washington Avenue
Loveland, CO 80537
(303) 669-7672

Established in 1977

Handwoven magazine, published by Linda Ligon of Interweave Press (see p. 196) is a useful and inspirational full-color magazine for weavers, spinners and other textile and fiber artists. The periodical contains many well-designed weaving projects with complete instructions and includes articles on dyeing and spinning, helpful hints, book reviews and profiles of fiber artists.

Write for current subscription rates.

Knitter's magazine, a full-color quarterly publication, presents an integrated approach to the craft of knitting. The magazine includes various projects that help the growth of knitting skills, as well as artist profiles and news of suppliers.

Write for current subscription rates.

Knitter's

Golden Fleece Publications
335 N. Main Avenue
Sioux Falls, SD 57102
(605) 338-2450

Established in 1979

The Knitter's Newsletter is a bimonthly publication that includes original knitting designs, a reader's column and classified ads. Edited by Hazel Lambert, an avid knitter and designer, the newsletter also features regular columnists that bring interesting patterns and information on handknitting to the reader.

Send for current subscription rates.

The Knitter's Newsletter

P.O. Box 175
Woburn, MA 01801
(508) 454-8483

Established in 1972

Kurenai: Japanese Embroidery Journal

Kurenai: Japanese Embroidery Journal is translated and published quarterly in cooperation with the Kurenai-Kai School of Japan. Edited by Dolly Norton Fehd, each issue contains articles by Master Iwao Saito and Mr. Shuji Tamura on Japanese symbolism, color usage and design. A calendar of events and a list of study opportunities are also included.

The current subscription rate is $18.00 per year; write for further information.

Kurenai: Japanese Embroidery Journal

10800 Alpharetta Highway
Suite 200 G-4
Roswell, GA 30076
(404) 578-6544

Established in 1987

Lace Crafts Quarterly, edited and published by Eunice Sein, is a full-color, 48-page magazine that includes articles on the history of lace, lacemaking techniques by hand and machine, sources of supplies, lace collections and conservation of lace. Every issue contains at least two actual-size patterns and complete instructions.

Write for current subscription rates.

Lace Crafts Quarterly

3201 E. Lakeshore Drive
Tallahassee, FL 32312-9982
(904) 385-5093

Established in 1988

Lacemaking Today, edited and published by Judy Green Davis, contains patterns, articles on all types of lacemaking, related crafts and profiles of lacemakers. The eight-page newsletter is published six times a year.

The current subscription rate is $10.00 per year; write for additional information.

Lacemaking Today

Bizarre Butterfly Publishing
P.O. Box 16186
Phoenix, AZ 85011
(602) 266-2426

Established in 1981

Needle & Craft

2509 W. Berry Street, Suite 7
Ft. Worth, TX 76109
(817) 921-3801

Established in 1978

Needle & Craft (formerly *Needlecraft for Today*), edited by Margaret Dittman and Charlie E. Davis, covers the entire field of needlecrafts. The full-color, 78-page magazine contains full-sized patterns for quilts, dolls, toys and wearable art along with an excellent, extremely accurate instructions section.

The current subscription price is $15.97 per year for six issues.

Needle Arts

The Embroiderers' Guild of
America
200 4th Avenue
Louisville, KY 40202
(502) 589-6956

Established in 1958

Needle Arts is the official publication of The Embroiderers' Guild of America (see p. 154). The full-color magazine contains articles on all types of embroidery, both traditional and contemporary. A past issue contained an article on Wilcke Smith, regional EGA chapter news, a historical article on embroidered quilts and information on hardanger embroidery and mounting and matting embroidered work.

A subscription of *Needle Arts* is included in the annual EGA membership fee; write for current rates.

Ornament

P.O. Box 35029
Los Angeles, CA 90035-0029
(213) 652-9914

Established in 1987

Ornament is a full-color 90-page quarterly magazine that covers the field of ancient, contemporary and ethnic ornamentation of jewelry and clothing. The magazine promotes original design, knowledge and research, features resources for the artist and encourages collecting. A recent issue contained articles on the wearable basketry of John McGuire and the beautiful hand-painted silk pieces by Ina Kozel, as well as articles on netsuke, Russian beads and collectible jewelry.

A one-year subscription is currently $25.00; write for additional information.

The Professional Quilter Magazine

P.O. Box 4096
St. Paul, MN 55104
(612) 426-9681

Established in 1975

The Professional Quilter Magazine is published quarterly for people who are serious about their quilting as a business. The magazine includes information on marketing, education, organization of a business, improvement of teaching skills and increasing profits.

Send $4.00 for a sample copy or write for more information.

The Rug Hooker: News & Views

P.O. Box 351
Kennebunkport, ME 04046
(207) 967-3520

The Rug Hooker: News & Views is edited by Joan Moshimer, who believes that rug hooking "is an art form and you should use it to express yourself freely." The magazine stresses experimentation, flexibility and enjoyment in the craft of rug hooking. A recent issue included patterns, information on mothproofing rugs and technical advice on dyeing.

The current subscription rate is $15.00 per year for five issues; write for further information.

Rugging Room Bulletin

10 Sawmill Drive
Westford, MA 01886
(508) 692-8600

Established in 1987

The *Rugging Room Bulletin* is a quarterly, 12-page newsletter edited and published by Jeanne H. Fallier. The bulletin contains patterns for hooked rugs and information on techniques, conservation of rugs, exhibits, historical topics, book reviews and color-planning ideas. (See p. 200 for the listing on books.)

A one-year subscription is currently $8.00; write for further details.

Sew News is a monthly fashion magazine for people who sew. A current issue contains useful information on sewing capes, holiday projects, wearable art, printing on fabric and machine methods for smocking.

The current subscription rate is $13.95 per year; write for details.

Sew News

PJS Publications, Inc.
P.O. Box 1790
Peoria, IL 61656
(309) 682-6626

Established in 1980

Kathy Sandmann, owner of Sewing Sampler Productions, publishes and edits a monthly newsletter devoted to fashion sewing. A current issue includes information on sewing suits, working with boiled wool, fabric and pattern news, reader tips and helpful hints. Ms. Sandmann also publishes a bimonthly newsletter devoted exclusively to sewing for children.

Send $.50 for a current brochure and price information.

Sewing Sampler Productions

P.O. Box 39
Springfield, MN 56087
(507) 723-6547

Established in 1985

Shuttle, Spindle & Dyepot is the official publication of The Handweaver's Guild of America (see the listing on p. 154). The magazine contains technical and inspirational features for weavers, spinners and dyers of all levels. Other information includes news of weaving and spinning guilds, exhibit calendars, reports on new equipment, suppliers and more.

The magazine is included in the HGA's membership dues, which are currently $25.00 for one year. Write for further information.

Shuttle, Spindle & Dyepot

The Handweaver's Guild
of America
120 Mountain Avenue, B101
Bloomfield, CT 06002
(203) 242-3577

Established in 1969

Spin-Off comes from Interweave Press (see the listing on p. 196), also the publishers of *Handwoven* magazine. A recent issue of the full-color quarterly magazine aimed at spinners featured articles on spinning wheels, sheep breeds, spinning sharlea and projects made from handspun yarns.

Write for current subscription rates.

Spin-Off

306 N. Washington Avenue
Loveland, CO 80537
(303) 669-7672

Established in 1977

The Surface Design Journal, edited by Charles S. Talley, is the official publication of the Surface Design Association (see the listing on p. 156). Published quarterly, the full-color magazine includes technical, historical and inspirational articles on surface design. Past issues have included articles on wearable art, painted warps for weaving, growing indigo in China, Indian block printing and computer graphics. A companion newsletter, also sent to SDA members, contains information on regional activities and an exhibition calendar.

Current membership dues are $35.00 per year or $25.00 for students with current identification.

Surface Design Journal

The Surface Design Association
4111 Lincoln Boulevard, Suite 426
Marina del Rey, CA 90292
(213) 392-2274

Established in 1975

Teaching for Learning

46-305 Ikiiki Street
Kaneohe, HI 96744
(808) 235-3775

Established in 1984

Teaching for Learning, edited and published by Charlene Anderson-Shea, is a quarterly newsletter published especially for fiber-arts teachers. The informative and interesting newsletter contains information on presenting yourself professionally, motivating your students, expanding your teaching opportunities, diversifying income, managing the business of teaching, gaining valuable publicity and using technology in teaching.

A one-year subscription is currently $12.00; write for further details.

The Textile Booklist

P.O. Box 4392
Arcata, CA 95521

Established in 1976

The Textile Booklist, published and edited by Kaaren Buffington, is "an international quarterly digest of book news and reviews in textiles, fiber arts, needle arts, costumes and related subjects."

Write for current subscription rates and more details.

The Textile Museum Journal

The Textile Museum
2320 S Street, N.W.
Washington, D.C. 20008
(202) 667-0441

Established in 1962

The Textile Museum Journal is the official publication of The Textile Museum in Washington, D.C. (see p. 170). The annual publication contains scholarly articles on historical textiles with emphasis on the geographic areas of the Near East, Central, South and Southeast Asia, and South and Central America.

The journal is provided to members of The Textile Museum only. Current membership fees vary; write for details.

Threads Magazine

The Taunton Press
63 S. Main Street
Newtown, CT 06470
(203) 426-8171

Established in 1985

Threads magazine, edited by Betsy Levine, is a full-color, 92-page bimonthly that covers the entire field of the fiber and textile arts. The publication takes a professional approach to these crafts, provides considerable technical how-to information, and features a wide variety of articles on knitting, sewing, soft sculpture, quilting, embroidery, fashion design, rug making, dyeing, weaving and beading. (See the listing for Taunton Press books on p. 202.)

The current subscription rate is $20.00 per year; write for additional information.

Treadleart

28534 Narbonne Avenue
Lomita, CA 90717
(213) 534-5122

Established in 1978

Treadleart, published and edited by Janet Stocker, is a bimonthly magazine that focuses on "sewing-machine artistry" and features patterns, techniques, hints and tips, new product and book reviews, profiles of sewing machine artists and class listings.

The current subscription price is $14.00 per year; write for further details.

Update Newsletters

2269 Chestnut, Suite 269
San Francisco, CA 94123
(415) 931-7370

Established in 1986

Update Newsletters include articles, news, innovative techniques and ideas for both serger sewing and general sewing. A series of *Update Booklets* also includes information on fashion sewing and serging.

Write for free information on both the newsletters and booklets.

VavMagasinet is the only imported European weaving magazine sold on a regular basis in the U.S. The full-color magazine focuses on Swedish weaving techniques and artists, and comes with an inserted English translation.

The current subscription rate is $25.00 per year for four issues; write for further information.

VavMagasinet (The Scandinavian Weaving Magazine)

1304 Scott Street
Petaluma, CA 94952
(707) 762-3362

Established in 1982

Vintage Clothing Newsletter, edited and published by Terry McCormick, contains technical and general information, personality profiles, networking opportunities and solid, useful information about vintage clothing. The newsletter serves as a means to foster "person-to-person contact between vintage-clothing lovers." Ms. McCormick is also the author of the *Consumer's Guide to Vintage Clothing* (Dembner Books, 1987).

The current subscription rate is $15.00 per year; write for details.

Vintage Clothing Newsletter

P.O. Box 1422
Corvallis, OR 97339
(503) 752-7456

Established in 1984

Weaver's Magazine, (formerly *The Prairie Wool Companion*), is published by Alexis Y. Xenakis and edited by Madelyn van der Hoogt. The full-color, quarterly publication for weavers endeavors to present weaving theory in clear language and emphasizes weaving with more than four harnesses.

The current subscription rate is $16.00 per year; write for more information.

Weaver's Magazine

Golden Fleece Publications
335 N. Main Avenue
Sioux Falls, SD 57102
(605) 338-2450

Established in 1979

Weavings of New England, published and edited by JoEllen Sefton, is a delightful quarterly journal dedicated to coordinating and sharing information on the fiber arts among the artists of New England and the surrounding areas. Issues are illustrated with charming old line drawings and contain regular articles on basketry, spinning, weaving, shows and festivals, workshops, museums, guild news and New England products.

The current subscription rate is $12.00 per year; write for further information.

Weavings of New England

P.O. Box 217
Sterling, CT 06377
(203) 774-2998

Established in 1986

Wool Gathering is published by Schoolhouse Press (see p. 200) in March and September of each year. Elizabeth Zimmermann decided to start a newsletter of her own in 1957 when she became disenchanted with the way other knitting magazines would "emasculate and louse up" her original designs. That newsletter has now developed into *Wool Gathering*, a semi-annual catalog of books, general information and original knitting designs by both Mrs. Zimmermann and her daughter, Meg Swansen.

Send $2.00 for a sample copy of *Wool Gathering*.

Wool Gathering

6899 Cary Bluff
Pittsville, WI 54466
(715) 884-2799

Established in 1959

Geographical Index

Subject Index

Editor: Christine Timmons
Designer: Steve Hunter
Layout artist: Marianne Markey
Art assistant: Iliana Koehler
Copy/production editor: Pam Purrone
Typesetter: Margot Knorr
Print production manager: Peggy Dutton

Typeface: ITC Garamond
Paper: Makers Matte, 70 lb., neutral pH
Printer and binder: Arcata Graphics/Hawkins, New Canton, Tennessee